SPECIAL PRAISE FOR *RAGE*

"Bill Denehy has an amazing story to tell. Stop what you're doing, start reading, and get ready for a life-changing experience."

Pat Williams
Senior Vice President, Orlando Magic
Author of *Coach Wooden's Greatest Secrets*

"*Rage* by Bill Denehy and Peter Golenbock is must reading for anyone concerned about issues of addiction, and it has a special application in the world of professional sports. Crisply written, Denehy's life story is an important one for us to share. Bill has opened his heart, and anyone who reads it will see the pain, tragedy, and ultimate triumph of this great person."

Richard Lapchick
Founder of the Institute for Diversity and Ethics in Sport

"I have been Bill's sponsor for eighteen of his twenty-one years of continued sobriety. Through the loss of his parents and his pet dog Schmucko, times of anger and resentments, and concurrently, the loss of his eyesight, his commitment to sobriety has never wavered. His resolve to live life to the fullest is inspiring."

Allan Webber
Retired Attorney, Orlando, Florida

"Bill Denehy is an interesting, complicated guy. His stories about his baseball days are utterly hysterical. His ability to treat and manage his drug abuse and alcoholism, as far as I'm concerned, puts him in the Hall of Fame. I really loved this book."

Greg Boger, MD
Physician/Partner at Florida Otolaryngology Group

"Nobody could have built a college program the way Bill did at the University of Hartford. We could have been—should have been—perennial powers, if only he hadn't been fired."

Ted Lombardo

RAGE

RAGE

THE LEGEND OF "BASEBALL BILL" DENEHY

Bill Denehy
with Peter Golenbock

CENTRAL RECOVERY PRESS

LAS VEGAS

Central Recovery Press (CRP) is committed to publishing exceptional materials addressing addiction treatment, recovery, and behavioral healthcare topics, including original and quality books, audio/visual communications, and web-based new media. Through a diverse selection of titles, we seek to contribute a broad range of unique resources for professionals, recovering individuals and their families, and the general public.

For more information, visit **www.centralrecoverypress.com**.

Publisher: Central Recovery Press
3321 N. Buffalo Drive
Las Vegas, NV 89129

19 18 17 16 15 14   1 2 3 4 5

ISBN-13: 978-1-937612-55-9 (paper)
978-1-937612-56-6 (e-book)

Publisher's Note: This is a memoir, a work based on facts recorded to the best of the author's memory. Central Recovery Press books represent the experiences and opinions of their authors only. Every effort has been made to ensure that events, institutions, and statistics presented in our books as facts are accurate and up-to-date. To protect their privacy, the names of some of the people, places, and institutions in this book have been changed.

Central Recovery Press makes no representations or warranties in relation to the medical information in this book. This book is not an alternative to medical advice from your doctor or other professional healthcare provider.

Cover design by David Hardy
Interior design and layout by Sara Streifel, Think Creative Design
Photo of Bill Denehy by Patrick M. Kittell. Used with permission.
Photo of Peter Golenbock by Wendy Grassi. Used with permission.

I'd like to dedicate this book to all the men and women in and out of recovery who still haven't found the right solution to stay abstinent from alcohol and other drugs.

And to my three girls, Heather, Kristin, and Marilyn.

Bill Denehy

Here's to my brother and sister, Robert and Wendy.

And to the other Golenbocks, Aunt Hazel and cousins Jeffrey, Susan, and Douglas.

Peter Golenbock

TABLE OF CONTENTS

INTRODUCTION

I'M BLIND, AND MY BELOVED BASEBALL HAS made me this way. I've always loved Ray Charles and wanted to be like him, but not like this. I wanted to sing like him, not be blind like him.

The reason I'm blind is that during my five-year professional pitching career, team doctors prescribed fifty-seven cortisone shots for my aching shoulder. I didn't know any better. This was before the dangers of cortisone were made public. I knew Sandy Koufax was taking them for his arm, and Sandy was my hero, so I figured what was good for Sandy was good for me. I found out years later that no one should take more than ten cortisone shots in a lifetime. I was later told that if you take more than ten shots in a lifetime, your corneas will grow weak and you risk going blind. I wish someone had said something back then.

I was one of the best young pitchers in the nation when I graduated from high school in 1964. I could throw a baseball ninety-five miles an hour. I once struck out twenty-four batters in a high school game. I retired forty-one batters in a row when I pitched in two American Legion games. Both outings were almost perfect games. Did you ever do something where you felt—where you *knew*—that you were the best in the whole wide world? That's how I felt when I was a teenager in high school.

When I came up to the New York Mets in 1967, I got more ink than Tom Seaver, the college kid from California. In our first games pitching for the Mets, Tom and I each struck out eight batters to set a rookie record that wasn't broken until 2012. My future was so bright that Topps even put us on the same baseball card, calling us Mets Rookie Stars of 1967. I was living my dream. It was a dream I got to live for about two weeks.

In my fourth start, I hurt my arm. I never saw it coming. I had never been hurt before. I threw a pitch and felt the intense grip of pain in my shoulder. Little did I know that my brilliant major league career was finished after exactly two months; after that I was just hanging on to my dream.

I would experience one more brief moment of fame that was very unusual at that particular time. The Mets traded me to the Washington Senators for their manager Gil Hodges. The Cleveland Indians had once swapped managers by trading Joe Gordon to the Detroit Tigers for Jimmy Dykes. However, no player in baseball had ever been traded for a manager. That trade was a first. Mets fans who remember me ask, "Oh, Bill Denehy. You're the guy who was traded for Gil Hodges, aren't you?"

"I am," I tell them with great pride.

I spent the next five years trying to hang on. For a short while I played for Ted Williams. I sat by his side in the dugout and learned about pitching from perhaps the greatest hitter who ever lived. Later I acted as Billy Martin's hatchet man in Detroit.

Billy wanted me to come into a game and hit a batter. To keep my job, and because I was something of a sadist, I was only too willing to do so.

I then pitched in the minor leagues, hoping beyond all hope that I'd be struck by lightning and my arm would come back. I never was, and it never did. You hear all the time how an athlete dies twice. The first time is when his athletic career comes to an end, and the second is when he leaves this world. Sometimes I think that the second death would have been preferable to what I went through.

I haven't had it easy in civilian life. I've had anger issues. I don't work well with others, especially assholes who don't respect me. My rages usually got me fired—and so did my drug use.

I toiled in the minors for a few years, uprooting my family and picking up a nasty drug habit, though I didn't see it that way. After baseball released me, I needed to make money, so I went into real estate. I soon discovered that sitting behind a desk felt more like a prison sentence than earning a living. I quit my lucrative sales job and took a job working for a pittance as a pitching coach for the Boston Red Sox in their minor league farm system. I loved my job. But I had two daughters to raise, and my long-suffering wife, Marilyn, wasn't happy with my low wages. Because of her harping, I went to management and demanded that I be made a manager so I could earn more money. I was let go. I was crushed.

Then I got a well-paying job as a radio talk show host, another job I loved, but as luck would have it, the station went bust nine months later. I was broke. My wife, two daughters, and I had to move in with her mother, who hated my guts, partly because I was seemingly incapable of holding down a steady job.

Hartford College hired me to coach college baseball, another job I loved. I took the worst college baseball team in America and built it into a powerhouse. But before I could realize the fruits of my labor, my anger got the best of me. I threatened to blow up an opposing coach's car, and a snooping, sniveling reporter put my comments in the papers. I was fired from that job too.

I got divorced, and my drug habit only got worse. I smoked marijuana incessantly, and I snorted cocaine with my buddies.

I moved from Connecticut to Florida to take another job in radio, leaving behind my ex-wife, mother-in-law, and two daughters. For ten years my ex-wife wouldn't speak to me or let me see my daughters. By then my drug habit had become so bad that I knew either I had to do something about it or I'd die. I entered a drug rehab program, began recovery, and got my life back, though I was still unable to control my rages.

One time at a recovery meeting one of the other attendees called me a liar. I went for his throat. The guy's lucky I didn't kill him. Another time in a Publix supermarket I asked for fresh, homemade peanut butter. They didn't have any. Four days in a row I went back, and finally I blew my stack. The cops came, and Publix management barred me from the building.

I was fired from my job at a golf shop for trying to strangle one of the other workers and because I wouldn't deliver his illegal drugs to him. Without a job, things got so bad that I had to ask the nonprofit Baseball Assistance Team (BAT) to pay my rent and give me money for food. They provided for me for a year and a half. I had to ask for help because baseball has royally screwed about 850 of us out of our pensions.

In 1981, the Major League Baseball Players Association made a deal with the owners not to include any players in the union who played before 1980 and who didn't play for five years or more. I played part-time in three seasons between 1967 and 1971. Since I don't qualify to join the union, I can't get a pension. Marvin Miller and Bob Boone conspired to really fuck me but good.

That would be enough to enrage anyone, but now I'm blind, and baseball is the reason. When I tried to get workman's comp, I was told, "You don't have any records of your fifty-seven cortisone shots. How do we know you had them?"

Those bastards! The baseball moguls are like the Holocaust deniers. Baseball is making so much fucking money. I just can't understand why they won't do the decent thing and help me out.

I don't want you to think this is a story of disappointment and loss. It's not. Well, yes it is, but it's also a story of great fun and amazing memories. My baseball stories are every bit as colorful as Jim Bouton's in *Ball Four*. I played with Tom Seaver, Tug McGraw, Frank Howard, and Gates Brown. I was managed by Roberto Clemente, Ted Williams, and Billy Martin. I had sex with Chicago Shirley; I almost got shot after a teammate picked up a stripper. My teammates and I once threw a dead shark into a motel pool and scared the hell out of a bunch of senior citizens. Tug McGraw and I slept with the same woman. And I almost hit Willie Mays in the head with a pitch.

My story is also a story of redemption. My ex-wife had her own problems with alcoholism, and she got help around the same time that I did. As a result, we have found each other again, and I have been able to reunite with my two talented daughters. I may be blind, but I can still see what's important.

My name is Baseball Bill, and I'm an addict. I'm going to talk about what my life was like when I was on top of the world, what happened to bring me into therapy, and what it's like to be in recovery today.

As you will see, my life may have been a mess, but it was never boring.

Being Tom Seaver was easy. Being Bill Denehy? *Not so easy.*

PART I

My Years *Before* the Downward Spiral

1

CHILDHOOD

I GOT HIGH FOR THE FIRST TIME when I was six years old. I went to the dentist's office and he gave me nitrous oxide, and I loved it. When I came home and my parents asked me how the visit went, I said, "I have good news and bad news." I was a pretty precocious six-year-old.

"What's the bad news?" my mother asked.

"I had sixteen cavities."

"What's the good news?"

"I didn't feel a thing."

The dentist had given me laughing gas, and I spent the whole time floating up near his ceiling and doing loop-de-loops in and around the dentist's chair, so there was no pain, and I *really* enjoyed it.

At age twelve I was an altar boy, and one of the benefits of the job was access to the wine that was supposed to be offered to Jesus. I noticed the friendliness of our three parish priests after they drank all His wine. The monsignor and one of the priests only took sips, but the second priest would drink the wine down to the bottom of the cup. I wanted to feel like the second priest. So, at the end of each mass, instead of pouring the wine out, I would drink it. I would drink all of it.

At age twenty I was carefree. I had been a high school pitcher and a star athlete with one hell of a fastball. I was six foot three, 200 pounds, and in American Legion ball I had almost thrown two perfect games in a row. It was all so easy. I just had to rear back and throw, and if the ball found the strike zone, the batter usually didn't stand a chance. I was clocked somewhere in the neighborhood of ninety-five miles an hour, but I had an easy motion, and batters told me it seemed the ball went much faster. When a pitcher throws a ninety-five-mile-an-hour fastball to the hitter, the hitter has to decide in 44/100ths of a second whether it's a ball or a strike, whether he should swing or "take" the pitch, or whether to hit the dirt.

At age twenty I drove to spring training in St. Petersburg, Florida, certain that I was going to make the big leagues. I had the same feeling of invincibility that I found from taking the laughing gas at the dentist and drinking the wine in church. As I drove my Oldsmobile Cutlass convertible down I-95 from wintry Connecticut to balmy Florida, I was just north of Jacksonville when the disc jockey on the radio said that he was about to play a song by the Rolling Stones called "Let's Spend the Night Together." He said, "It has been banned by the FCC." The Rolling Stones were in sympathy with the devil; the Vietnam War was raging; it was the winter of '67.

In 1967 I had every reason to be optimistic about my future. The year before I had pitched for Double-A Williamsport, and

I had a nine-win-and-two-loss record with a 1.97 earned run average. I had been named Pitcher of the Year in the Eastern League. I was promoted to Triple-A Jacksonville, and even though I hadn't pitched very well there, I was sure I'd make it to the majors.

I was cocky, though I never saw it as cockiness. I felt I was self-confident. Everyone else said I was cocky. I wondered why the Mets had bothered to send me to the minors at all. I had some trouble getting my breaking ball over, but in my mind I felt I had big-league talent and should have already started my professional career with the big boys.

I wasn't the only phenom on the Mets' roster. The Mets had a number of excellent young pitching prospects in the minor leagues, including Tom Seaver and Jerry Koosman. Scouts swore I was just as talented as they were, if not more so. In fact, in the Mets' 1967 yearbook, "Billy the Kid" Denehy got more press than the fair-haired Tom Seaver, the all-American college star from California who was certain to make the jump from Triple-A ball to the Mets.

I arrived at the spring training complex in St. Petersburg, Florida, in the afternoon, bounded into the clubhouse, and said hello to those coaches and players I already knew. The manager of the Mets was stone-faced Wes Westrum, a former New York Giants catcher. Wes had replaced the legendary Casey Stengel after Casey broke his hip falling off a barstool and got too old to manage.

I found my locker, and I was getting into my uniform when the Mets' general manager, Johnny Murphy, came by. I was stoked that Mr. Murphy, once a great Yankee pitcher, thought enough of me to pay me a visit. I took it as an omen.

"You arrived a half hour ago," he said, "and since you arrived everyone has been talking about you. You probably don't have a clue as to why." He was right.

"It's those fucking sideburns of yours," Murphy said. I was sporting mutton-chop sideburns. I had let them grow over the winter, and now they had reached almost to my jaw.

"If you want to be in uniform tomorrow," said Murphy, "you need to go directly to the shower room and cut them way back." I didn't have a problem with that.

When spring training began, Westrum let me know that I was only there for a look-see. He had set his rotation, and I wasn't in it, and so at first it didn't appear I'd pitch much, but fate has a way of rearranging things. Fat Jack Fisher was supposed to pitch a game against the Cincinnati Reds, but the morning before the game was to start, Jack got a phone call that his young daughter had been injured in a fall. When I arrived at the ballpark that day, Wes informed me I was going to start.

I didn't have a lot of time to think about it. I didn't even know most of the players on the Reds.

Who are these hitters? I wondered. I warmed up and went out to the mound.

I certainly knew the first batter, Pete Rose, who ended his career with 4,256 hits to break Ty Cobb's all-time record. Pete Rose didn't faze me. I threw Pete three straight fastballs for three straight strikes, and Charlie Hustle, as Rose was called back then, returned to the bench.

It seemed *so* easy. I stood on the mound, and would think I was Superman. To this day I can still imagine those fastballs I threw past Pete Rose. Strike one, strike two, strike three. Have a seat.

Holy shit! I thought to myself. *I just threw three fastballs past Pete Rose. Wow! This is easy.*

Before my three innings were over, I had struck out six of the nine Reds batters I faced, and we're talking about some great hitters: Tony Pérez, Vada Pinson, Lee May, Leo Cárdenas, Tommy Helms, and Pete Rose.

Westrum, who didn't talk much to his players, came up to me after the game and said, "That was impressive. Let's see if you can do it again." I gave up exactly one run in the twenty innings I pitched during spring training. I led all Mets pitchers in strikeouts and ERA, and that included all of the Mets starters and the rookies Seaver and Koosman.

There was a game against the Kansas City A's (before the Athletics moved to Oakland) in which Tom and I split the pitching duties. Tom pitched the first five innings. I pitched the final four. We held Kansas City to five hits and won the game 8–1.

When I read the papers the next day, Westrum was quoted by Dick Young, the influential but not easily impressed *New York Daily News* reporter, as saying that both Tom and I had made the team.

I kept the clipping. I have memorized it. Young compared our pitching styles and our strengths. Young commented that when the regular season started, either Tom or I could well be the fourth starter in the Mets' rotation behind Jack Fisher, Bob Shaw, and Don Cardwell. *Shit*, I thought to myself when I read that, *Tom and I have better stuff than any of those other guys.*

As I mentioned in the Introduction, as proof of how highly we were regarded, Topps, at that time the only baseball card company, issued a card with my mug and Tom's side by side. At the top of the card, which was number 581, it read: *1967 Rookie Stars.*

We were both supposed to have long and brilliant careers. Tom won 311 games over a twenty-year career. My brilliant career would last exactly two months. But for those two months, I was everything my hometown press clippings predicted I would be.

In my first start as a Met, I struck out eight Phillies to set a Mets record that stood until 2012. I had a blazing fastball and a wicked curve, but the Mets had a pathetic-hitting team, and I lost three close games. Then in May I took the mound against pitching great Juan Marichal and the San Francisco Giants. A teammate handed me a "black beauty" to give me an adrenaline boost. I had never had a "black beauty" before, but I took it because I trusted him.

With my body bursting with adrenaline, I pitched three shutout innings, and then in the fourth I threw a pitch that changed the entire course of my life. If I had known what was going to happen, I would have taken the pitch back. But life doesn't work that way. One day you're headed for greatness, and the next day you're falling into a deep chasm with no end in sight and nothing to break your fall. I threw Willie Mays a hard slider, and it felt like someone stuck a knife in my shoulder. My days of excellence were over pretty much before they began. I would hang on to my professional career for parts of four more sorry seasons, and in my final season in Detroit I assumed the reviled role of designated headhunter for Billy Martin.

As I said, Tom Seaver, the other guy on my rookie card, won 311 games with an ERA of 2.86, pitching himself into the Hall of Fame. I, on the other hand, finished my career with a one-and-ten record and a 4.70 ERA.

And yet, compared to Tom Seaver, my life was far more entertaining and interesting. Tom was a real good guy. Seaver, born with a silver spoon in his mouth, now has the complementary silver fork, silver knife, and Silver Cloud. He has triumphed in everything he has done.

Tom was the perfect addition to King Arthur's court; he was Sir Lancelot. I, on the other hand, was Robin Hood, a fun-loving, practical-joking scoundrel with unlimited potential and a deep-seated mean streak.

With my career over in my mid-twenties, I had to figure out how I would live the rest of my life, and that hasn't been easy. I suffer from the disease of addiction. I have a wicked temper, and I was born with a self-destructive streak, which would ensure that my life after baseball followed the arc of my baseball career, with promising beginnings followed by crushing disappointments and failures. In each attempt to do well, I would come tantalizingly close to a roaring success, only to find myself empty-handed. My hot temper and insistence on never settling for less than being the best would contribute greatly to those failures. I weep to look back on it. Many have no idea how hard it is for me to stand before the world and share any of this.

Then, five years ago, at age sixty, I began to lose my eyesight, and now, because of the steroids I took as a player, I am blind. I realize that throughout my whole life I never had a Plan B, which means a rewarding career *outside of baseball*. I've had to struggle to gain similar satisfaction and still make the good money I was accustomed to making in baseball.

I was a dreamer. And time after time I figured that if I could come up with some grandiose idea, some magical plan, I could provide my family with all the trappings of success for a person no longer in major league baseball. I felt driven and under tremendous pressure to succeed, in part because my ex-wife's mother thought I was a loser. I suffered great agony having never been able to prove her wrong. The more I pursued those dreams, the more I chased the illusion, the deeper I got into drug abuse, and the more I separated myself from my morals and my ability to be a good husband and father.

When my two daughters played softball, I did not coach them, preferring instead to stand behind the center field fence and smoke joints with a couple of the other parents. To this day, my younger daughter still holds some resentment toward me because I didn't teach her the sports that I excelled in when I was in high school.

In June of 1992 I flew to Connecticut on vacation and watched my daughters play high school softball, but I didn't play catch with them. I didn't participate in their warm-ups. I stood behind the center field fence, smoked my pot, and watched the games. The next day, I was leaving to fly back to Florida and took both girls to breakfast. I asked them whether there was something we didn't do this time that we could do the next time we got together.

Kristin said, "Not really." She always kept her real feelings inside. Heather said, "Yeah, play catch, Dad."

That was June 15, 1992, and on the plane back to Florida I vowed that I would never have another drink or drug. I have been in recovery since that day.

But before I talk about my recovery, let me share some of my history. The root of my anger and my trouble with women began with the nuns in Catholic school. These sex-starved sadists never should have been allowed around children. I thought they were a menace to society.

Forgive me, father, for I have sinned.

2

LESSONS OF YOUTH

EXCEPT FOR THE FACT THAT I WAS the victim of physical and verbal abuse in Catholic school, abuse that took me years to get over, I had a great childhood. I was raised by two loving parents and several adoring aunts and uncles.

But my greatest trauma, one that caused me to feel great shame and guilt, came when I was ten years old. Richie Barone was my best friend. We were in Little League together. We lived in Middletown, Connecticut, and one winter's evening I went to visit Richie at his house. After a delicious spaghetti dinner, Richie's dad asked him to go out on an errand.

We left Richie's house and headed into town. We had the choice of taking the long route around Pameacha Pond or taking a shortcut across the ice. My father had warned me never to walk across the ice during winter. The pond had heavy currents, and the ice wasn't always solid and safe.

Richie was stubborn, and he insisted he would take the shortcut across the ice.

I stayed on land and made my way home. Richie didn't return home that night. He fell through the ice and drowned.

A wake was held for Richie two days later. For the first time in my life I felt deep-down anxiety. I walked into the funeral parlor and was confronted by Richie's dad, who grabbed me and started shaking me.

"How could you let your best friend walk across the ice by himself?" he shouted.

"I'm sorry," I said. "I couldn't stop him."

The incident scarred me so deeply that I didn't attend a wake or funeral until I was out of high school. Years later, Richie's dad apologized to me, but I could never get it out of my mind that I could have done something to save Richie from his fate.

The death of Richie Barone haunted me for years. I would have conversations with him.

"Rich," I'd say to him, "I don't know if I'm going to go into the NBA or major league baseball, but you're coming with me. You may not be able to physically get there, but I'm going to get there, and spiritually I'm going to take you with me." I always had the thought that I was doing it for *us*, not just for me.

The highlight of my childhood was playing in Little League. In Middletown, Connecticut, when I was growing up, players were typically from ten to twelve years old. Ten-year-olds sat on the bench for most of the game. At age ten I would bug my coach, a man by the name of Roy Huffman.

"When can I pitch? When can I pitch?"

Finally a game was well out of hand, and Coach Huffman let me pitch. The batter stepped in, and my first toss hit the top of the backstop. I was nervous at first, but I settled down and got out of the inning. The following year I began pitching regularly. I had grown and put on weight, and no one threw as hard as I did. I was the best pitcher in the league, leading the Jaycees to the city championship.

In the championship game, the Jaycees played a team coached by a former high school coach by the name of Ed Collins. Ed's son, Pete, was one of my close friends. Every time we moved a runner into scoring position, we squeeze bunted, and were successful every time. After the game, Ed Collins complained that Coach Huffman "wasn't playing real baseball." It's what a lot of losing coaches say after they've been beaten by a squeeze bunt. We didn't care. We won.

Winning is the most controversial word used in youth sports. Are young players supposed to have fun playing the game, or are they there to win?

Go to any Little League game and ask the parents that question; you will automatically start an argument that may well break out into a fistfight. That's how strongly each side feels about the issue. The parents of the less talented players always opt for fun. The parents of the best players always opt for winning. My dad made it clear that the Denehys were there to win.

My dad and his brother used to reward me for winning. If I won, Uncle Amos would give me five bucks or my father would buy me a hamburger or a chocolate milk shake. Or maybe he'd say I didn't have to mow the lawn that week.

If we lost, the story was "Losers get nothing." The tone was soft, but what stuck in my adolescent brain was that winners were good and losers were *bad*. There was never a time, in any sport that I played, where playing fair and square was a consideration.

In one game I was playing catcher and a batter named Paul LaBello hit a home run to beat us. My first thought was that our pitcher fucked up, that though I had given him a target inside, he had thrown it right down the middle and had lost the game for us.

After the game ended I was so pissed off we had lost that I kicked a soda can down the middle of the road all the way home, holding up traffic. It was an early indicator of my proclivity toward rage, and while I was raging, I was out of my gourd. I had no idea what I was doing, no sense of how I was affecting anyone else around me.

Aunt Jody, who watched me kick the can right by her house, later said to me, "Bill, you have a terrible temper, and you ought to know better than that."

I didn't have the words to explain it, but I couldn't accept losing. Losing made me crazy.

When I put that uniform on, I was there to win. I was going to do anything I could to win, and if I didn't win, I was not a good sport about it. From a self-esteem viewpoint, winning was good and losing was horrible.

Nobody ever said to me that the joy of the competition was what was important. If I had to hit you in the head with the baseball to win the game, that was okay, so long as I won. If you got hit, you should have gotten out of the way. If you were standing at home plate, and I could either slide around you or run over you, I ran over you. It's the way I played the game.

If I had trouble controlling my temper, my time at St. Mary's Catholic School didn't improve my disposition. In fact, how I was abused by the nuns only made me more resentful and angry. I don't really know why I was even there but for the fact that my grandfather was one of the school's founders.

For disciplinary purposes, the nuns would put a dunce cap on you, make you stand in the corner, or beat you with a ruler.

They tried to humiliate you. A friend of mine told me about the Catholic school he went to. He said the nuns would make him kneel down on upside-down bottle caps and say the rosary. Today they would be arrested and thrown in jail. But back then, well, people tended to look the other way as long as the children received a good Catholic education. If you were punished, you probably deserved it.

When I was in the seventh grade I was given an IQ test. The nun-teacher presented me with a dozen pairs of words. For instance, one pair of words might be basketball and arena. Or another pair might be book and library. I had to read the twelve sets of words and memorize them, and the nuns would discuss another topic for five minutes. Finally, after five minutes, I was asked to recall the twelve sets of words from memory. I was tested three times. I couldn't remember one damn word.

The second part of the test consisted of listening to a three- or four-paragraph story about two people meeting, and after talking about something else for five minutes, the nun asked, "Where did they meet?" I'd think hard and have to say, "I don't remember."

The third part of the test consisted of a number of pictures—a family at a picnic, a mother holding up a sweater at a department store—and I'd be asked to study the pictures. That part I was able to do. But as for the other parts of the test, I wouldn't be able to answer correctly, and the nuns would always make fun of me.

I always got the feeling that I was somehow stupid. I felt shame and humiliation, because I couldn't keep up with the class. I internalized that shame. That feeling would remain with me throughout my life. If someone made the mistake of saying, or even implying, that I was stupid, that person would soon regret it.

I remember the nuns beating me and trying to make me cry. This was a Catholic thing. Christ suffered on the cross, and you had to suffer too. I grew up during a time when my father said, "Big boys don't cry." So whenever the nun hit me with a wooden ruler, I would grit my teeth, but I would never cry. I was determined to take the pain. You could whack me, but I wouldn't give them the satisfaction of crying.

After a beating the nun would say, "If you go home now and show off your swollen hand, your parents are going to want to know why, and once you tell them, they're going to beat you too." This was a secret I was forced to take home with me. As a result, I would keep my hands under the table during dinner. I will always remember the fear and guilt I felt. The anger I felt at being physically abused was great, and the thought formed in my mind that I wasn't about to take any shit from anybody.

One time I was class monitor and slugged a student after he refused to say the rosary. I was sent to Sister Superior's office. "You've been in trouble a lot," said Sister Superior. "Take down your pants, bend over the desk, and I'm going to give you a few whacks with the yardstick."

"No, you're not," I said, and I began to run around Sister Superior's long desk. I grabbed her lunch box sitting on the desk, and I fired it at her. My control wasn't very good, and the lunch box sailed through a window, shattering the glass.

The next thing I knew, I was sitting in the priest's office with my father. The priest told me he'd give me one more chance. I could stay at St. Mary's as long as there wasn't another incident. I told my father we should leave.

I left St. Mary's emotionally scarred, and it wasn't until years later that I understood the toll those beatings took on my psyche.

Later, when I went to public school, a group of kids who enjoyed fighting came after me.

I enjoyed fighting at first, but I wasn't very good at it, and I used to get the piss beaten out of me. I didn't have visible bruises and cuts; I could cover up my face. But one time my clothes got ripped. When my mother told my father about the ripped shirt, my father took me down to the YMCA the following weekend to meet Willie Pep, the boxing champion.

Willie was from Middletown, and my father knew him. He introduced me to the champ.

"Would you say a couple things to my son so he can defend himself a little better?" asked my dad. Willie said to me, "When it looks like you're going to get in a fight, the first thing I want you to do is grab the guy's ears and smash the top of your forehead into his nose as hard as you can. That will break his nose, and if it doesn't, his eyes will water, and he won't be able to see. And then kick him in the nuts as hard as you can, and after he goes down, just keep kicking him."

All the while, my father was saying, "Whoa, whoa, whoa," and finally he said, "Willie, can you teach him how to box?"

"I can get him into the ring and teach him how to box," said Pep. "*I'm trying to teach him how to survive.*"

It was a lesson that I would never forget. One afternoon I was taking my usual beating when I decided I wasn't going to take it any longer. I realized that I was just a pissed-off, angry, abused kid. And I decided that I wasn't going to be abused again. I picked up a tree limb, struck the first kid who came after me, and kept beating him and beating him until the kid was pleading for mercy. After that day, I didn't have to fight that kid again.

3

THE BUMPY ROAD
TO THE PROS

MY ADOLESCENCE WAS FURTHER FILLED WITH FRUSTRATION, resentment, and anger because my high school basketball coach was a prick who resented how good I was, and that I was a lot smarter about basketball than he was. I also felt a deep frustration in baseball because as a sophomore in high school I had trouble throwing strikes. Then, when I was a junior and my control improved, I was kicked off the baseball team when I deliberately hit a kid in the head with a pitch. For some reason, my coach wasn't too happy about it.

I could throw the heck out of a baseball, but my first love was basketball. As a sophomore I was six feet tall, a solid 180 pounds, and I could shoot and dribble the ball like Meadowlark Lemon.

My sophomore year I started on the Woodrow Wilson High School varsity team.

Before my first game, my father, who himself had been a basketball star, wanted to talk to me in private. He told my mom he wanted to take me to the game. Dad and I drove the five miles to the high school, and as I started to get out of the car, he grabbed me by the arm and said, "Son, I'm only going to give you one piece of advice: If somebody whacks you, whack him back harder."

I took his words to heart.

My junior year, against New Britain High School, one of the New Britain players stole the ball from me and drove in for a layup. On the next play a pass came to me close to the basket, and a New Britain player by the name of Dave Rybczyk slammed me into the padding three feet beyond the end of the court. I grabbed him, and we started swinging before cooler heads broke up the fight.

Another of my dad's sayings was "Don't get mad. Get even."

I did both.

I'll get even, I swore to myself at the time.

When baseball season came around I was on the mound facing New Britain, and in the first inning, who should come to bat but Dave Rybczyk. My first pitch was a fastball that hit him squarely in the head. Rybczyk went down. I had no remorse. My feeling was that since he had started the fight in basketball the previous season, he had it coming to him. It was part of my Catholic upbringing, because it says in the Bible, "An eye for an eye and a tooth for a tooth." I settled for a broken helmet and a concussion. I stood over him and shouted, "I told you I'd get you, you son of a bitch."

My baseball coach, Gene Pehota, was standing behind me, and he heard what I said, and he kicked me hard in the ass, removed me from the game, and kicked me off the baseball team.

A day or so later, my father and I asked Coach Pehota to let me back on the team.

"I can't have Bill doing this," he said to my dad. "As hard as he throws, he could kill somebody. We can't have him throwing at people. He's not going to play the rest of the season."

And so I, one of the best pitchers in Connecticut, had to sit out my junior year of high school. I had to wait for American Legion ball to start during the summer to play ball again.

I like to say I got my temper from my grandpa, James Denehy, a fine Irishman and an alcoholic. He was once the head of public works in Middletown. I never met Grandpa Jim, but his wife, Anne, once told me that when a new mayor was elected, Grandpa was fired. According to Aunt Anne, after getting canned, Grandpa walked a block to the Elks Club, proceeded to get snockered, then headed back to his office in City Hall, where all the maps containing the locations of the sewers and water pipes in Middletown were stacked. Grandpa collected them, put them on the concrete steps of City Hall, and set them ablaze in a public display of spite and malice.

"Unless you have copies of these," said the new mayor, "we're going to put you in jail."

Some copies did exist, but not all, and every so often there'd be a leak in a water pipe or a sewer, and no one would know what to do because there weren't any maps of it.

Addiction is in my genes. Like my grandfather, I wasn't afraid to pull the trigger. And like Grandpa, I didn't have any remorse.

I rejoined the Woodrow Wilson High School baseball team my senior year. I could bring it, and the rest of the team was a nose-to-the-grindstone bunch of overachievers, but we had no idea we would be state champions at the end of the season.

Getting thrown off the team for hitting Dave Rybczyk didn't curb my sadistic tendencies. The coaches didn't know that my teammates and I devised a sick, potentially deadly game. A number of our players bet a dollar for the chance to pull a number out of a hat. The center fielder was position number eight, and the player who picked the number eight out of the hat won the pot. My job was to drill the center fielder of the opposing team with the ball. For me, it wasn't much different from the dunk tank game you played at the state fair, only in this game I was hitting my target with the ball. We did it twice. Both boys I hit ended up with bad injuries, so we talked it over and decided to stop.

In one game against Southington High School, I retired the first eight batters; the ninth batter was the center fielder, and I nailed him in the arm but good. "What the hell was that for?" Coach Pehota wanted to know. He had no idea the kid writhing on the ground was the batter designated to get drilled.

Somebody once said, "You could kill someone." I said, "When I put that uniform on, I'm here to win the game." I was once asked by Don Lombardo, a close friend, "What would you do to win a game?" "Fuck the rules" was my answer.

I dominated my senior year. I pitched 151 innings and struck out 288 batters, only fourteen strikeouts shy of striking out two batters per inning. I finished the year with a seven-win-and-two-loss record, helping Woodrow Wilson High win the 1964 Connecticut High School State Baseball Championship. Then I had a perfect record of nine wins and no losses in American Legion ball for the Middletown, Connecticut team. None of this gave me much pleasure, though. I was a perfectionist and wasn't able to throw strikes as easily as I wanted.

I threw real, real hard, and I didn't let up; but I was wild. If anyone was going to see potential in me, it was from pure velocity.

In my first high school game, as a sophomore, I pitched against New Britain. I faced nine batters; seven walked and the other two batters got hit.

Against Middlefield that same year I faced five batters; two batters walked and the other three got hit. My coach came to the mound and asked my catcher, "What kind of fastball does he have?"

My catcher, Tom Serra, who would later become mayor of Middletown, replied, "I really don't know. Every one he's thrown has either hit the backstop or he's drilled someone with it."

Serra saw I was having trouble focusing. He told me, "I'm going to hold my glove over the middle of the plate. Just throw the ball to me, and we'll win."

And that's what I did. In the summer of my sophomore year, pitching in an American Legion game, I struck out nineteen batters and walked seventeen. That's a lot of batters where nobody hits the ball. It made for very boring—and frustrating—baseball.

My coaches and my catchers would tell me, "Just throw it over the plate. Just let them hit it," but I wasn't able to do that, and it was killing me. The culprit was bad mechanics, but either the coaches didn't know how to fix it or I was too stubborn to adapt. I didn't know what the word *mechanics* meant. I certainly never heard of it when I was in high school.

I threw straight overhand, and I pitched great on a high mound with a steep pitch, but too often when the mound wasn't high, I wasn't able to get on top of the ball and throw it over the plate. On a flat mound I was high and wild inside to a right-hander. Righty batters were taking their lives in their hands against me.

Still, I threw a mean fastball at over ninety miles an hour, and even though I didn't know it at the time, major league scouts were paying attention. They came to my games trying to be anonymous, but I learned to spot them because they'd huddle together in the stands with their clipboards and speed guns. The speed guns were kind of a giveaway.

One night in my junior year my father asked me, "What are you doing tomorrow night?"

I responded and he said, "We're going to the Yankee Silversmith," which was a fancy Middletown restaurant where the Wesleyan professors liked to eat. We only went to that restaurant on special occasions. I asked him why.

"Because the Boston Red Sox are taking us out to dinner."

The baseball scouts had been watching me since I was a sophomore. Bots Nekola and Charlie Wagner scouted me for the Boston Red Sox. Harry Hesse of the New York Yankees contacted me, as did Len Zanke of the New York Mets.

Bots, the Sox' top scout for New England, and Broadway Charlie Wagner, who had once been Ted Williams's roommate, were the Red Sox scouts who hosted me and my family. Eating at a fancy restaurant in the company of two major league scouts was a little overwhelming for me. One of the first things Charlie Wagner asked me was "Do you like shrimp cocktail?"

"If you're going to be a big leaguer," said Wagner, "you gotta have shrimp cocktail." And he ordered me one. Eating shrimp cocktail was one of the highlights of the visit.

Three-quarters of the way through my American Legion season junior year, Bots and Charlie invited me to a Boston Red Sox tryout camp for high school juniors and seniors.

I was scheduled to pitch a game one night, but I wasn't able to participate. Bots brought me out to the bullpen, and he told me, "Listen, I just want you to throw a little bit, not even hard, and I want to show you something."

Bots said he didn't think that I was getting the most of my ability by throwing straight overhand. He had me drop my arm angle down to three-quarters.

"Just throw across your body," he told me.

"Take a pitching rubber and look at the third base side, where you'd place your push-off leg," he said. "If you draw a line from where your toes are toward home plate, in order to throw across your body all you have to do is stand to the third base side of that line."

I was getting instruction from a former major league ballplayer, and I tried to do as he said. My pitching problems had nothing to do with my motion or my release point. What the change in angle did was to set up more of a rotation and a closing-the-door effect—as opposed to my previous up-and-down motion. Once I moved my left leg toward home plate and to the left of that line he showed me, it opened up my chest and hips. The result was that I could be more of a power pitcher. It may sound complicated, but what he told me was actually very simple.

"I think you'll have more movement on your fastball if you pitch this way," he said.

I returned home, and that night in my game against Cromwell American Legion, I pitched using the motion Bots showed me. Throwing three-quarters motion, rather than up and down, I found I could get the ball down, and I threw a lot more strikes than I ever did before. I threw a no-hitter against Cromwell, retiring the last twenty-one batters in a row.

I went back to the Red Sox camp the next day. Bots asked me, "How did you like that?"

"Pretty good," I said. That was an understatement. I had never pitched better in my life.

In my next start against East Hampton, I used the same motion. Thanks to Bots Nekola's advice, I was throwing nice and easy, and I retired the first twenty East Hampton batters in a row. With two outs in the top of the seventh, I was one strike away from throwing a perfect game. Coach Pehota called time and came out to the mound.

"A bunch of scouts are sitting here," he said, "and you haven't thrown a really good curveball all game long. You have two strikes on this guy. Snap off a really good curve and show them you have that pitch, too."

Pehota's intentions were good, but as I look back on it now, I wish he had stayed in the dugout. On the next pitch I snapped off a curve as instructed and hit the batter in the foot. There went my perfect game. But in those two games, using the motion suggested by Bots Nekola, I went from a guy with a wild fastball to a pitcher who retired forty-one consecutive batters.

I went from this hard-throwing, grunting, 120 percent-throwing fastball motion to this 75 percent, sidearm, easy-whipping motion. When I pitched those two no-hitters, it was like I was playing catch in the outfield before the game. I actually felt let down, because I wasn't getting the rush from having to exert myself, even though the results were better. It was almost like it was *too* easy.

Before the end of summer, the Red Sox brought me to Fenway Park, where I got to meet Carl Yastrzemski. Bots had signed him. Carl, who was in civilian clothes, took me up to Tom Yawkey's box and introduced me to Mr. Yawkey. Mr. Yawkey asked my parents to have lunch with him while Carl welcomed me to the Red Sox, and he showed me around the clubhouse and introduced me to the players.

"Bots is really high on you," said Yaz. "We'd like you to be part of the organization."

The Red Sox showed a lot of interest in me. With that interest, and my being Irish, I really should have signed with them. But I was strangely noncommittal, in part because my favorite team was the New York Yankees, and because my heart was actually set on becoming an NBA basketball star.

My secret goal was to be a shooting guard for the Boston Celtics. All I had to do was beat out Sam Jones. I had been so wild on the mound that baseball wasn't fun for me yet. I also thought, despite the attention of the Red Sox, that I couldn't really believe anyone would be interested in signing me as a pro baseball player.

As a guard on the Woodrow Wilson High School basketball team I was a brawny, six-foot-three 180-pounder. I was a magician with the ball who could dribble between my legs and behind my back, pass, and stuff the ball into the basket two-handed. I just loved the game of basketball.

When I was a junior in high school, we played a basketball game at the Waterbury Arena against powerful Wilby High School, which was among the top five schools in the state. We had no business getting within fifteen points of Wilby, but somehow at the end of regulation play, the score was tied.

In the overtime period, we scored first and quickly got the ball back. Wilby called time.

Our coach, Jim Sullivan, told us, "Stay with our offense," but when the team walked back onto the court, I called my teammates together and told them, "Listen, they're in a zone defense. We have the ball. Let's stay as far away from the zone as possible. Let's just hold the ball."

At the time, there was no shot clock in high school basketball. I thought that holding the ball was the smart way to go. The whistle blew, the ball was passed to me, and I just stood out on the perimeter, holding the basketball underneath my arm. I did this for three and a half minutes. I couldn't believe that Wilby was staying in their zone defense. I guess they figured we'd have to do something eventually.

With only thirty seconds left in the game, Wilby changed to a man-to-man, and at that point we went to our man-to-man offense. The ball was again passed to me; I made a layup, and was fouled. When I made the free throw, we led by five, and it was enough to seal what was an incredible, improbable victory. The joy I felt was unrestrained.

The upset of Wilby was a sterling victory, and I was fiercely proud of my role in it.

After the game ended, the thrill of victory lingered. The sportswriters went to talk to a smiling Coach Sullivan. Sullivan took the credit for our holding the ball; I couldn't believe it.

The storyline should have led with how senior guard Bill Denehy's brilliant strategy had won the game against Wilby, but instead Coach Sullivan hogged the glory. His lack of morality angered me so, and my joy was dimmed considerably.

As we were boarding the bus to go back to Middletown, I was one of the last players to get on. I was still aglow with the thrill of the upset when Coach Sullivan pulled me aside and said to me angrily, "Listen, I'm the coach. Don't you ever pull that shit again."

Didn't we just win the game? I thought to myself.

In my rage over what he said, I was also thinking something else: *My cleverness was what earned my team an improbable victory over a team we had no right to beat, and this lying son of a bitch refused to acknowledge my role in it.*

Coach Sullivan and I had never had much of a rapport, and we never would.

My senior year at Woodrow Wilson we had three players who were six foot three or taller, and we won the conference basketball championship. We should have won state, too. The ego and pigheadedness of our coach kept us from going all the way.

The first time we played rival Middletown High School, we won by twenty points. Middletown High was a much faster team. Before our second meeting I went to Coach Sullivan and said to him, "Listen, we're a big, bullish team. That's why when we play small teams, we kill them, because they can't run with us and they aren't as strong as we are. Middletown is a small team, and the next time we play them, instead of playing our usual offense, why don't we bully them?"

Coach Sullivan, once an excellent finesse player in his own right, wasn't comfortable playing rough, and he wasn't about to play the game that way. "I'm the coach," he told me. "I know you went to basketball camp for a couple of years and you think you know basketball, but I'm the coach, and we're going to play it the way I set it up."

I bit my lip and held my tongue. In the rematch against Middletown, we did it his way; they held the ball, and they beat us. Middletown went on to win the state championship, a championship that could have been ours, if not for Coach Sullivan.

A new conference MVP award was inaugurated that year, and after our loss to Middletown in the conference championship, they held a ceremony. The award was presented to Middletown High School's Bill Brown, who had eighteen rebounds and twenty points.

Before the announcement of the winner, players from both teams lined up on the court, and I was standing there stewing about the fact we had lost when I heard Brown's name announced as the MVP. I walked off the court in a blind rage and made a beeline for our locker room.

Spectators whispered that I had left because I hadn't won the award, but that wasn't it at all. I couldn't have cared less about the award. I walked off the court because I was so fucking pissed off that we had lost a game that we should have won. Jim Sullivan didn't do anything to help us win, we lost, and *that* pissed me off royally.

That week Sullivan called me and the other two captains of the Woodrow Wilson High basketball team into his office.

"We want to send a letter to Middletown wishing them luck in the tournament," he said.

To his face I told him, "They're our biggest rivals, and I didn't feel we played them to the best of our capabilities, and I refuse to sign it." He talked about sportsmanship. "It has nothing to do with sportsmanship," I said. "It has everything to do with winning." And I walked out.

My anger was so great that I also refused to go to the end-of-season party with my teammates. A couple of friends brought a case of beer. We walked into the woods and got drunk.

I told my two buddies how fucking pissed off I was that we had done nothing to change the offense. I told them exactly what we could have done to win the game. Yes, I had gone to Bob Pettit's basketball camp for two years and I had learned a lot. But was that any reason for Sullivan not to listen to me? I will never forgive Coach Sullivan for as long as I live.

I didn't play college basketball, despite my size and talent, because I wanted to go to St. Bonaventure University to play both basketball and baseball. But during my senior year, St. Bonaventure announced it was dropping baseball from its curriculum.

I had had dreams of playing college basketball, but after St. Bonaventure dropped baseball, I decided to concentrate on becoming a professional baseball player. Sounds silly, but that's how kids think sometimes. Baseball was starting to be fun, and after going from wild and inconsistent to domineering on the pitcher's mound, I wanted to see what the pros had to offer.

After the money offers to play baseball started to come in, I thought, *Why am I going to go to school? To get a job? I can start a job right now and start making some money.*

When baseball season rolled around my senior year, I approached the game with more maturity. For reasons I will never understand, I abandoned the easy three-quarter motion Bots Nekola had taught me. Maybe it was *too* easy. Maybe I felt I wasn't working hard enough. Maybe I was self-destructive. I can't honestly say why. But I returned to my overpowering overhand fastball, and my senior year I was a force to be reckoned with.

Woodrow Wilson needed to beat Middletown to get to the state finals. I pitched fourteen innings, striking out twenty-six batters in that game. On that day, in my mind, I asked myself who else was in my class as a pitcher. Christy Mathewson, Bob Feller, and Sandy Koufax came to mind.

In the Connecticut State Tournament we won our first two games, and then I threw a one-hitter against Northwest Regional High School, led by pitcher John Lamb, who would later play for the Pittsburgh Pirates, and we won the game 3–0. I could have had a no-hitter, but our shortstop fielded the ball and slipped as he made the throw.

That game was played on a Wednesday, and the final game of the tournament against Seymour High School was to be played on a Saturday. It didn't occur to me that I wasn't going to pitch, but our coach, Gene Pehota, announced that John Hudak would start the game.

Pehota explained to the local reporter, "Bill has a chance to play professional baseball, and he just pitched eleven innings, and we don't want him to hurt his arm."

Just about every player on the team and many of their parents went to Coach Pehota and told him his reasoning was bullshit.

"We're playing for the state championship," they told him. "You can't do that."

Nevertheless, Coach Pehota stuck to his guns. But it rained on game day, the game was postponed until the next Monday, and I was named the starter.

Seymour High was located somewhere in the Naugatuck Valley, about fifty miles away. We had never played them before. I only knew about one player they had, a fine outfielder and left-handed pitcher named Milt Cochrane. I struck out the first ten batters I faced. Once I did that, it was just a question of whether we were going to score. Seymour didn't have a chance. We walked away champions of all the Class B high schools in Connecticut.

After the game we drove the bus past rival Middletown High blasting the horn, and we kept blasting it all the way down Main Street. No one expected us to be in the championship game in the first place. My great disappointment is that, to this day, our team has never gotten the acclaim that the 1964 Middletown High School basketball team got when they won it all. There was no parade and no celebration. Our team isn't even in the Middletown Hall of Fame.

After my senior baseball season was over, I was asked to come to Springfield, Massachusetts, to work out with the Springfield Giants, the Double-A farm club of the San Francisco Giants. Carl Hubbell, one of the greatest left-handed pitchers of all time and the head of minor league development for the Giants, asked me to try out. In the 1934 All-Star Game, Hubbell had struck out in succession Babe Ruth, Lou Gehrig, Jimmie Foxx, Al Simmons, and Joe Cronin—five of the best hitters of their era. Ruth, Gehrig, and Foxx were three of the greatest hitters of all time.

My father called Hubbell and told him, "We're supposed to play Rockville. You can come and see Bill pitch on Sunday against a real team."

Hubbell agreed to come to the game.

On that day I had a live, crackling fastball. My adrenaline was flowing, and I struck out twenty-four of the twenty-seven batters I faced. Afterward, I wondered why I couldn't have that kind of stuff all the time. But that day I had it. I was throwing pitches to a left-handed batter on the outside part of the plate, waist high or cock high. I wasn't on the black.

I thought, *Here it comes. See if you can hit it. You can't fucking touch it.*

I don't know if I was hyped up because I knew Carl Hubbell was coming to see me or what, but I just had an exceptional fastball that day, and I had it throughout the entire game. I was throwing just as hard in the ninth inning as I was in the first.

I thought, *Take a deep breath, because here it comes, baby.*

After the game I was on a high, waiting to hear what Carl Hubbell had to say about my performance. I waited.

Carl Hubbell never showed up. I was crushed. I felt let down like the cast in the movie *Waiting for Guffman.* I later heard from another scout that Hubbell hadn't made it to the game that day because he was playing golf.

My success against Rockville wasn't a fluke. In a game against Niantic, the score was 0–0 for fifteen innings. We won on a squeeze bunt in the top of the fifteenth.

In the American Legion tournament, my Middletown team lost the opener and we had to start from the loser's bracket. I think we would have won if I had pitched the opener. We played Rockville in game two, and in that game I struck out fourteen of the eighteen batters I faced.

The next night John Hudak started for us against East Haven. He was pitching well when he was hit on the elbow with a pitch and had to come out of the game. I relieved John and struck out thirteen of the fifteen batters I faced. In eleven innings, I had struck out twenty-seven batters, which, to this day, is still the Connecticut state tournament American Legion record. Unfortunately, the legion tournament imposed an inning limit, and I was only allowed to pitch one more inning. We lost to Bristol, who went on to represent Connecticut in the New England tournament.

I was hoping to sign with the Yankees, and I had that opportunity. John DeNunzio, the baseball coach of Middletown High School, was a bird dog for the Yankees. If John found a prospect, and that prospect was signed by the Yankees, he got some money. John told the Yankees about me, and I was invited to come to Yankee Stadium for a look-see.

I visited Yankee Stadium with my dad, and it was a good bonding experience. I brought my spikes and gloves and wore a red undershirt, the color of our legion team. I was met at the press door and taken down into the Yankee clubhouse. The equipment guy asked me what size pants I wore, and I told him a thirty-six waist, and the only pants they had with a thirty-six-inch waist were Yogi Berra's. I wore Yogi's pants and a Yankee uniform top. I walked around the corner to the trainer's room and saw a Yankee player standing on top of the trainer's table. I could only see him from the waist down.

He has the most pathetic-looking legs I ever saw, I thought.

He was getting big rolls of elastic bandages wrapped around him. I was escorted back to the clubhouse, to dress in the ball boys' stall. Then I was told, "We made a mistake. You're not supposed to dress back here. We're going to move you."

They took me to the locker closest to the trainer's room in the Yankee clubhouse, which belonged to Mickey Mantle.

"You're going to get dressed here," I was told.

"Are you sure?" I asked.

"Yeah, Mickey wants you to dress here."

"Mickey?"

"Yeah, he's in the trainer's room. He saw you coming in."

That's when I realized the player standing on the trainer's table with the gimpy legs was Mickey Mantle.

I was dressing when Ralph Terry, who pitched for the Yankees, walked over to me and introduced himself. He said, "Listen, if you're going to dress here, you have to look like a Yankee. We don't have red undershirts on here. Put on one of mine." He gave me a navy-blue-and-white undershirt to wear.

I was then introduced to Bill Dickey and Whitey Ford, two legendary Yankees. Dickey was going to catch for me. Whitey, one of the greatest Yankee pitchers ever and the Yankee pitching coach for that year, was coming along for a look-see.

The three of us went out to warm up. Bill Dickey had caught for the Yankees for twenty years and was elected to the Hall of Fame, and here he was, catching me. I wondered whether Dickey would be able to catch me. I was eighteen years old. What did I know? And Dickey caught me like I was throwing butter. I was throwing real hard, but he had great hands, and caught everything so easily.

I threw my fastball from a windup, and then threw my fastball from the stretch. Whitey wanted to know whether I had any other pitches.

"Yeah, I have a slider," I said.

"Oh, he has a slider," Whitey said sarcastically. "The kid has a slider. Let me see it."

I threw it, and Whitey said, "Holy shit, you *do* have a slider." I had learned a slider through reading an instruction book written by pitching great Sal Maglie.

I threw a little more. I was concentrating, throwing strikes and hitting Bill Dickey's target, and without my noticing him, a batter had wandered toward the plate.

"Do you mind if I step in here?" he asked.

It was Mickey Mantle. Aw, fuck. I thought, *All I need to do is hit Mickey Mantle with a pitch, and I'm in serious trouble.*

As Mickey stood there, I threw a half dozen pitches. Mickey never said a word, and when I was done, I went back inside the clubhouse. My father was in the stands, and while I was throwing, an usher walked up to him and asked who I was. He must have been one of reporter Dick Young's stool pigeons, because the next day a story about my workout appeared in the *New York Daily News.*

"Congratulations," said Whitey. "It looks like you have a good arm. I hope you sign with the Yankees." I was waiting for a visit from someone from the Yankee front office, but no one said a word to me before I left.

Toward the end of my American Legion season, Len Zanke, a scout for the New York Mets, asked me to try out. I drove down from Middletown to Shea Stadium. I was having my tryout, warming up on a mound between the visiting dugout and home plate, while the visiting team, the San Francisco Giants, took batting practice.

Two Giants players, Willie Mays and Willie McCovey, took a particular interest in me. I wanted to say to them, "If you like what you see, you could have had me. I had one of the best games of my life, and your scout Carl Hubbell didn't bother to show up." But I didn't say it.

Every time the catcher would throw the ball back to me, I'd turn around and go back to the mound, and I could see Mays and McCovey moving from the batting cage, getting closer and closer.

After I was finished throwing, I went into the Mets clubhouse, and I got to meet Mets manager Casey Stengel, who talked so fast I couldn't understand most of what he said. He was chattering away, and I was nodding and thinking, *What the fuck is this guy saying?*

Casey was talking a mile a minute and shuffling his feet; he was funny and entertaining. I was only able to understand, "Listen, we don't have any super pitchers, so if you sign with us, you can get here within two years." I thought about my previous offers to play.

Several months earlier, the Chicago Cubs had offered to sign me for $75,000. Another prospect was involved. In short, he got the job and the money, and I didn't.

The Boston Red Sox had offered me $25,000, much lower than I expected. For some reason, I never felt a connection with the

Red Sox. If only Bots Nekola had followed through. My Aunt Jody, a die-hard Red Sox fan, was heartbroken. Until the day she died, Aunt Jody wanted me to be a Red Sox.

I turned down Boston because several of their starting players did not take the field for infield practice before a game against the Yankees. I was in the Red Sox clubhouse when it was time for the Sox to take infield practice. First baseman Dick Stuart, the worst-fielding first baseman I ever saw, should have taken infield practice every day, but that's not the kind of player he was. I had the impression that the Red Sox didn't care about winning. And since winning was an important part of my psyche, it was easy to cross the Red Sox off my list.

Harry Hesse, the head New England scout for the Yankees, came in with an even lower offer—$15,000—and he wouldn't go any higher.

Harry told me, "You're going to get a World Series check every year." Harry turned out to be *very* wrong about that. This was the fall of 1964, and the Yankees, having just been purchased by CBS, wouldn't see the World Series again until 1976.

The Mets offered me $22,500. Two days later I signed the deal. I had great expectations. The downside of having great expectations is that when they don't come to fruition, you're left feeling angry and disappointed.

My dad and I had agreed that if I signed with a team, any team, that team had to send me to the Instructional League. When my dad proposed that to Wid Matthews, the Mets' head of scouting, Wid tried to convince us that I would be in way over my head, and that they didn't want me to start my pro career on a negative note.

Matthews then asked Len Zanke, who was also in the room with us, "Can he pitch down there?"

"Absolutely," said Zanke.

My dad told Matthews, "We want Bill to be ready for the next full season. The instructional season will help him learn the tricks of the trade that might help him pitch better in pro ball. It's important to us that this is part of the offer."

I was the only player in winter ball with *zero* professional experience.

At the time I signed, I couldn't understand why my signing bonus wasn't higher. The Cubs were going to offer me $75,000 and that seemed about right.

Looking back now, my family and I made a mistake in dealing with the ball clubs. We thought if we used the threat of my going to college to play basketball against my signing a professional baseball contract, we could get more money. I told the baseball scouts all through the summer that I was considering going to college, and I suspect that some organizations questioned whether I was really serious about playing baseball.

It haunted me that my signing bonus was so low. *Why?* I kept asking myself. *I had a great summer, a great year. What reason could it be? I pitched two no-hitters my junior year in American Legion. It was a full year of great pitching.*

It isn't fair. I'm not appreciated. Coach Sullivan didn't appreciate me, and now the Mets weren't showing me much appreciation for my skills with their middling offer.

Despite my deep disappointment, I still had a world of confidence in my ability. I was eighteen years old and I was on my way to the big leagues. When I arrived at the Mets' Instructional League camp, I had a chip on my shoulder the size of a boulder. I asked myself, *Why couldn't I pitch tomorrow with the Mets?*

You motherfuckers, I thought to myself, *I'll show all of you.*

SUPERSTAR IN
THE MAKING

I WAS A STARRY-EYED EIGHTEEN-YEAR-OLD FLYING FROM Middletown, Connecticut, to St. Petersburg, Florida, for the two and a half months of Instructional League play in September of 1964. I had never been on an airplane before. I was a little anxious and didn't know what to expect. A couple of friends told me that when they flew from Hawaii to Vietnam, they imagined what was going to happen when they hit the ground. I figured that going to Instructional League had to be easier than going to Vietnam.

The purpose of the Instructional League was severalfold: A young pitcher on a major league roster might go down there to learn another pitch; a young major league hitter might go down there to learn to hit to the opposite field; and for top prospects in the minor leagues, it was a chance to get some excellent instruction and compete against high-caliber players.

Because my father insisted that the Instructional League be put in my contract, I would be the only player without a single inning of pro experience.

When I got there, I was surprised and shocked to see that there were several pitchers who could throw as hard as, if not harder, than I could. And they had more polish, because they had played some Single-A ball.

When I walked into the clubhouse, I was met by Eddie Stanky, the head of the minor leagues for the Mets. Eddie had been a star second baseman for the New York Giants under another shit-stirrer manager, Leo Durocher. Stanky took one look at me, and the first thing he said to me was "You're fat."

I had spent the summer eating hot fudge sundaes and drinking milk shakes, adding weight, because I was told that I should bulk up before going to camp. What no one told me was that the added weight should be made of muscle, not flab.

"First thing we have to do," Stanky said to me, "we have to get you in shape."

Stanky gave me a nylon shirt with a rubber inner lining, and he put me through an exhausting regimen of sprints and pickups. Day after day, Stanky, or another coach, made me field 100 balls in the Florida heat while wearing that goddamn rubber shirt. Slowly, but surely, my weight dropped from 220 pounds down to 180.

Stanky was a great, great instructor, but he was also a ballbuster. One time he took me to dinner. I thought, *Great, free food.* We got in his car and he drove us to downtown St. Pete, where we stopped at Morrison's Cafeteria.

I walked down an aisle of food past hundreds of different items, and as I pushed my tray along, I figured I'd order a couple of hamburgers, some ham, and a little potato salad, but then Stanky stopped me.

"I'm going to order for you," he said, and he ordered me a plain piece of chicken and a salad, and for dessert he said I could have a little cup of Jell-O or a little cup of fruit. That was my dinner with Eddie Stanky. And I hadn't yet pitched a game.

Where were the mashed potatoes? Where was my chocolate cake?

Eddie had been a firebrand, and in one of the first pieces of advice he gave me, he told me, "When you look at pitching, consider a loaf of bread. If you get the hitter out, then that loaf of bread goes to your family. If you don't get him out, the batter's family gets the loaf of bread."

Stanky also told me I would never become a major leaguer unless I learned to throw a batter a first-pitch breaking ball for a strike.

"And you have to learn how to pitch under pressure," he said.

I was warming up just before I was scheduled to start a game. Eddie walked up to me and said, "Okay, first pitch, curveball." He squatted down beside me. I threw a curve; it was way out of the strike zone.

Later in the season when I was playing in the minors for Single-A Auburn, Eddie visited, and he asked me, "Have you gotten any better throwing first-pitch breaking balls for strikes?"

"Yeah, I have," I said.

"Let's find out," Eddie said. "I'll give you a $300 sharkskin suit if you throw a first-pitch curveball for a strike."

The first batter stepped in. I threw a curveball. "Ball," said the umpire.

I didn't miss by much, and I didn't get my sharkskin suit.

The first game I pitched in my professional career was against the Washington Senators' Instructional League team in Plant

City, Florida. I struck out the first batter on a fastball eye-high—he wasn't a professional. I walked a couple of batters, but got out of the inning without giving up a run.

A couple of days later Johnny Murphy, the general manager of the Mets, invited me for a bullpen session. Murphy had been a star pitcher for the New York Yankees during the 1930s and 1940s, seven times leading the American League in wins by a relief pitcher. John had pitched in eight World Series, and he was meeting with me to tell me he didn't like my pitching motion because I fell off the mound after every pitch.

John taught me to drag my back foot as my pitching arm came forward. Dragging the back foot had been part of the Yankee way of pitching. By dragging the back foot a pitcher is forced to bend at the waist, compact his motion, and keep from falling off the mound.

John was wearing a sport jacket and tie and cordovan shoes as he showed me what to do. After I tried it once, Murphy wasn't satisfied. He grabbed my glove, motioned for the catcher to come halfway, and demonstrated the technique, dragging his expensive leather shoes through the dust.

After Murphy's pitching lesson, I returned to the dugout where my manager, Don Heffner, said to me, "It's obvious to me that Johnny Murphy really likes you."

"Why's that?" I asked.

"Because he just ruined a hundred-dollar pair of shoes to teach you that motion."

I was so green that I didn't know how to sign a baseball. I picked up a box of balls and signed them, but the next day I was called into Don Heffner's office.

Don said, "Let me explain something to you. If you look at a baseball, the place for the team's superstar or the manager to sign is where the seams come closest together. The other players sign somewhere else on the ball. You haven't even played a game yet. You might want to think about signing on the stitches."

"I didn't know," I mumbled.

Soon after Murphy's lesson, Jerry Kraft and I combined to throw a no-hitter against the Detroit Tigers' Instructional League team. I pitched five innings, Kraft pitched two. My performance focused even more attention on me.

My Instructional League experience was drama-free. I pitched pretty well that winter.

In one game against Minnesota, a hard-hitting team, I was batted around pretty good, but by the next time I faced them I had become more secure with my new motion of dragging my trailing foot as I delivered the ball home. Then, in a game a few days after Thanksgiving, the New York brass, including Johnny Murphy and Eddie Stanky, came down to watch their prospects. I pitched four innings of one-hit baseball against those same Twins, striking out seven batters.

I returned home to Middletown, Connecticut. I was inspired to stay in shape, so I worked out five days a week at the Wesleyan University indoor college facility. When February rolled around, I reported to Mets' spring training minor league facility in Homestead, Florida, just south of Miami. I worked out with the Williamsport team. The Mets were hoping I could start my career in Double-A.

Homestead wasn't a town for nineteen- and twenty-year-old baseball players. It's probably why the Mets picked it. It had an army base and not much else. Manager Solly Hemus, another hard-bitten old-timer, had no curfew. One night a number of my teammates and I decided to drive to Miami and have some fun at the Fontainebleau Hotel.

Tug McGraw, his brother Hank, Kevin Collins, Terry Christianson, and I had a good time drinking and dancing. On the way back, somewhere south of Miami at two o'clock in the morning, we saw a sign for The Marina.

"Hey, let's check this out," said Tug. Hank, our driver, headed for the wharf.

From the distance we could see a large, black shark, hanging from a hook. Tug had an idea. We walked to the dock. Tug asked the fishermen on the dock if they wanted the six-foot-long creature. One of the fishermen asked, "Unless you cut it up and eat it, what are you going to do with it?"

Tug, with a gleam in his eye, asked the fisherman if we could have the shark. We had all been drinking, so that probably had some effect on our decision making.

The five of us lugged the smelly, oily, ugly, scary, toothy, leathery, three-hundred-pound sea creature over to our car and put it into the trunk. The shark's head and tail hung out the back of the trunk, but it was so heavy that the shark was in no danger of falling out. We drove back to Homestead with the shark in tow.

We knew that Joe McDonald, the Mets' director of scouting for the minor leagues, liked to get up early in the morning and swim in the hotel pool. Joe was very pale—we called him the "White Ghost"—but we liked Joe well enough. Tug decided—with my encouragement—to invigorate him for his swim. Under the dark of night we placed the lifeguard stand into the deep end of the pool and stood it up with the armrest just below the water. Then we dumped the dead sea monster, with the big, jagged teeth, into the water and sat it on the armrest of the submerged lifeguard stand. Satisfied with our work, we went to bed.

At seven o'clock the next morning, my three roommates and I were awakened by blood-curdling shrieks of horror coming from the pool area. We leapt up, expecting to see a frightened Joe McDonald, only to learn that a church bus filled with senior citizens had beaten him to the pool. The church folk had jumped in, and when they looked up, they were confronted by "Jaws" staring them in the face.

"Oh, shit," we said to each other.

Sheepishly, we drove to training camp. We sat in the dugout, waiting for the other shoe to drop, when Joe McDonald confronted us.

"I have a pretty good idea who did this," he said. "I'll go a lot easier on you if you just admit to it."

The White Ghost called us the "Five Irish Mafia." He paced up and down until he stopped directly in front of me. He looked me up and down, kept on walking, then stopped and stared at Tug. He stopped in front Hank, in front of Kevin, and in front of Terry, and of course we were the five involved. We ran all afternoon as punishment.

One of the teams we played during Mets' spring training was the University of Miami. Ron Fraser, the longtime coach of Miami, kept calling the Mets, asking if they would play an exhibition team against his talented college kids. Finally, Joe gave in.

The Miami team traveled to Homestead, and the three pitchers who manager Whitey Herzog chose to throw against them were three of his best minor league prospects.

Before the game I was standing with Tom Seaver, who had played at the University of Southern California. Tom was interested in what kind of team the University of Miami was fielding, and was curious how they would fare against some of the hardest throwers they would see all season long. Tom had a boyish way of giggling and laughing, and he was saying to the Miami players, "Wait until you see our guys."

I got along really well with Tom. He didn't have a big ego. He was funny, very cerebral. He was a California guy, a college guy, and he was far more mature than I was.

I didn't hang out much with Tom because he was married to his college sweetheart, Nancy, and after games Tom went straight home. Nancy was sweet and charming.

Against Miami, Whitey pitched Dick Selma for the first three innings. I pitched the second three innings, and a skinny eighteen-year-old by the name of Nolan Ryan pitched innings seven, eight, and nine. Selma threw real hard, and then I came in, and when Nolan's turn came, he blew them all away. Nolie was a twig, but his wrists were as big as his waist. He threw 100 miles an hour; his fastball clocked at 100, his curveball clocked at 100, and his changeup clocked at 100.

Those Miami college kids couldn't hit Selma or me, but they had never seen anyone like Nolie. Those poor guys; I'm sure that after the game they went back to Miami asking themselves, "Is there any way we can play another sport?"

The Mets decided that I was still too raw to begin my career in Double-A, and rather than send me to Williamsport, they assigned me to Single-A Auburn, in upstate New York. Auburn played in the New York-Penn League. I hadn't been hit hard in the spring, but I didn't throw a lot of strikes either, and I had yet to master my new pitching mechanics.

When I arrived in Auburn, I focused on becoming a major league ballplayer. I made sure I got my rest, at least at first. I would get to bed early two days before I pitched. The night before, I might go out and have a drink or two with my buddies, but it was only a couple of drinks, and then I was off to bed.

All I wanted to be was a major league ballplayer. That was the expectation I had for myself. I had read all the articles about my potential, and I was determined to fulfill that promise. I knew I'd only get one shot, and I wanted to make the best of my opportunity.

In one of my early starts for Auburn, I pitched against the Wellsville Red Sox. When I warmed up, I had great stuff. My ball was tailing, my curve was sharp, and I was throwing strikes. I started the game with two strikeouts, but then I couldn't get anyone else out, and manager Clyde McCullough had to come to the mound to get me. I went into the clubhouse, had a beer, then another, then another, and by the time the game was over I was tipsy. After the game, McCullough called me into his office. Not only was I drunk, but I was feeling sorry for myself, down in the dumps, and despondent.

Clyde and I both were staying at the Auburn Hotel. Clyde was another old-timer. Twenty years earlier he was the scout who had brought Jackie Robinson to speak to Branch Rickey before Rickey signed Robinson to play for the Brooklyn Dodgers and break major league baseball's color barrier. Clyde had a world of experience, and he saw how uptight and nervous I had been, and he wanted me to relax and not be so grim about my job.

Clyde said to me, "I'm going to be in the lobby at five o'clock in the morning, and if you come in one minute before five, I'm going to fine you one month's salary. I don't care what you do, but it would be best if you went out and had a good time. Here are the keys to my car. See you later."

"Okay, Coach."

I spent most of the night drinking, and I came in as the sun was coming up. I spent much of the rest of the next day throwing up. I had my washboard abs from throwing up after drinking too much. That day was as painful as any day I ever spent. I drank some chicken noodle soup, but not much else.

I arrived at the ballpark, and Jimmy Callahan, our trainer, told me that Clyde wanted to see me. I walked into his office, and Clyde looked up from his desk, and he said, "You look terrible."

"Yeah," I said. "I wouldn't mind if you let me stay in the clubhouse during the game and sleep it off."

"I'd like to," Clyde said, "but you're pitching tonight."

I went out and pitched six innings, which was as far as I could go before keeling over. It was my first win in pro ball. Clyde's message to me was that I was too uptight. I was too focused on making it to the big leagues. I wanted to win *too* badly, and I needed to relax.

"I don't want you doing this before every start," he told me, "but every so often between starts you need to go out with the guys and have a few beers and relax."

Clyde was warm, sincere, and funny.

He told a story about how he had once played for the Chicago Cubs. It was opening day and he was out in the bullpen. It was so cold, he said, that he and a number of the Cub players carried glass flasks in their back pockets, and they'd take a nip every so often. He was called on to pinch-hit in the eighth inning. He went up to the plate and hit the ball off the ivy of the Wrigley Field outfield wall. He slid into second base, and he could feel something warm running down his leg. It was the whiskey. The flask broke into pieces during his slide.

"I spent the next two hours in the training room pulling shards of glass from my ass," he said.

I loved Clyde. He was as good a manager of first-year players as you could find in the game. He was easygoing and had an infectious smile, and yet he'd give you the rough-tough voice when he felt he needed to. He was a real players' manager.

I kept my nose clean during my year at Single-A Auburn, though I did find myself at the wrong end of a gun.

One night, Bob Johnson and I decided to drive from Auburn to Syracuse to have some fun. Bob was a starting pitcher with tremendous potential, but he was also a magnet for trouble. He had a long scar along the side of his face, and he told me that one time in Chicago he got caught up in a race riot. He also had had his front teeth knocked out.

He was a nice guy if he liked you, but if he didn't like you, watch out! For example, Bob developed a burning hatred for the scout who had signed him. The scout had given him $10,000 to sign, but then gave another pitching prospect, Dennis Musgraves, a bonus of $100,000. Bob, Musgraves, and the scout were together in the Instructional League one year, and Bob and the scout were watching Musgraves warm up.

"You gave that motherfucker $100,000 and only gave me $10,000!" Johnson said to the scout. "My changeup is faster than his fucking fastball. I ought to kill you," he said as he chased the terrified scout into the clubhouse.

We arrived in Syracuse and drove to a strip club where we began drinking zombies, which contained ten different types of liquor. If you could drink five zombies, the drinks were on the house. Clyde McCullough had shown me that I could get good and looped and still pitch, and so Bob and I both decided we'd accept the zombie challenge.

There was an acrobatic pole dancer performing, and she did things on that pole that I haven't seen again to this day. She could flip over and do things that are hard to describe. Bob and I were drinking pretty heavily, and he started talking to this pretty young stripper who was sitting at the bar, and before I knew it, Bob said to me, "This gal is going to go back to Auburn with us."

"How is she going to get back to Syracuse?" I wanted to know. Syracuse is a good twenty-five miles from Auburn.

"Who gives a fuck?" Bob said.

Bob and I, with the stripper close behind, headed for the parking lot. I started to open the car door when a man with a gun jumped out from behind a car.

"What are you doing with my wife?" he wanted to know. "What's going on?"

Bob and I were standing together, and the man pointed the gun first at Bob and then at me. Both of us had the same bright idea: When the gun was pointed at the other guy, we'd attack him. The gun was pointing at me when Bob made his move. Bob was catlike, and he punched the husband in the face before the man could pull the trigger, knocking him out cold. The woman ran off, and Bob and I jumped in my car and drove back to Auburn.

In the newspapers the next day it was reported that a man had been attacked by two men who broke the man's jaw, his collarbone, and his nose. But, in reality, it was only one man.

The Single-A Auburn team would travel from town to town by bus. The bus didn't have great air conditioning. Clyde would sit in the front of the bus, wearing a shirt and boxer shorts. On the trip from Auburn to Jamestown, the longest of the season, I walked to the front of the bus and said, "Skip, a couple of the guys and I have to take a piss."

"Good idea," Clyde said. "I have to take a piss too. I'll show you how to do it."

"You guys thought we were going to stop," he said in a loud voice. "We're not going to stop." He was laughing when he said it. Then he said, "We can't afford to stop the bus. We have to get to the game."

"So how do we do it?" I asked.

Clyde walked down the two steps leading to the door of the bus and had the driver crack the door open, and he peed out the opening as we traveled down the highway.

"That's how you do it," Clyde said. And when any of us had to pee, we did the same thing. I often wondered what the cars traveling behind us must have thought when streams of urine splashed across their windshields.

Under Clyde's supportive tutelage, I finished the year at Auburn with a thirteen-win-and nine-loss record. It was a great learning experience. I pitched in the rotation on a regular basis. Clyde let me pitch. I pitched well even in the losses, most of which were close games.

Against Jamestown I was pitching a perfect game going into the bottom of the sixth inning. The opposing pitcher was up, and I ran up a three-ball-and-no-strike count. Clyde called time and came to the mound.

Clyde said, "For God's sake, if you're going to lose the perfect game, don't walk the son of a bitch."

My first pitch after that was a strike, and my second pitch was a strike, and on the third pitch, the Jamestown pitcher hit a line drive back up the middle that struck me in the face. I was knocked out of the game, and for a couple of days my face was swollen. Oh yeah, I lost my perfect game.

Once I got the okay from the doctor to play again, my next challenge was to pitch without fear of getting hit by a batted ball. The first time back on the mound, I pitched and ducked, pitched and ducked, pitched and ducked, until Clyde came out to the mound to talk to me.

"You can't pitch that way," he said. "Throw naturally."

I hadn't realized what I was doing. Clyde got me through the game, and I had a terrific year.

5

GAINING EXPERIENCE

NOT LONG AFTER I RETURNED HOME FROM my first year at Auburn, I received my draft notice. The Vietnam War was raging, and I knew that if I was drafted my professional career would be over before it began. I preferred not to have to give up playing baseball. I called Johnny Murphy and asked him what to do.

"No problem," said Murphy. "Call the governor of Connecticut and let him know, and he'll take care of it."

When my dad came home, I told him about Murphy telling me to call the governor.

"That doesn't sound right," Dad said.

Instead, my dad called a local Irish Middletown politician who was the head of the Democratic Party. The man suggested that I come and see him.

The politician lived in a big mansion on High Street. He and I sat in a large sitting room.

"Just go down to the National Guard tomorrow and enlist, and you'll be all taken care of," he said. The next day I went down to the National Guard office and got in line. When I returned home, my dad asked me what had happened.

"They didn't take me," I said. "I'm number 252 on the waiting list, and if I'm number 252, I'm going to be drafted. There's something wrong."

"Let me call him again," said his father.

I returned to the politician's house.

"Did you speak to Captain Dzailo?" he asked.

"No."

"They must have forgotten to tell you," he said. "Go in tomorrow and talk to Captain Dzailo. He'll take care of you."

I returned to the National Guard recruiting office and asked to see Captain Dzailo, who said he was expecting me. I signed the papers, and the following day I found myself at Fort Dix, New Jersey, getting my hair cut for the National Guard.

The National Guard enlistment consisted of four months of boot camp at Fort Dix followed by six years of weekend service in New Jersey, rather than two years of trekking through the rice paddies while getting shot at in Vietnam.

Captain Dzailo had fixed me up, all right. I owe you, captain.

I was an excellent marksman with a .45-caliber pistol, and I was adept at hand-to-hand combat. In fact, of all the soldiers in my battalion, hundreds of men, I finished with the highest proficiency score. I had a 97.5 score out of 100 for my skill shooting a .45 caliber, an M-16, and a mortar; for fighting hand to hand; and for my proficiency in medical training. I had the highest score in the battalion. I'm damn proud of that. I still have the trophy.

We learned hand-to-hand combat, a skill I really loved. It was a perfect vehicle to unleash my aggression and pent-up anger. One of the soldiers I fought was Boston Red Sox outfielder Tony Conigliaro. Tony was cocky. He came at me with a rifle. I parried, stepped to the side, and hit him with my elbow right in the forehead, almost knocking him out.

Tony was pissed. Now it was my turn to go at him with a rifle, and I figured he was going to try to knock my block off. The sergeant had said to me, "When you thrust with a rifle, drop your head down so the steel helmet will be facing him."

Sure enough, I went after Tony C with my bayonet, and he parried me perfectly, and then he stepped to the side and gave me his best shot with his elbow—right into my steel helmet!

I was made platoon leader, and two of my squad leaders were Tony and Billy Rohr. Billy was a young kid who pitched for the Red Sox. They were great guys.

We had to go on bivouac. It was winter in New Jersey, and it was absolutely freezing. Tony came up with the bright idea that I needed to sneak into the officers' tent and steal some coal. Not that *he* had to sneak in—*I* had to sneak in. Tony said, "We could burn the coal in one of our steel helmets inside our little pup tent and stay warm."

I snuck inside the officer's tent, swiped ten pieces from a huge pile next to the stove, hid them in my jacket, stole some matches, and snuck back to our little tent.

Tony put the coal in his helmet and lit it, and we went to sleep. The next morning we awoke to find that the coal had burned a large hole in our tent.

"Okay, you wise guys," our superior officer said, "you're sleeping with a hole in your tent."

"This was your idea," I told Tony. "You're sleeping under the hole."

Two nights later it snowed. I woke up at six o'clock in the morning when the bugle blew, and I looked at Tony, and all I could see were his nostrils. The rest of his face was covered with snow.

One evening in January Tony and I were invited to leave our little pup tent, where we slept on the hard ground, and enter the warm tent of the superior officers. We were told, "The son of the general is having a Little League banquet, and the general wants to know if you two will come and speak."

"Of course we will," I said.

Tony wasn't quite so willing.

"Oh no," said Tony. "I'm not doing this for nothing."

"I think we should just go," I said.

"I'll tell you what," Tony said to the general's assistant. "If we can get a weekend pass, we'll do it."

I thought to myself, *They are going to throw us in the brig.* But they didn't.

Instead, they gave us weekend passes. Tony and I spoke at the Little League banquet at Fort Dix, New Jersey, and then spent the weekend in New York City.

Tony, an idea man, was always looking for ways to escape the freezing bivouac.

"If we join the boxing team," Tony said, "we could get off bivouac for a couple of days. Let's join the boxing team."

"I don't want to join the fucking boxing team," I said.

"We'll join the boxing team, and we'll fight each other, and we'll just play patty-cake," Tony said. I was stupid enough to agree.

The boxing program was in the evening. We had to box three three-minute rounds. I was a heavyweight. Tony was a light heavyweight. As soon as we put on the trunks and the boxing gloves for the first time, they split us up.

The boxer I was scheduled to fight came from Europe. He was about five foot ten, 225 pounds, and he looked out of shape. I had seen him around the PX before. He didn't seem very imposing. I figured that for three rounds I'd shuffle around and jab him.

My opponent turned out to be the heavyweight champion of the army.

I covered up the best I could.

I didn't realize until afterward that when I covered up my face, he hit on my biceps hard, and pretty soon I couldn't hold my arms up to protect my face. So by the end of each round he was just beating the shit out of my face. Oh God. My face was like a piece of hamburger.

After the second round I told Tony, "If I make it through this fight, I'm going to kill you." That fucker hit me more times than I could count. I had dozens of bumps and bruises on my arms where he kept pounding them. He hit me on my side and he hit me on the side of my head, and after he was done with me I had cauliflower ears the size of the largest piece of cabbage you've ever seen in your life. For three rounds he battered the living shit out of me.

I kept thinking, *Ring the bell. Oh*, please *ring the bell.*

And that was the last time I listened to one of Tony's crazy schemes.

My company commander was an American Indian with a chip on his shoulder. He hadn't gone through West Point, but had come up through the school of hard knocks. He wanted to prove he was tough.

Our company went on bivouac again. On the last day, everyone got up at six o'clock in the morning. At eight o'clock in the morning, trucks arrived to take the men back to their barracks. But our company commander had other ideas.

"My company will run home," he said.

The barracks were twenty miles away. He told me, "You're in charge, and I expect *everyone* to make it."

We were a National Guard unit. We had lots of snotty-nosed lawyers. These weren't the type of guys you wanted to bivouac with, never mind go to war with. Halfway home, several of the men informed me that they wouldn't be able to go the distance.

"We have to make it," I told them.

"I can't walk," one guy whined.

"If I have to beat the living shit out of you, or have another guy drag you along, you're going to make it," I told him.

"Yeah, let's see you make me," one of the other men said to me.

That really pissed me off, and I hit him alongside his head with the butt of my rifle. The man rolled down a small embankment, and I faced the rest of the men and snarled, "Next."

The man had a concussion, and two other men helped him make it the rest of the way home. One of his buddies carried his gun. Another carried his equipment.

We started at nine o'clock in the morning and arrived at our barracks at six o'clock at night. It was brutal, but we got everyone back. We covered roughly twenty-five miles in nine hours.

My four months of National Guard training ended just in time for me to go to spring training. In fact, I had exactly one day to report for the first day of spring training at the New York Mets' camp in St. Petersburg.

By 1966 the Mets had shed their most notable flakes and characters, including Choo Choo Coleman and Marv Throneberry. But that year they did feature first baseman Dick Stuart, a power hitter who played first base as poorly as, or even worse than, Throneberry had. Stuart's nickname was Dr. Strangeglove, and the irony was that Stuart's lousy attitude had been the reason I hadn't signed with the Red Sox, and here he was playing with us.

We had a weigh-in, and I was waiting in line behind Dick. We had to strip down and get on the scale, and when trainer Gus Mauch saw how much Stuart weighed, he slapped him on the rump and said, "Holy shit, look at the size of that ass."

Stuart stepped down and said, "Gus, it may be big, but wait until you see this ass tie into a fastball."

In one of the intersquad games, a pop-up was hit down the first base line, and Dick circled under it like only he could. He put his glove up, but caught the ball in his bare hand. You talk about a guy who was made for the role of designated hitter—the rule adopted by the American League in 1973 that let one batter in the lineup do nothing but bat.

Unfortunately for Stuart, the DH wouldn't be instituted for another six years.

On opening day of spring training, the Mets faced Bob Gibson and the St. Louis Cardinals. The Mets scored five runs off Gibson in the three innings he pitched.

I was sitting on the bench next to outfielder Al Luplow during the game.

"I hope I'm not speaking out of turn," I said to Al, "but Gibson doesn't look too impressive to me." I didn't realize it, but the veteran Gibson was working on a particular aspect of his mechanics and wasn't caring too much about the results.

Luplow, also a veteran, put his hand on my shoulder and said, "I don't know how long you're going to be here, kid, but if you stay here long enough and you catch him at the end of spring training, you'll see quite a difference."

Three weeks later, on a Friday night, when the Mets faced Gibson again, he gave up one hit and struck out twelve in seven innings. *What happened in three weeks?* I thought. *Jeepers. Wow!*

Toward the end of spring training, the Mets sent me down to Double-A Williamsport, Pennsylvania, managed by former Pittsburgh Pirates outfielder Bill Virdon. After the Mets released Wes Westrum, they should have picked Bill to be Westrum's replacement. In Bill, they would have had a terrific manager. Bill was a strict disciplinarian and he worked players very hard. He was no-nonsense. He was a guy you could talk to—he wasn't aloof—but you had to befriend him. He wasn't a players' manager in the sense of him befriending you. You had to go seek him out.

Bill worked the pitchers hard. I'd start on the right field line, run out to center field with the baseball, and throw it to him; then I'd run to left-center field and he'd toss it back. If I loafed, he'd throw the ball way over my head and I had to run as hard as I could to catch it. With Bill, there was no jogging. One time Bill sharply criticized me, and I commented that he should ease up on me because I had been pitching so well.

"My job," Bill replied, "is to get every ounce of potential out of you, and that's what I intend to do. It's nothing personal, Bill. You seem to react better when someone's on your ass than when someone is more lenient. Unless things change, this is the way I'm going to treat you."

After four months in the Army Reserve, I reported to Williamsport in the best shape of my life. My weight was down to 185, and I was in top shape. I had my stuff, and I had the pleasure of throwing to catcher Lloyd Flodin, who was great at handling pitchers.

Lloyd had great hands; he caught everything, and we had great communication.

During one game Lloyd wanted me to throw a sidearm curveball. We didn't have a signal for it, so Lloyd dropped his fingers down to the dirt, and in the dirt he made a half circle that started at the side of the plate and curved back toward the middle of the plate. He nodded at me, and I instinctively knew what he wanted. I threw a sidearm curve for strike three. Lloyd laughed for most of the rest of the inning when the two of us returned to the dugout.

"That has to be a baseball first with that signal," Flodin said to me. "I'm dumb enough not to run out to the mound to talk to you about it. I'm drawing the sign in the dirt, you pick it up, and you throw a strike!"

Lloyd was terrific. Unfortunately, Lloyd couldn't hit, and he never made it to the majors.

At Williamsport I had a solid infield behind me. Terry Christianson, a pitcher at Auburn, was moved to first base, where he did a nice job. Ken Boswell, who would soon move up to the Mets, was at second. Kevin Collins, another future Met, was at shortstop, and bonus boy Jim Lampe played third. Lampe was an outstanding fielder and a solid hitter, but he had one serious shortcoming that kept him from reaching the majors: He couldn't catch a pop-up fly ball during night games. Jim wore really thick glasses, and at night, every time a pop fly would go up in the air, he'd yell, "I can't see it. I can't see it." I don't know how they signed that kid. They must have just scouted him during the day. If the shortstop couldn't run over and make the play, the ball would just hit the ground.

One of my finest performances came against the Elmira Pioneers, managed by Cal Ripken, Sr. I was warming up before the game, and Bob Johnson, who had moved up with me from Class A, was watching me throw.

"Are you really going out to the mound with that shit?" Bob wanted to know. "Jesus Christ, we're going to have to take the married men off the infield. I can catch that fastball with my bare hands. We're in trouble here."

But there's a difference between warming up and pitching in the game. Bob was taunting me about my fastball as I warmed up, but once I got out there, I struck out sixteen batters. The only hit I gave up was to Felix Delgado, the Elmira pitcher, a swinging bunt down the third base line that we let roll, and it ended up sitting on the foul line.

I may not have been throwing very well in warm-ups, but once I got into the first inning, man, my juices just kicked in, and that was the best game I pitched in the Eastern League that year.

My most memorable weekend during my season with Williamsport came after I met a stunning stewardess on one of the team's flights. She had been Miss Alabama, she was living in New York City, and I couldn't believe it when I asked her for her phone number and she gave it to me. She warned me, though, not to come over without calling first.

After I called her to see if she'd be around, I decided to go to New York to see her.

After a Sunday afternoon game at Williamsport, five teammates—Hank McGraw, Kevin Collins, Lloyd Flodin,

Jay Cardin, and yours truly—flew to the Big Apple. The plan was to fly back to Williamsport early in the morning the next day, just in time to catch the team bus going to Elmira.

The five of us arrived and checked into a hotel. I then took a cab to the girl's apartment without calling first. When I knocked on her door, she was taken aback, to say the least. It was like what happened to George Clooney in the movie *Up in the Air.*

"What's going on?" I asked her.

"A guy I've been dating just called," she said, "and he's coming over, and I don't think you should be here when he comes."

"I don't mind meeting him," I said naïvely. "What's he going to do, beat the shit out of me?"

Then I said, "What's his name?"

"Tucker Frederickson," she said.

At the time, Fredrickson was the starting halfback on the New York Giants football team. The girl had gone to Auburn, as had Frederickson, and they were going out.

"I guess I probably won't want to meet him," I said.

She apologized sweetly, and I closed the door behind me. I walked to the elevator just as it was opening. Tucker Frederickson, all 240 pounds of him, exited it.

"Hey, Tucker, my name is Bill Denehy," I said. "I'm in the Mets organization. I want to tell you, I'm a big fan."

We shook hands, and then I slid into the elevator as fast as I could.

"Down, please."

I returned to our hotel, dateless, and a couple of my teammates and I went barhopping. The next morning we flew back to Williamsport, but because the plane was late, we found ourselves driving up to the clubhouse just as the other players were getting on the bus. We had to go into the clubhouse to get our game gear and throw it on the bus, but Virdon had decreed that the bus was to leave at 4:30 p.m. While we were gathering our gear, we could hear the roar of the bus engine, and to our dismay, when we looked out the window we could see that the bus was leaving without us. We ran outside, waving to the driver, but all we could do was watch as the bus drove out of sight.

Somebody suggested that we drive to Elmira, which was an hour and a half away.

We arrived in Elmira only to discover that the game had been rained out. It had been called even before the players dressed. The five of us then jumped back into our car and drove to the clubhouse in Williamsport, waiting for the bus to arrive with the rest of the players.

After the bus arrived and the players were putting their gear back in their lockers, Virdon told the five of us he wanted to see us.

"First of all," Virdon said, "I'm fining the five of you $200 each for missing curfew on Sunday night."

"What do you mean, missing curfew?" we asked.

"How did you make curfew if you guys were in New York?" asked Virdon.

Someone told him, I thought.

Virdon continued, "I'm fining you $200 for missing the bus on the way up to Elmira, and I'm also fining you $200 for missing the bus on the way back from Elmira, because you didn't ask permission for all you guys to drive back."

That was $600 each player—almost a month's salary.

We weren't happy about it, but Bill had a way of being so nonchalant about saying "We're taking $200" that all we could say was "Okay."

He took it out of our checks over a period of time. With all those fines, at the end of the season we had the best team steak dinner you can imagine. I was able to attend the Williamsport team dinner at the end of the season, because even though I had been promoted to Triple-A Jacksonville in July, my stay there would be cut short and I would be sent back to Williamsport a month later. I will explain *that* story a little later. So after the season in Williamsport I was looking to move up, and the Mets agreed.

After I compiled a seven-win-and-two-loss record at Williamsport, the Mets hierarchy decided to see how well I could pitch at the next level, Jacksonville, Class AAA, just one stop below the big leagues. Among those playing for Jacksonville were highly rated prospects including pitcher Tom Seaver, second baseman Ken Boswell, and first baseman Ronnie Allen, Philadelphia Phillies slugger Richie Allen's younger brother. There were also over-the-hill players like pitchers Craig Anderson and Larry Bearnarth, a St. John's University product who had spent time in the big leagues. They had been sent down to the minors, but they still had dreams of getting back to the majors.

Another of my Jacksonville teammates was starting pitcher Tug McGraw. I thought the world of Tug. He was just a real good friend.

In one game in which Tug was called upon to pitch in relief, he walked to the mound and began throwing his warm-up pitches. The hitter stood near home plate while Tug was warming up, trying to time Tug's pitches. From the stretch position, Tug wound up and threw the ball as hard as he could *at the guy*—and he just nailed him. The benches cleared. We were stunned. I had never seen a pitcher drill a batter in the on-deck circle before.

I was invited to move into an apartment with Tug, Kenny Boswell, and pitcher Floyd Weaver. Tug's bed was in the walk-in closet. He hung his clothes in there, and that was his room.

Tug and I were close, but few knew just *how* close. We were both having an intimate relationship with the same girl. Tug would entertain her during the day, and I'd bed her at night after the ballgame. Both of us knew about it and didn't mind.

She was a pretty girl. She was only about seventeen at the time; we were nineteen- and twenty-year-olds. I'd come back from the ballpark, she'd come out from Tug's "closet," she and I would go out someplace, and then we'd go back to my room. It was weird and odd, but funny and so much fun at the same time. You would think one of us would get pissed off, but we were *very* happy with the arrangement. The next year, after both of us made the Mets, the girl showed up in spring training in St. Petersburg. I don't know whether Tug brought her in or she came to see him.

Tug was a so-so starter at Williamsport and Jacksonville, and it was only later that he shone as a reliever. Pitching in relief, he could use a lot of that pent-up energy he had and pitch on a daily basis, rather than once every five days. The switch to reliever fit his profile perfectly.

Tug was a lot of fun to be around. He was a lot of laughs. My rookie year with the Mets we went on a road trip to San Francisco. We got to the hotel, and Tug had balloons, which he filled with water. He opened a window, and we bombed people who were walking along the sidewalk below with water balloons.

Tug's brother Hank was the complete opposite of Tug. Unless you knew they were brothers, you wouldn't think they came from the same mother. Hank wore sandals when the rest of us wore shoes. Hank had long hair, longer than the Mets liked, and reported to spring training wearing a small earring. They ordered him to remove the earring, which he did, but after games he'd put it back on, and they held that against him.

Hank was a good outfielder and catcher, but he never hit well enough to stay in the big leagues.

My manager at Jacksonville was Solly Hemus, a former big league infielder for the St. Louis Cardinals. The hard-bitten Solly was from the old school.

He had one rule: Don't leave the clubhouse until all the beer is drunk.

Solly believed that you needed to sit down after every game and talk about baseball with the older players, and they would tell you about life in the big leagues. I hadn't been a heavy drinker, and so I would only have four beers before departing the clubhouse.

After a game in Richmond that we lost, somebody—I want to blame Larry Bearnarth—decided we all needed to go to a whorehouse. About ten of us jumped into a couple of cabs and went to an old stucco house that had five or six rooms that were converted into bedrooms.

When we got in the waiting cabs to leave, we could hear sirens. As we were going up the street, the cops were coming down the street in the opposite direction. All of a sudden four cop cars slammed on their brakes in front of that house, and the cops jumped out and rushed the place. It was being raided! We kept on going.

One reason I didn't pitch very well at Jacksonville was that I suffered a hamstring injury not long after I got there. The ground in Jacksonville was sandier and looser than a normal field. During a game, I threw a pitch, slipped, did a split when I threw the ball, and pulled something in my back leg. It wasn't enough to keep me from pitching—back then you pitched with injuries—but it affected me, because the injury was to my right leg, my push-off leg.

My record at Jacksonville was zero wins and four losses. Part of the problem was that my catcher, Greg Goosen, and I weren't simpatico. Greg was awful to throw to, and because of that I didn't enjoy pitching in Jacksonville. It's funny because Jason

Varitek of the Red Sox got so much acclaim, but if you watched him, he moved around a lot behind the plate. If he had been my catcher, I would have put stakes in his feet. He had way too much movement, bouncing from the outside corner and standing up. How was I supposed to set up for a target like that?

Goose was like Varitek, except that Goose couldn't catch the ball. At least Varitek could catch the ball and frame it. And he could throw. Goose couldn't catch and he couldn't throw. He had a good arm, but was big and slow. Goose could hit Sandy Koufax's fastball, but he was limited in his catching ability.

Someone might ask how Tom Seaver won twelve games that year pitching to Greg behind the plate. A whole staff can pitch to a catcher, and one of the pitchers won't want to pitch to him. It happens. Today pitchers demand a different catcher. I wasn't like that. I never asked to pitch to someone else, but I had a tough time pitching to Goose. I had him the whole year at Auburn, that was bad enough, but to have him in Triple-A *too*? I must've pissed somebody off.

Because he didn't throw well, Goose would call a lot of fastballs to give him a better shot at throwing out a runner. I had a good curve and a good slider, but Goose didn't mix them in enough for me to utilize my fastball in a way that I could get the best results.

But that wasn't the reason I only lasted one month at Jacksonville. I made a strategic error. One night Tug and I went to a party along with quite a few of our teammates, and at the party we met this really pretty young girl. One thing led to another, and she came home with me. We were in my bedroom, when all of a sudden there was a banging on the front door of my apartment. I heard, "Get your clothes on and get out here immediately." It was her dad—Jacksonville general manager Danny Melendez!

We got dressed; he grabbed her by the hand and started walking out. He turned around, looked at me, and said, "I'll see you in my office at nine o'clock tomorrow morning."

I arrived at nine o'clock as ordered, and Melendez said but one sentence to me.

"Here's your plane ticket back to Williamsport."

It wasn't the end of the world. I was actually relieved. I didn't enjoy playing at Jacksonville. Goose was awful to throw to. Williamsport still had my old catcher, Lloyd Flodin. My first game back in Williamsport, I pitched nine innings and had a complete game. It was as though I never left. I pitched one more game, and I won that one too. I finished my season at Williamsport with a nine-win-and-two-loss record. My ERA was 1.97. As far as I was concerned, 1967 would be the year I would start for the New York Mets.

6

THE BIG TIME

AFTER THE 1966 SEASON I JOINED THE New York
Mets' Instructional League team for the second time, and
this time I no longer was a rube. My manager was Whitey
Herzog, who would later become one of the greatest big league
managers ever. Unfortunately for the Mets, Whitey would go
on to manage the St. Louis Cardinals. I was partly, if indirectly,
responsible for that trade.

I pitched well. I was outstanding, really. I started a game against
the Boston Red Sox in Sarasota, a game attended by the Mets'
top brass. I was winning a shutout in the bottom of the ninth
inning with a runner on third base. A batter hit a ground ball
toward the first baseman. Pitchers are trained to cover first base
on all batted balls hit to the right side. I had a brain fart and

failed to cover first, and the batter beat the first baseman to the bag, allowing the tying run to score.

I don't recall who won the game, but I certainly remember that after the players got on the bus for the return trip to St. Petersburg, manager Whitey Herzog stood up and announced that he wanted the entire infield, including me, to report to the park at ten o'clock the next morning.

Monday was a day off, but Whitey wanted us to practice fielding balls hit toward first base. So for forty-five minutes he hit balls to the first baseman, and my job was to cover first base. Then he hit grounders to the second baseman, where the first baseman would range far to his right, and my job was to cover first base. Then he hit balls to the first baseman, who threw to the shortstop at second, and my job was to run over to first to take the relay throw. Then we had bunts down the third base line where my job was to field bunts. Whitey finished the practice with another ten hits to the first baseman, where my job was to cover first base.

I can tell you right now, if I'm listening to a game on TV or radio and the play-by-play announcer says the ball is hit to the right side, if I'm in a lounge chair, one foot is heading toward first base.

During my two months in the 1966 Instructional League, I was rooming with Bob Johnson, my tough-guy buddy who played ball with me at Auburn and Williamsport. Bob and I always got along. We were in St. Petersburg, staying at a motel just north of Al Lang Field. We practiced at Huggins-Stengel Field, about two miles north of our motel. Neither one of us had a car, which was no big deal. To stay in shape, we decided to buy a couple of bicycles. We biked to and from the ballpark every day.

One Friday night Bob came up with a clever idea. He said, "Let's see if we can go downtown, pick up a couple of gals, and bring them back to the room on our bikes."

I had never done that before. That sounded interesting. We got as far as getting two girls to go outside the bar and walk over to where they thought our car was going to be.

We said, "You're going to sit on the handlebars, and we're going to pedal you home." That's as far as our clever idea got. They didn't trust a couple of drunken ballplayers taking them back to our motel on bicycles. What were we thinking?!

We pedaled back to the motel. We arrived a little past our 1:00 a.m. curfew, and when we got there, we could see Whitey Herzog checking rooms. *Oh shit, how do we get to our room?*

The motel had two wings of rooms, and Whitey was checking rooms on the far wing; our room was on the near wing. We were hoping he'd go around the corner so we could rush up the stairs, run into our room, and get by him without being seen.

We went up the steps, and we could see Whitey going around the corner, and that was our chance. Bob went first. After Bob reached our room, I could see Whitey turn and head in my direction. I was behind Bob but hadn't reached the room yet. I was hoping I could hide until Whitey walked by, but where was I going to hide?

I jumped in a big linen basket and pulled the sheets over me. I tried to stay as quiet as possible. I could hear Herzog walk past, then it got quiet, and then I could hear him walking back. He was just outside the corridor. But somehow he knew. His footsteps got closer, and I could hear him stop in front of the linen basket. He pulled away the sheets, and there I was.

"What are you doing?" Whitey asked me.

I didn't know what to say.

"Don't you think you should sleep in your room instead of sleeping out here?"

"That's a good idea," I said.

"Get the hell out of there and get in your room. In fact, I will walk you back to the room."

Whitey walked me back, and when I opened the door to our room, there was Bob Johnson in bed with the sheets up to his neck. He blinked his eyes.

"What's going on?" Bob asked.

"Mr. Denehy, I will see you tomorrow morning at 9:00 a.m. at the ballpark," Whitey said.

Herzog walked away, and Bob said, "Do you think he's gone?"

"Why?" I asked.

"*Because I have to get undressed.*"

Bob was in bed with all his clothes on, including his shoes.

I said, "You bastard."

"You got caught," Bob said. "You can't squeal on me."

The next day Whitey didn't say much.

"You broke curfew," was about all he said, and I did sprints and pick-ups as punishment.

That was the same year I didn't cover first base. I sure made a big impression on Whitey Herzog.

After Instructional League play, I went home to Middletown, Connecticut, for the winter. In February I drove my Oldsmobile Cutlass convertible to Florida for spring training. Though was ordered to cut my sideburns, I had an exceptional spring training. The highlight for me came when pitching coach Harvey Haddix, who had once thrown a no-hitter against the National League champion Milwaukee Braves for twelve innings, only to lose in the thirteenth on a home run by Joe Adcock, suggested that I change the grip on my fastball.

The Cat, as Haddix was called, suggested that I abandon my two-seam grip and try a four-seam grip. Haddix was certain I would have more control over my pitches. I tried it, and it was as though something magical happened to the baseball when I threw it plateward.

The new grip gave me another three miles an hour, maybe more, and it allowed me to pitch *upstairs* to hitters. I no longer needed to keep my pitches low, and I had more options.

What baffled me was how I was able to throw so hard while throwing so *easy*. I couldn't believe how much I improved. In the Instructional League I was pitching with the seams, trying to keep the ball down, trying to get ground balls, and whenever I'd get the ball above the waist, I'd get hit. When your sinking fastball *doesn't sink*, it's very hittable, and left-handers hit my low-and-away fastball if they reached for it. They also hit me pretty good to center field. But when I started to grip across the seams, now I was throwing up higher, above the waist, and they weren't hitting it. Left-handers were now fouling off my low-and-away fastballs. I was throwing much harder, and with much more life on my fastball.

I wondered, *Did a genie sprinkle fairy dust on my arm?* I couldn't believe how much velocity I was able to get on the ball and how much easier it was to throw a pitch. I no longer had to struggle so hard. I attributed it all to Harvey Haddix.

My first clear indication that I was in the Mets' plan for the 1967 season came when I was approached by Sy Berger, the gentleman who ran the Topps baseball card company. He told me that for 1967 Topps was going to include a series of cards that had photos of two top prospects on the same card. One such card, he said, would feature the photos of Tom Seaver and me.

Sy told me, "We'll send you a catalog, and you can pick out a gift."

And so Topps put Tom and me on the same card. Today the card is worth five hundred dollars. I call it the Bill Denehy rookie card.

In spring training I pitched every fourth day, a routine that gave me comfort. But once the regular season began, the Mets switched to a five-man rotation, the brainchild of Whitey Herzog, who was the Mets' director of player development. The Mets should have chosen him as manager after Gil Hodges died in 1972, but Donald Grant, who ran the Mets at the time, chose Yogi Berra instead.

Whitey was a brilliant baseball man. A lot of people said the Mets went to the five-man rotation because of Tom Seaver, because he liked to pitch every five days. But the truth is that the improved rotation should be credited to Whitey, who figured out that if there were five pitchers in the rotation, it would give the minor league system the opportunity to develop one more starting pitcher in the big leagues. As far as I know, the Mets were the first team to switch to the five-man rotation.

The change was certainly good for Tom Seaver. For me, it wasn't so hot. I really pitched better starting every fourth day. My arm was more lively when I pitched on three days' rest versus four. When I had that extra day's rest, I felt that I overthrew a little bit, and when I did that, my ball tended to "straighten out." Curveballs and sliders shouldn't straighten out. When the season began, the Mets' rotation included Jack Fisher, Tom Seaver, Bob Shaw, veteran Don Cardwell, and, finally, me.

Tom pitched the second game of the 1967 season against the Pittsburgh Pirates. He won the game, pitching very well and striking out eight batters; this was a new strikeout record for a Mets rookie pitcher.

Three games later, I took the mound against the Philadelphia Phillies in Connie Mack Stadium. I hadn't pitched in ten days, and my arm was too rested. I didn't have my good fastball, but I did have a sharp curve and wicked slider that day. Even though I lost two to nothing, I struck out All-Star outfielder Johnny Callison three times en route to tying Seaver's new rookie strikeout record with eight Ks (strikeouts). The record we shared stood for forty-five years until 2012, when Mets rookie Matt Harvey broke it with eleven strikeouts against the Arizona Diamondbacks. I sent Matt a telegram congratulating him.

My catcher, Jerry Grote, was an excellent defensive backstop who had an accurate, powerful arm. Grote was very demanding. He forced his pitchers to focus and concentrate. If you didn't concentrate, he would walk out a few feet in front of home plate and throw his best fastball right at your nuts. It was his way of saying, "Concentrate on what you're doing. Hit my target." Jerry was a very good catcher. He was also one of the grumpier players ever to don a uniform.

He was from Texas, and he seemed like he had a chip on his shoulder all the time. He hung around with Seaver and Buddy Harrelson, the shortstop. I didn't see a lot of him socially. Jerry didn't like the reporters and TV guys at all. I didn't find out about his "media phobia" until years later.

My second start for the Mets came a week after my first. Two days before that second start, I was shagging fly balls in the Shea Stadium outfield when I sprained my ankle. At the time, we shared Shea Stadium with the New York Jets. They used to resod the field all the time. The sod hadn't completely taken. I went back to catch a fly ball in right field, slipped on a piece of loose sod, and twisted my ankle badly.

I walked off the field, and the trainer put ice on my ankle. Two days later, right before I was to go out on the field to pitch, the trainer gave my ankle a shot of Novocain, taped it up, and sent me out. I pitched nine innings in a losing cause.

In a strange way, because I wasn't completely healthy, I didn't overthrow, and as a result I actually threw harder. I pitched beautifully against the powerful Phillies, and the score was tied at one run each in the ninth inning. Dick Ellsworth was pitching for the Phillies.

In the top of the ninth, the first batter got on base, and the next batter was Richie Allen, one of the best and most dangerous hitters not elected to the Hall of Fame. Jerry Grote came out to the mound to talk to me.

"You've been getting him out all day with sliders and fastballs," said Grote, "so let's start him out with a curveball, because he might not be looking for it."

That sounded good to me, and I threw Allen a curve that I hung eye-high. Richie Allen hit that sumbitch completely out of Shea Stadium. He hit it over the outfield fence, over the bleachers, and over the little parking lot where the Phillies' team bus was parked.

By the time that ball stopped rolling, it was close to Sheepshead Bay. I stood on the mound with my mouth open and watched the ball bounce into the main parking lot. That ball had to have gone eight hundred feet, if you take into account air time and roll. I got beat 3–1.

A few days later I was shagging balls in left field in Wrigley Field in Chicago. Tommy Davis and a couple of other guys were out there with me, and they were cracking up like a bird had just taken a shit on my head. Tommy was laughing like crazy, pointing me out to the other guys, and they were pointing and laughing too.

"Okay, guys, what's going on?" I wanted to know.

Tommy walked over, and he said, "I know you like Richie Allen, but this is a little ridiculous."

"What is?" I wanted to know. "What's ridiculous?"

"Turn around," Tommy said, and when I did, he ripped off my back a large photo of Richie Allen that someone had taped there when I wasn't looking.

"Look," said Tommy.

"Who did that?" I asked in mock anger. No one seemed to know.

I would bet that it had to be Tommy who pulled the prank. He was one of my favorite teammates.

I had never been to Chicago, and it was there that I was introduced to a woman known by ballplayers all over America as "Chicago Shirley." My warm welcome from Chicago Shirley was arranged by my two buddies, Ron Swoboda and Eddie Kranepool.

Ron and Eddie both enjoyed playing pranks on me. I remember one time, during my second stay in the Instructional League, we were in the clubhouse when Ron bet me that he could lift me up, and two other players, with just one finger. Ron was a strong guy, but I thought, *There is no way he is that strong.*

To do the stunt, Ron said, I had to be perfectly balanced for it to work. The weight had to be distributed just right. Jerry Kraft, one of our pitchers, lay down to my right, and pitcher Larry Bearnarth to my left. It would be Ron's job to pick us all up.

Ron had me lie on my back on top of them, entwining my left leg with Larry's two legs and my right leg with Jerry's two legs. Faceup, while on top of them, I had to put my left arm around one guy's neck and my right arm around the other guy's neck. Each guy then grabbed one of my wrists with both hands.

I had to be immobilized, I was told.

"Wait, wait," I said. "My right leg is still too loose. It has to be tighter."

"No problem," they said. Jerry tightened his grip around my right leg.

Ron stood over me and with one finger motioned like he was going to reach down and lift us up by my belt.

Ronnie bent down, and while Jerry and Larry made sure I was held down and unable to move, he unbuckled my belt, unzipped my pants, pulled down my pants and underpants, and bombarded me with mustard, shaving cream, ketchup, relish, honey, and aftershave in one disgusting mess as everyone in the locker room laughed their asses off.

What was funny was that Ron and Eddie never let me forget that I was so naïve that I told them, "My right leg isn't firm enough. It needs to be tighter."

"Okay. No problem."

I had fallen for their pranks before, so I was leery when, on our arrival at the hotel in Chicago, Ron and Eddie informed me that this woman, who broke in all the rookies who came into the National League, was coming up to see me later that night. "It's part of the rookie ritual," said Ron. "It'll be very enjoyable," said Eddie. The two of them were winking at me and at each other.

"You have to remember this is the big leagues," said Ron, "and when we say she's something special, we mean it."

I was expecting someone who looked like Tina Louise or Jane Fonda or Ann-Margret.

"Go back to your hotel room," said Eddie, "and around seven o'clock tonight there'll be a knock at your door. Chicago Shirley will be there."

I returned to my room. I showered and put on enough cologne to kill all the mosquitoes in Chicago, and waited impatiently for the clock to strike seven. At seven o'clock on the dot, there was a knock. I rushed to the door, I opened it, and there was this older woman wearing overalls with the brand name over her left breast, and sandals.

"Hey, Sweetie," she said. "I'm Shirley."

I just stared at her overalls. I don't even remember what she looked like. It was like God had struck me blind. I thought to myself, *This is a hotel, not a farm. Did she lose her cow?*

"Aren't you going to invite me in?" she asked.

"I guess so" was all I was able to mumble. I had just turned twenty-one years of age, and I was totally overwhelmed that this older, experienced woman had been sent to my hotel room to have sex with me. She came in, and she said, "The first thing I do, I like to get you relaxed, so I'd like to give you a massage."

She told me, "Take off everything."

"What do you mean by everything?" I wanted to know.

"*E-ver-y-thing*," she said.

"All right" was my weak response, and I got naked and lay on my stomach on the bed, and she began giving me a massage. I have to say, she was a big league masseuse.

"Turn over," she said, and when I did I could see that she wasn't wearing her overalls anymore. She proceeded to service me, and when we were done, we talked. She was a schoolteacher and said she would invite players to speak to her class.

She's a schoolteacher? I thought. *What class is she in? I want to be in her class.*

She said she liked baseball players, and particularly hockey players.

"I've slept with every player in the National Hockey League," she said. "I've also slept with whole teams of baseball players."

I was morbidly curious, so I asked her, "Who was the best you ever had?"

There wasn't even a pause before she answered, "Pete Rose."

"Why Pete Rose?"

"Because one day I was up in Pete's room, and after I had sex with Tommy Helms, Pete and I were playing around, and he took some scotch and poured it on my privates, and he went down and played a little submarine."

When she left, I could only think how nice she had been.

The next morning, when I walked into the lobby, Ron and Eddie and a number of my teammates were waiting for me. Ron and Eddie must have told them how they had set me up, because they were all snickering and laughing and covering their faces.

"How was your night last night?" Ron wanted to know.

I didn't even know what to say.

On a Wednesday night in early May of 1967, I took the mound against the powerful San Francisco Giants, a team that featured the slugging of Willie Mays and Willie McCovey, who had watched me so closely when I had tried out with the Mets as a high school kid three years earlier.

Before the game, Yogi Berra, a Mets coach at the time, handed me the baseball to warm up with. I was confident I was going to win. I was *always* confident that I was going to win, even though the Mets hadn't been hitting well that season. In fact, Dick Young suggested that I sue the Mets for lack of support. My record was one win and seven losses, but I was only getting one or two runs a game.

"Okay," said Yogi half-jokingly, "go out and pitch a shutout to get us a tie."

Yogi didn't have much confidence we would score against future Hall of Fame pitcher Juan Marichal. Just before I was to go out and warm up, my roommate, Don Cardwell, handed me a black pill. "Take this," he said. "It will add three feet to your fastball."

Don was a great guy. He was a veteran pitcher and very helpful. I didn't think anything of it. I had no idea what it was. So I took it. The pill was an amphetamine, a "black beauty."

As I walked through the bowels of Shea Stadium toward the bullpen, I began to feel hyper. I had an extra bounce in my step, and I seemed to be more alert. I felt very positive and upbeat, and when I started warming up, I was throwing fastballs that were popping out of my bullpen catcher John Sullivan's glove.

I felt like I was throwing to a kid in my backyard, nice and easy, and whoosh. *Holy fuck.*

I went out to pitch in front of the fifty thousand fans in attendance that night at Shea Stadium, and along with the natural flow of my adrenaline, my normal nervousness and excitement, I had a powerful amphetamine surging through my veins. Once the game started, I was rushing my delivery. I didn't have the composure and rhythm I normally had, but boy, when I let it fly, that ball was going.

I retired the first two Giants. I stood with my back to the plate, and I could hear the public address announcer saying, "Now batting. Number 24 for the San Francisco Giants," and the crowd noise became so loud that I couldn't hear the rest of the announcement.

Standing at home plate, swinging the bat and bouncing up and down, was Willie Mays, the future Hall of Famer who would conclude his career with 660 home runs.

Before the game I had met with several of my teammates including my catcher, Jerry Grote, and we went over the Giants hitters. I was a rookie, so I listened. Grote told me about the likes and dislikes of Tom Haller, Jim Ray Hart, Willie McCovey, and Willie Mays.

"Fuck Willie Mays," Grote said. "First time up let's throw right at his face and knock his ass down. Let's see if he can hit your pitches after that."

The meeting broke up. It was the first time on the big league level I had even heard someone talk about knocking someone down.

Mays stepped up to the plate. I looked at Grote behind the plate. If Grote flipped his thumb, that was the sign for me to knock down the hitter. Grote set up inside the plate and flipped his thumb. I took a deep breath. Then I fired the ball as hard as I could right at Willie Mays's face.

Mays dropped to the ground, and my first thought was that I had killed him.

I couldn't see where the ball went. I didn't know what happened. But Mays went down, and for a while he stayed down. Slowly Willie got up, stared at me, checked his body parts, and made sure everything was still there. And after that knockdown, I found facing Willie Mays was no problem at all. He couldn't have been easier to get out. I don't even remember him hitting a foul ball off me.

When I came to bat, I expected Marichal to knock me down, but he didn't throw a single pitch close to me. That night Marichal pitched a one-hitter, and the only hit was a fly ball to center field that Mays came in on but couldn't get. It took one hop. Mays said he lost it in the lights. A couple of days later, Mays and Marichal got into a fistfight in the dugout. We were sure the fight was over Marichal not retaliating after I knocked down Willie Mays.

In the fourth inning, Willie Mays came up again. With two strikes, I rushed my delivery, throwing a hard slider for strike three, and as I threw the ball I felt as though someone had stuck a knife into my shoulder. The pain was awful. It felt like when they miss the area they're supposed to numb with a painkiller during an operation—like someone sticking a knife into my shoulder without the painkiller. I bent over, the trainer came out, and I walked off the mound. My arm was throbbing too much for me to go back out there.

I was scared. I had had a tired arm before. But this time it was different. The excruciating pain was right behind my shoulder, where the triceps tendon attaches. It was part of what's now known as the rotator cuff. But this was 1967, and it would be another seven years before a doctor by the name of Frank Jobe would attempt what is now known as "Tommy John" surgery. But in 1967 there was no known operation to fix it.

The Mets' doctor, Dr. Peter LaMotte, took a series of X-rays, and he could find no structural damage to my arm. I was placed on the fifteen-day disabled list, and for six days did no throwing at all. I was given a cortisone shot.

The Mets drove to West Point to play an exhibition game against the Army cadets. I went with them. I went out to the bullpen to see if I could throw. I couldn't throw a ball thirty feet. I felt a constant, aching pain and weakness. The ball was so heavy; it felt as though I was lobbing hand grenades.

Over time I was able to throw farther and farther, and after coming off the disabled list, I made a couple of relief appearances. I returned to the rotation against the Atlanta Braves, a hard-hitting team featuring Joe Torre, Rico Carty, Hank Aaron, Felipe Alou, and Clete Boyer. On a sunny Sunday afternoon in Queens, I went seven and one-third innings and beat the Braves for the lone victory of my career.

I actually felt and pitched pretty good that day. I had good velocity. In that game Torre hit a home run, a triple, and a double. With one out in the seventh, Torre again came to bat.

"Keep the ball down and away," Wes Westrum, the manager, told me.

I got the count to three balls and two strikes, and then threw a slider down and away that could have been called strike three, but umpire Augie Donatelli called it a ball. Torre headed for first base, and Westrum walked to the mound and asked for the ball.

As I walked off, Donatelli was bending down, dusting off home plate. On the way to the dugout I took the "banana route," passing close by Donatelli, and I screamed at him, "Jesus Christ, I'm busting my balls. That should have been a strike."

Augie casually turned to me and said, "Hey, rookie, look at it this way. At least I held him to a single."

We flew to Los Angeles for a series with the Dodgers, then had two games at Houston, with the next stop in San Francisco, where I was scheduled to pitch on a Saturday against the Giants. We played the Dodgers the Tuesday before the series with the Giants. I threw some warm-up pitches between our at bat in the top of the first and the Dodgers' at bat in the bottom of the inning.

The Dodgers loaded the bases in the bottom of the first inning.

"Get warm," I was ordered.

I had just come off the disabled list, and had pitched seven innings just two days before.

Why is Westrum sending me into a game? I wondered.

I was skeptical, but I wasn't the type to question my manager. He wasn't close to the players and wasn't a players' manager, but he wasn't a hard-ass either. I think Wes felt a lot of pressure as manager. I also thought Bill Virdon should have gotten the job instead.

Westrum did silly things. After the game against the Braves, we flew out to Los Angeles for a Sunday game. We had the Monday off, and Ron Swoboda, Ed Kranepool, and I took a trip to Disneyland.

The next day, Tuesday, we played the Dodgers. I was warming up, getting ready for my start in San Francisco in the upcoming series, when our starter got in trouble.

"You're going to go into the game to get out a hitter," I was told.

My arm already was tender from having pitched two days before. I trotted out to the mound, and I toed the rubber when the plate umpire called time. I asked him why. "I want to take a couple of minutes so we can get His Highness seated," he said. His Highness was Frank Sinatra.

I wasn't used to the steep pitch of the mound at Chavez Ravine—it was perfect for Sandy Koufax, but not me. I wasn't ready to pitch on such short notice, and I was lousy. I allowed all three base runners to score. Worse yet, I reinjured my arm. The intense pain returned, though I didn't tell anyone. After the game, Westrum called Swoboda, Kranepool, and me into his office.

"From now on, Disneyland is off limits," he told us.

The first stupid thing Westrum did that day was put me in the game. The other stupid thing he did was tell us we couldn't go to Disneyland. *It was Disneyland, for crying out loud!*

Westrum was my manager, but I had the same relationship with him that I had with my high school basketball coach—no relationship.

The following Saturday at Candlestick Park, I pitched pretty well. Juan Marichal gave up thirteen hits but didn't give up any runs. He had the bases loaded every inning, it seemed, but we just couldn't score. The score was 0–0 in the seventh, and I allowed two hits, and Westrum came to the mound and took me out of the game.

Jack Hamilton came in, and Willie McCovey hit a home run, and we lost 5–0. For me it meant another loss in a game we might have won.

At least three of my losses came when I left either when it was tied or the game was close, and then the reliever came in and threw gas on the fire.

One of my last appearances was against the Chicago Cubs. In early June we played them in Chicago at Wrigley with the wind blowing out. Their center fielder, Adolfo Phillips, hit four home runs in the doubleheader, with three in the second game.

I was sitting on the bench next to Westrum when he grabbed me and said, "I don't care if you get beat twenty to nothing. When you pitch against Phillips the next time, that fucker better not get a hit."

I faced the Cubs at Shea, and in that game Adolfo came up to bat in the first inning, and I knocked him down as good as I did Willie Mays. It was a replica of how I pitched Mays. Every time he came up to bat, I knocked him down.

Leo Durocher, the Cubs' manager, said he was going to personally get me.

Leo, who was accused of stealing Babe Ruth's watch when they were both with the Yankees, was a tough character. Later in my career I played with Ted Savage, an outfielder with the Cubs, at the time managed by Durocher, when he dropped a ball with two outs in the ninth inning to lose the game.

Ted told me he had no intention of coming into the clubhouse and listening to Leo rip him up and down and call him all sorts of names, so he waited where the bat boy sat in the outfield until the park cleared. They were shutting off the lights, and he was sure that everyone had gotten on the bus and gone back to the hotel. He figured he'd be able to dress in peace and quiet.

He said he opened the clubhouse door, and Durocher grabbed him and yanked him down onto his knees. Durocher was yelling at him, "You fucking cocksucker, you. You cost us the fucking game, for God's sake. I don't want to fucking trade you. I don't want to fucking send you anywhere. I'd like to fucking kill you. How can you drop an easy fucking fly ball?"

Ernie Banks, the Cubs' longtime star, got between them. Ernie was mild-mannered, and said to Durocher, "Hey, Leo, the kid feels bad enough. You don't need to jump down his throat."

"Oh, here he is, Mr. Fucking Cub," said Leo, "sticking up for his teammate. I want to see you dive for just one fucking ball— one time—before you spout off. Do you ever fucking get dirty out there?"

Eventually Ted took a shower and left. The next day the Cubs played the Cardinals. Ted told me that in the first inning of the game, Lou Brock, the first batter for the Cardinals, hit a ground ball between Ron Santo at third base and Don Kessinger at shortstop. As the ball rolled into the outfield, if you looked over at first base, there was Ernie Banks, his first baseman's glove outstretched, pretending he was diving for a ball. Ted said he laughed all afternoon.

In my game against Adolfo Phillips, Leo Durocher, and the Cubs, a game I lost by a run, I learned a painful lesson about guessing. Billy Williams was at the plate, and I threw him a curveball, a changeup, and a curveball, and I had him at one ball and two strikes.

Grote gave me the sign to throw a fastball inside to the left-handed Williams. There was no one on base, and I went into my windup, and when I got to the top of my delivery I could see that Billy was taking his front, right leg and pulling it into the bucket so he could open up his hips and clear them as he looked for an inside fastball.

Looking back, I couldn't stop my motion, though I should have. When I saw what he was doing, I knew I shouldn't throw that pitch, and I didn't throw it far enough inside. I put it on the corner, and Billy hit a line drive that bounced off the scoreboard at Shea Stadium. He hit a ballistic fucking frozen rope. I had pitched well against the rest of the team, including Ernie Banks and Ron Santo, and I knocked down Phillips every time, but I didn't win the game because of Billy Williams.

I made a few more starts, but my arm was hurting, and I was lackluster. I had a clause in my contract that if I remained with the Mets for ninety days, I would get a $5,000 bonus. On day eighty-nine, as luck would have it, Johnny Murphy, the Mets' general manager, sent me down to Triple-A Jacksonville.

How could you do this to me, Uncle Johnny? was how I felt.

I was only able to go back to Jacksonville because Danny Melendez was no longer the general manager, so he couldn't screw with me and trade me as he did previously for trying to date his daughter. While at Jacksonville, I managed to pitch to a 3–3 record despite the constant pain. I figured that if my two idols, Sandy Koufax and Mickey Mantle, could play through the pain, then I could too. Koufax must have had a tremendously high pain threshold. So did Mantle. The pain brought me closer to those guys. I would tell myself, *You know what, I might not be able to throw as hard as Koufax, but if he took forty shots, I can too.*

If my arm was killing me, all I had to do was picture Mantle with his seventy-year-old legs getting wrapped so he could play. I was determined to be every bit as tough as they were. I decided I could fight the pain, the agony. I could grit my teeth. I could take the cortisone shots.

And why would I do this? My two idols did it before me, and I hoped that the shots would get me back to the big leagues. Of course, I didn't know that when I turned sixty years old I would go blind because of the cortisone. No one at the time mentioned the downside, though when Koufax retired, he said, "I'm pitching high with an upset stomach, and no one can tell me what the long-term consequences will be." God, if they're giving it to Koufax, the greatest pitcher of my era, why shouldn't they give it to me? And why shouldn't I take it?"

Because, Bill, you might go blind.

If someone had said that, I wouldn't have listened.

When I was in grammar school the nuns told me that if I kept masturbating, I would go blind. I didn't pay any attention to them, either.

While pitching for Jacksonville, I complained about my sore arm. I was sent to a local hospital where dye was injected into my shoulder. If there was a tear, the dye would bubble up.

A bubble appeared. Though the source of my pain was kept hidden from me, the doctors said there was a tear in my terris minor, which is located in the rotator cuff. After the injection, it hurt so badly. It felt like they put acid in my shoulder.

I was told to go home for the remainder of the 1967 season, rest, and don't pick up a ball.

I left for home on August 1, 1967.

Being an ex-major leaguer, at home during the baseball season, isn't much fun. My friends and complete strangers would ask me, "What are you doing here? Aren't you supposed to be in L.A.?" and "What's wrong with your shoulder?"

The worst part of the injury was the uncertainty. I worried. I wondered, *What if I can't throw hard ever again?*

I also second-guessed myself. *Would I have gotten hurt if I hadn't taken that amphetamine before the game? Would I have gotten hurt if Westrum hadn't thrown me into that game in the first inning against the Dodgers?*

I was emotionally distressed, and angered at having taken that pill. I don't blame Don. He was a good teammate, a good roommate. He was trying to help me out. If he had said to me, "I want you to lick the stomach of a chameleon four times, bite off his head, and swallow it," I would have done it.

My biggest problem was that the Mets didn't tell me about the tear. They wouldn't tell me what was wrong. And yet the terrible pain in my shoulder persisted.

In September I returned to Shea Stadium to meet with Dr. LaMotte, who gave me another cortisone shot. The shot was to be my last experience as a New York Met for quite some time.

7

MY ARM IS KILLING ME

I PICKED UP THE *NEW YORK DAILY NEWS* in November of 1967 and read a column by Dick Young saying that at the winter meetings in Mexico City the New York Mets were trading right-hander Bill Denehy to Washington for Senators manager Gil Hodges.

Mets general manager Johnny Murphy called a couple of hours later. Johnny said the Mets were close to making a deal with Washington. We were getting Gil Hodges as manager, and the Senators would get me. There were other Mets players involved in the deal, but the Senators weren't interested in them.

I told Johnny, "My arm is still hurting, John."

"That's for them to worry about," said Murphy; he was the same guy who had sent me to the minors on day eighty-nine so he didn't have to pay me a $5,000 bonus for remaining with the Mets for ninety days. The trade was made, and was a baseball rarity where a player was traded for a manager.

When Washington Senators GM George Selkirk welcomed me to the team, I told him my shoulder was still sore. A month before I left for spring training, he sent me to meet team physician Dr. George Resta. Dr. Resta injected four vials of cortisone into my aching shoulder. Dr. Resta, in addition to being the team physician of the Washington Redskins, was reportedly referred to as "Dr. Feelgood." He was confident that he could take care of my shoulder.

I was a twenty-two-year-old ballplayer with a painful pitching arm. I'd have undergone anything the good doctor prescribed for me.

Today an MRI can pinpoint the exact spot of an injury. In those days doctors had to guess. Dr. Resta gave me Xylocaine to deaden the pain and then gave me two shots of cortisone.

Imagine yourself as a human pincushion. They just pump that needle in there until you flinch. When you flinch, that's where they inject the cortisone. They jab and jab, and when you flinch again, you get another shot. And they do this until you stop flinching. Well, guess what? Every time Dr. Resta shoved that needle in, he put a hole in the tissue.

I didn't know it then, but his regimen of more than fifty cortisone shots would destroy my arm. And, of course, nobody seems to have kept any records of those shots. I believe the shots contributed to my addiction, and I firmly believe they also resulted in my going blind.

When Washington traded Gil Hodges in exchange for me, it worked out rather well for the Mets, who, under Hodges's tough but caring leadership, won the World Series in 1969. I, on the other hand, pitched exactly two innings for Washington in 1968, giving up four hits, walking four, and allowing two earned runs, before I was sent down to Triple-A Buffalo.

My manager with Washington was Jim Lemon, who had a dry sense of humor but wasn't close to the players. He didn't bring any enthusiasm, spirit, or inspiration. He was just there.

Sid Hudson was the pitching coach, and it was Sid who had been responsible for my trade to Washington. Sid had seen me pitch several times before I got to the Mets and was impressed. We got along very well.

When spring training began, I was throwing with a little pain. Every pitcher throws with soreness in his elbow, shoulder, or back. The soreness eventually works itself out. If you're lucky, it doesn't get worse. The pain in my arm was tolerable, perhaps because of the cortisone.

I pitched opening day of spring training against Mel Stottlemyre and the New York Yankees. I faced Mickey Mantle in the bottom of the first inning. I ran the count to three balls and two strikes. I threw him two straight fastballs that he fouled off, and then I threw him an off-speed curveball that he missed by three feet. I walked off the mound clapping to myself.

After I left the game I was jogging in the outfield when I ran into Mel Stottlemyre.

I told him that I admired his sinker and slider. He told me I threw the shit out of the ball.

I was amazed. I didn't think I was throwing that well. Obviously, Mel thought so.

I pitched well in a spring training game in Pompano Beach against the Baltimore Orioles. It was a hot day, and my arm felt good. Curt Blefary hit a home run, and the next batter was Frank Robinson, the only player in history selected as the Most Valuable Player in both the American and National Leagues. My first pitch got away from me and almost took his head off.

This time I hadn't done it on purpose. I wasn't trying to hit him with the ball.

When Frank got back in the batter's box, I could see he was tiptoeing to the plate, taking tiny steps. I threw him a curve, and he took it for a strike. He crept closer. Obviously he was looking outside. I threw him another curve, and again he took it for a strike. I then threw him a slider that broke down on his hands, and he swung and missed.

Curt Blefary took a few steps from the dugout and started yelling at me. Frank grabbed him and dragged him back into the dugout. Frank was a class act and one of the great hitters of his day.

During the short time I was with Washington, it was uneventful except for the fact that I proposed to twenty-year-old Marilyn Waylock, and she accepted. My attitude toward women was formed in my youth, and as I think back to my childhood and teen years, I should explain how that attitude was formed.

When I was a boy in the sixth grade, my father forced me to take dancing lessons at the local YMCA. He told me, "Son, if you learn how to dance, you'll always be able to go to a dance and dance with the girls rather than stand in the corner." The dancing class consisted of three unathletic Jewish kids and me. I thought it was a dumb idea.

But when the junior high school dances started, I was able to ask a girl to dance because I knew how to dance while all my friends stood hesitantly against the concrete brick wall of the gym. I was a little shy, but because I could dance, even if I didn't ask a girl to dance, a girl would ask me, and so I could go to a dance and have a really good time.

I went to all the dances and all the proms, but I didn't have a steady girlfriend in high school. I didn't give away my athletic sweater or my class ring, even though I took Sherry Scott, Miss Middletown, to the senior ball.

The nuns also had a lot to do with shaping my attitude toward women. Those nuns made me mistrust women. Because of them, I didn't trust girls the way I trusted guys. If there was a party, I'd bring a date, but I wasn't the sort to hang on the phone every night just to chitchat. I couldn't talk on the phone because I had to do my homework. I worked my ass off to be an average student. I was never rejected by girls. I was always the chaser. I didn't like being chased, and I say that because I didn't have much chemistry with the girls who chased me.

Not until I met Marilyn Waylock did I start to look closely at my attitude toward women. I had been squarely focused on sports. That all changed when I met Marilyn. But we would never have met in the first place if it were not for her brother and my good friend John Waylock. She was his much younger sister, and when we met I was new to the Mets.

The winter after signing with the Mets I was playing in the Instructional League. I was shooting pool with John Waylock when his younger sister Marilyn popped in to tell him she was going out with her girlfriends.

"Who's that?" I wanted to know. She was cute as hell. She had shoulder-length blond hair and nice legs, and it was, *Oh wow, who's that?*

He introduced us.

A day later I called Marilyn on the phone and asked if she wanted to go for a ride down at the beach. She was sixteen, and

I had just graduated from high school, and she didn't want any part of me. I had gone to Wilson High, and she had gone to Middletown High, and the two schools were archrivals. I had played against her brother in basketball, and I had elbowed him a couple of times, and she held that against me. She had a low opinion of me because I played for Wilson.

I talked to her on the phone for half an hour in the hope she would change her mind. Finally I said, "This is the way it is. I'm coming over in fifteen minutes. Be ready."

We began dating. She was working full-time during the day in a car parts store, and at night she studied at Middlesex Junior College in Middletown; I enrolled there to be near her. When we started getting serious, I did what a lot of young guys do who feel stuck in a relationship: I wanted to date other coeds. So we decided we weren't going to date each other exclusively. Marilyn started dating a player on the Middlesex basketball team. We broke up before I went to my second spring training with the Mets. We still wrote to each other, though, and when I'd come home, we'd go out.

On the day I pitched my first game in the big leagues, I received a telegram from Marilyn. It said: "Good luck on your first professional baseball game. Love, Marilyn."

She visited me during my short time with the Mets.

The following April, after I was traded to the Senators, Marilyn flew to Washington, D.C., to visit. I was rooming with Joey Coleman, Dick Bosman, Barry Moore, and Frank Howard, the gentle giant who everyone called Hondo. Hondo slept on a mattress in front of the air conditioner, which he would turn down to about forty degrees. He would take out his teeth and lie there stark naked.

I met Marilyn at the airport, brought her back to my apartment, and asked her to marry me. She said yes. The first person she showed the ring to was Hondo, who said to her, "I'll bet you think he's the greatest guy in the world." She nodded.

"You're wrong," he said. "I'm the greatest guy in the world."

Marilyn called her parents with the news of our engagement. She asked her father for permission to marry, and he said, "Of course."

When Marilyn told her mother, the first words out of her mouth were "I hope you're kidding." Her mom wanted Marilyn to continue her education and graduate from college. She had been accepted to a four-year school when I asked her to marry me, and back then you didn't marry and stay home and go to school. Marilyn wanted to be a full-time wife, and she figured she could go to school whenever. Unfortunately, whenever never happened.

Her mother was not happy. She did not want us to get married. Marilyn was only twenty years old when we got married. We were both very young. Her mother had to sign the marriage certificate, and she told Marilyn, "I have a *bad* feeling about this." That's how my relationship with Marilyn and her mother started off. From that day forward, her mother hated my guts.

I married Marilyn because I was attracted by her looks and because we got along well together. I told myself she was the right one for me, but I also wondered whether she thought the same way.

Marilyn's sister Ellie was twelve years older than she was. Ellie was treated like a princess, while Marilyn was treated like the stepsister. Two weeks after we announced our engagement, her sister announced hers, and she insisted on getting married before we did. Marilyn's parents told us they could only afford to pay for one wedding—Ellie's wedding—so we went ahead with our big wedding anyway. Marilyn and I paid for the food, the band, and the restaurant; my parents paid for the liquor.

The priest who married us was a blond-haired guy named Al Kislick. In the Catholic Church you have to have a talk about sex before you can get married. He said, "Come to the rectory, and we'll go over this and go out to dinner."

All of the Catholic priests I knew drove black cars except Father Kislick. He had a light-green Buick Riviera. He took us to a country and western bar. He wasn't wearing his clerical garb, and when he went in there, he said, "I come here to listen to the music. No one knows me as Father Al. They just know me as Al." And when we entered, he was greeted by "Hey Al, how you doing?" from both men and women.

We were having dinner, and he said, "Where you going on your honeymoon?"

We named a couple of places.

"I have a place you ought to look into," he said. "It's called Pools and Pavilions. It's in the Virgin Islands, and it's really great. Every pavilion has its own pool. It's a great place to relax. You're by yourself. You can swim anytime, day or night."

Marilyn and I looked into it, and that's where we chose to go for our honeymoon. We were married on February 1, 1969. Ron Swoboda and Tug McGraw and about three hundred other people also attended.

After he married us, and just before we left for our honeymoon, Al told us, "By the way, when I go down there, I don't go as Father Al. I go as Al Kislick. I go to relax and enjoy myself."

We flew down to the Virgin Islands and went to check in at the hotel. The woman at the check-in desk asked, "How did you find us?"

"A good friend recommended this place," I said.

When we returned from our honeymoon, I bought Marilyn a miniature schnauzer we named Fritzie. I didn't want her to be alone when I went on the road. I didn't want to have kids right away, so I got her a dog.

I signed my 1969 contract with Washington for $10,000, which I thought was low, and I told GM George Selkirk that I thought it was too low.

"If you make the Senators team and remain with the club for thirty days, I'll give you another two thousand dollars," he promised me. I stayed on the team for the thirty days, and when I added up my pay from the first two paychecks, it didn't add up to $12,000 a year. I went to see Selkirk.

"You promised me if I made the club and stayed thirty days, I'd get $12,000."

"I don't remember that," Selkirk said. "We didn't put it in writing."

Bastard.

Right after our conversation, I was sent down to the Senators' Triple-A team, the Buffalo Bisons, where I posted a nine-win-and-ten-loss record with a 4.87 ERA. I pitched better than my ERA would suggest. I had a couple of really bad games when my arm was killing me, but most of the time the pain was bearable and I pitched well. Because of the cortisone shots, the pain in my arm was manageable all year. In fact, in the last game I pitched that year, I faced the Yankee farm club, the Syracuse Chiefs. They had John Ellis, Jim Lyttle, Bill Melton, Jim Hegan, and Ross Moschitto, and were a damn fine team. I threw ninety-four breaking balls, eighty-two for strikes, and I struck out the first ten batters I faced to set an International League record. All I could hear in my head was the voice of Eddie Stanky and how he kept telling me how important it was for me to throw curveballs for first-pitch strikes. I did that all afternoon. I finished with seventeen strikeouts. Eddie, I couldn't have done it any better.

I lost the game 2–0 when Johnny Ellis hit a fly ball; our left fielder Sam Bowens put his glove up, had it, hit the wall—and the ball bounced out and over the fence.

The baseball life was tough on Marilyn. She was from a small town. She would go to the ballpark and sit by herself because she didn't know anybody, and it was very difficult for her because she felt so isolated and alone. Being away from home scared her, and things were worse when the Bisons went on road trips and she had to stay behind. It took her a while, but she gradually made friends with a number of the players' wives, and that made things a little easier.

I was sure that with my performance in Buffalo the Senators would put me on the forty-man roster and bring me up to Washington, which was in last place, and give me a start or two. Instead, they sent me home, and I returned to Middletown and got a job working in a haberdashery store. I was hired by Camp's, an upscale clothing store that sold suits and sweaters to the Wesleyan University professors and local businessmen.

During the winter, my arm just got worse. I don't know why; I can't think of an event that caused it. Perhaps it was the cold. Perhaps it was because I hadn't had a cortisone shot since September. I wouldn't get another shot until February when spring training would start up again. Most likely it hurt because I wasn't throwing during the off-season. When I started to throw again, the adhesions and scar tissue tore, and I constantly had tendonitis.

Just before spring training I flew to Washington, D.C., to spend the weekend doing National Guard duty, and I was able to get a few more cortisone shots. I was sitting in the trainer's room of the clubhouse waiting for Dr. Resta to arrive. All of a sudden, an entourage of people poured in, and I could hear a booming voice. In walked Vince Lombardi, who had just been named the new coach of the Washington Redskins.

He stopped and we talked.

Lombardi smiled, gave me a pat on the head, and said, "Good boy." So I got a "good boy" from Vince Lombardi, one of the greatest coaches in National Football League history, and I took it to mean "You could have played for me, son."

He walked through the clubhouse, and I never saw him again.

When I went to spring training in 1969, the new owner of the Washington Senators was Bob Short. I don't know whether Mr. Short had heard rumblings, but he called a meeting of the players and told us, "I've got an open door. Anybody who has any complaints about anything that's ever happened here, I want to hear them now."

About fifteen guys, including me, went to see him. I told him how George Selkirk had promised me an extra $2,000 if I stayed with the team for thirty days and how he had reneged on his promise. My dad taught me that if you say you'll do something, or if you shake hands on something, a deal is a deal and a man's word is his bond. Maybe that's old-fashioned, but there were certain values my father instilled in me, and that was one of them.

Other players told similar stories, and a few days later Short fired Selkirk as general manager. When he was fired, half the Washington team was very happy.

The Senators' manager that year was Ted Williams. The first time I met Ted, the pitchers were at the practice pitching field, and we were practicing covering first base on balls hit to the right side of the infield. He walked over to us and addressed all the pitchers.

Ted said to us, "All right, I have a question for you guys. Who are the dumbest sons-a-bitches in all of baseball?"

We asked ourselves, *What kind of question is that?*

Ted said, "You guys are. And I'll tell you why. Can anybody tell me why a curveball curves?"

Someone guessed that it was the wind. No one knew the answer.

Ted said, "You guys don't know what you're talking about. And this is your profession. You're trying to make a living doing this, and you don't even know *why* a curveball curves." Well, that statement really pissed me off. After practice I went to the library, and I looked up why a curveball curves. What happens is that when the ball attains a certain speed, the air flow underneath the ball will lift it. In the case of a curveball, the spin is *downward* and the air will pull the ball downward. It's called Bernoulli's principle.

The next day I went to see Ted, and I told him I had the answer to his question.

"What are you talking about?"

"Why a curveball curves," I said. "It's Bernoulli's principle."

He laughed.

"All right," he said, "I have at least one fucking guy interested enough in his craft to go and check it out."

From that point on, Ted and I got along really well. Ted liked players who wanted to learn about our craft. Every game I didn't play, I would sit right behind him. I didn't take notes, but I was a mental sponge and I soaked up whatever he was talking about. It was like memorizing a four-year college course in baseball in just six weeks. I really enjoyed the time I spent with him, and I learned a lot about pitching and about hitting.

Ted couldn't stand Mike Epstein, our first baseman. He liked him as a person, but as a hitter, Ted thought that Mike never got to the point where he could make a calculated guess as to which pitch was coming next. He just couldn't anticipate what the pitcher would likely throw.

Ted schooled me on how to think like a hitter. One day in spring training I was sitting on the bench with Ted, and Epstein was at the plate facing Dave McNally of the Orioles.

Ted said to me, "Here's what Mike should be thinking: He's going to try to get ahead of him. He's going to throw him an off-speed slider just on the outside part of the plate, a strike pitch. You have to look for a slider, and hopefully he'll get it a little too high, and if he gets it up, you drive the ball."

Sure enough, McNally threw a slider, and Mike took it for a strike.

"Aaaaaaah," said Ted. "There was a ball he could have creamed."

Ted then said, "Now he's ahead of him. What's he going to do? He's going to run a fastball in on his fist, move him off the plate. So you're going to take this pitch, unless he makes a mistake over the middle of the plate. You should be thinking, *middle out.* Anywhere in, you take."

McNally threw a fastball inside. Epstein took a big swing and missed.

"Aaaaaah," said Ted. "Jesus Christ."

Ted continued, "Now he's got him no balls and two strikes, and you're in a defensive situation. What's he going to use for a strikeout pitch? He'll drop down and throw a big, wide curveball. You want to get a little closer to the plate. You want to get to the point of not trying to pull the ball. You're going to hit the ball back up the middle."

Of course, McNally threw Mike a curveball, and Mike tried to pull it, swung, and missed for strike three.

"Aaaaaaaahhhhhhhh," growled Ted. "*Jesus syphilitic fucking Christ.* That's what I'm talking about. *Fucking dumb hitting.* He didn't have a plan when he went up there."

Ted also had specific ideas about how pitchers should pitch. Ted's ideas were black and white. "This is what you should be as a hitter and as a pitcher," he would say.

"Unless you're Bob Feller, you have to throw a fastball that moves."

Ted got rid of Joey Coleman because Coleman couldn't throw a slider. Ted believed the slider was the toughest pitch for him to hit, and if it was tough for him to hit, everybody who pitched for him had to have a slider. If you didn't have a slider—and Joey didn't have one—you couldn't pitch for him. Joey was sent to Detroit. His first year there he won twenty games. Go figure!

I think if I had had a healthy arm, I would have loved pitching for Ted. My whole career I talked to hitters and asked what pitches they had trouble hitting, and I would make adjustments from there. I'd tell myself, *Here's what the batter did the last time I faced him. Here's what I got him out with. Here's what he's probably going to do this time.*

I expected Ted Williams to have a good knowledge of hitting, but I was surprised by how much he knew about pitching. He knew the difference between a two-seam fastball and a four-seam fastball, how each broke, and the advantages of each. He knew what gave hitters trouble, and how to get them out. Of all the coaches in the big leagues, I learned as much about pitching from Ted as I did from all of my pitching coaches combined.

All through spring training, one of our coaches, Nellie Fox, a future Hall of Fame ballplayer himself, kept trying to bait Ted into a base-hitting contest. Nellie was a really good infielder, a terrific bunter, and a line drive hitter. Finally, at the end of spring training, before we made the final cuts, Nellie was all over Ted to have a hitting contest. And he baited him.

There was one thing about Ted Williams: You *could* get to him.

"All right," said Ted. "Enough's enough."

Nellie hit first. He walked into the batting cage, and he got seven hits before he made three outs. He hit line drives, mostly to the outfield. So now it was Ted's turn. He popped up the first pitch, and then he hit a weak ground ball. Nellie was laughing.

"Only one more out," Nellie taunted. "What are you going to do? To beat me you have to have eight straight hits."

Ted dug in a little deeper at the plate, gripped his bat a little more firmly, crouched a little more, and proceeded to bat out eight straight hits. The eighth hit was a line drive that bounced off the right field wall. And then he walked outside the batting cage.

"Nellie, I just want to tell you," said Ted, "in your best times, you wouldn't be a big pus pimple on my ass as a hitter."

Right after that I was sent to the minor leagues. I usually pitched well in the spring, but from the first day I threw in spring training of 1969, my arm was really bad. I only had one good outing before I was sent from the big league camp to Buffalo, where I started the season on the disabled list. The cortisone shots were poking holes in my tissue, and my arm was getting worse. In addition to giving me shots each month, Dr. Resta gave me a prescription to get Xylocaine and cortisone shots if I needed them during the season. I could go to a hospital emergency room and tell them I had bursitis in my shoulder. I used the prescription once in Toledo and once in Columbus. When I was in Buffalo, I would cross the border to Canada to get shots from a doctor there. Our trainer was also a hockey trainer, and the doctor in Canada was his buddy.

Our trainer became concerned about the number of cortisone shots I was getting, and every time I'd get one, he'd report it to Dr. Resta just to cover his ass. But he could see I was having a tough time. In Canada, the doctor also put me on a machine that gave me electrical stimulation. It shot electric currents into my shoulder. I was desperate. I would have tried anything.

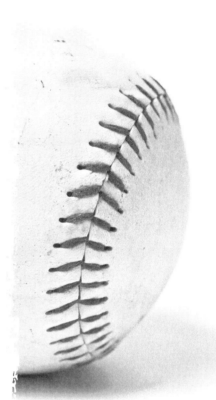

8

DMSO BRINGS
ME BACK

AFTER STARTING THE 1969 SEASON ON THE disabled list, I drove back to Buffalo. I pitched a game against the Rochester Red Wings, the Baltimore Triple-A club. The only reason my pitches sank was because I didn't have enough velocity for them to stay straight. The ball curved because it couldn't go in any other direction. I also had the "at-'em ball" thing going. Every time they hit a line drive, it was right *at* somebody. It was pathetic. I threw slop to the plate, and these guys hit ground ball outs and pop-ups.

I pitched eight innings and gave up two runs. I was so embarrassed, I wanted to walk off the mound. I wanted to scream, "You hitters are fucking pathetic. You really suck. Because I know how bad I'm pitching, and if I'm pitching this bad, you guys must really suck."

When I faced a good hitter in my heyday, I could have challenged him with my fastball. I had movement and velocity and I could throw an inside fastball and know I wouldn't get hurt. But now I knew that if I threw my fastball, I needed to have a screen in front of me.

I didn't have an answer. And no one could tell me what I should do to get better.

I went round and round with the doctors.

"What should I do?" I'd ask.

"Just keep pitching. We'll give it another shot of cortisone."

Where's the end of the tunnel? I kept asking myself. *When will it ever get better? Does it ever get better?*

Toward the middle of the 1969 season with Buffalo, I had taken so many cortisone shots that they couldn't even put in the Xylocaine because there was so much scar tissue in my shoulder that I wasn't flinching when they put in the cortisone.

I pitched a couple of more games, and finally I pitched a game in Rochester, New York. Someone in the big leagues had made a diving catch, and while he made the catch he had his index finger outside his glove, caught his finger in the turf, and broke his wrist. I don't remember who he was. But it prompted a memo from the big leagues that said no one could pitch or play with a finger outside his glove.

I understood at the time that it was a precautionary move, but I had been doing it as long as I could remember. You can catch a ball and not hurt your index finger.

Then one day I was pitching a game in Rochester. I was pitching okay. Suddenly Hector Lopez, my manager, a former Yankee infielder, ran out to the mound and started yelling at me.

"What the fuck are you trying to do? Are you trying to embarrass me? I stuck up for you. I've always been in your corner, and now you're pulling this shit?" he said.

"What are you talking about?" I asked.

"You're pitching with your finger outside your glove," Hector said.

"Hector," I said. "I forgot."

We got into a screaming match on the mound over this stupid finger-outside-the-glove memo. I lost whatever magic I had that day. I walked a couple of guys, gave up a couple of runs, and was taken out of the game. When I walked off the field, instead of staying in the dugout, I walked down the right field line to our clubhouse, and some guy from the stands yelled, "You suck." I took my shirt off and threw it right at him.

"If you think you can do better," I said, "you go out there and fucking pitch."

I got fined for that outburst. A few days later I was traded to the Cleveland Indians for Lee Maye. I was ordered to report to Portland, Oregon. That's clear across the country.

I flew out there and went to the hotel to register. Then I went to the bar and I saw a guy I thought I knew. I walked up to him and said, "Are you on the team?"

He reached out his hand; it was pitcher Sammy Ellis.

Sammy and I became good friends. When people ask me, "Where were *you* when men walked on the moon?" I can say that on July 20, 1969, Sammy Ellis and I sat at a bar in Portland, Oregon, drinking and watching Neil Armstrong walk on the moon.

I had a couple of starts with Portland and pitched okay. My record was one win and three losses in seventeen games. What I remember most about my time in Portland is that I had my first real flare-up of rage. I wasn't aware of it at the time, but cortisone is a steroid, and patients who take too many steroids can't control themselves when they get angry. Rage can lead to murder, suicide, and forms of mental illness. Studies show that people who exhibit rage often are those who have trouble controlling their temper and are prone to acts of violence in the first place. When it first occurred, I had no idea what was happening to me. People who exhibit rage are rarely aware of what is happening to them.

Kurt Bevacqua was the hitter. He checked his swing and hit the ball over the first baseman's head with a couple of runners on base. When he tried to stretch it into a triple, we got him in a rundown.

From my perspective, it was a longer-than-needed rundown. I was taught that a rundown should be no more than one toss. *I raged.* After my team made three tosses trying to tag him, I got all pissed off, jumped into it, got the ball, and tagged Kurt hard in the face with it.

While he was having some fun running back and forth to avoid being tagged, I wasn't in the fucking mood to get involved with his hijinks. I hit him pretty hard, and we went at it pretty good.

Before the end of the season, the Portland Beavers made a trip to Hawaii. Hawaii is a long way away; we spent a week or more there, and our manager, Red Davis, allowed us to bring our wives. I brought Marilyn. The trip to Hawaii was like a second honeymoon.

After the plane took off for Hawaii, we started to hear a bird tweeting in our plane.

The bird was a parakeet belonging to Red Davis's wife. She snuck it on board and kept it in a cage, and that damn bird chirped through the entire plane ride. Once we found out whose bird it was, we kept our mouths shut and finished the flight to the constant chirping of that damn bird.

When we got to Hawaii, they put the bird in quarantine.

In Hawaii, Davis told us he would be checking curfew every night.

"We're here to play ball," he said. "We're not here to have fun. I don't want to see any suntans."

Shut the fuck up, we were thinking. We're in Hawaii for ten days. We're going surfing. We're going fishing. We're getting on a sailboat. We may never come to Hawaii again. Fuck the games. We'll go see Don Ho at night. So let's not even worry about curfew.

We won one game out there. But we had a terrific time. Marilyn and I went to see the sunken battleship USS Arizona at Pearl Harbor, and we went scuba diving in 100 feet of water. At that depth, they told us, if we had a malfunction, we should go to the instructor and buddy-breathe to the surface. If that happened, we had three minutes to surface.

I ran out of air. And I did what they told me. When I discovered that I was out of air, I told the instructor, he made a motion, and we took turns buddy-breathing. I took a deep breath of air, then blew it out; he took a breath, then I took another breath. We surfaced without incident.

Back on shore we were walking off the pier, and there was a fourteen-foot sailfish hanging that someone had obviously caught. It was beautiful.

"Take a picture of me with that sailfish," I demanded.

Marilyn didn't want to. She was adamant. She didn't think it right that I was taking credit for catching that fish when I had nothing to do with it. We argued. Finally, Marilyn said, "I'll take the picture."

I have it somewhere. The whole time she was telling me, "You better not tell anyone *you* caught this fish."

"Who's gonna know?" I said.

Did my rage instigate this argument? Some steroid users become egotistical. Otherwise caring people become "it's-my-way-or-the-highway" dictators.

When we got back to the states, Marilyn flew back to Connecticut. There were only a couple of weeks left in the season, and my arm was just killing me. I was desperate. I had joined a health club in Portland. I got into the sauna and put some hot stuff on my shoulder, hoping the pores were open so the hot stuff would creep in and make the pain stop.

One of the other health club members asked me what I was doing, and after I told him about my arm, he said to me, "You need to go to the University of Oregon and see Dr. Stanley Jacobs. You need to get some DMSO."

DMSO is dimethyl sulfoxide, whose use as a killer of chronic pain was discovered by Dr. Jacobs at Oregon Health Sciences University of Portland in 1961. DMSO reduces inflammation and is an antioxidant. It was the first nonsteroidal painkiller discovered since aspirin. It has never been approved by the FDA, much to Dr. Jacobs's dismay.

Desperately seeking relief, I went to see Dr. Jacobs. He gave me two gallons of DMSO, a foul-smelling liquid that is used primarily as a commercial solvent, which I used faithfully all winter long. I started using DMSO in August. At first it didn't dull the pain, but it helped to break up the adhesions, so I started throwing better again, and after a few months I could throw without much pain. For me it was a miracle drug. It allowed me to pitch, at least for a little while, without excruciating pain.

Toward the end of the year, I called Len Zanke, who had signed me from the Mets, and I said, "Len, I'm throwing good again. Why don't you come and take a look?"

He did, and he reported back to the Mets, and the Mets purchased my contract. I had dropped down to Double-A ball in the Cleveland Indians' minor league system. They had assigned me to Chattanooga. It cost the Mets $12,500. Johnny Murphy did it; he got me back. My sense was that he did it because he liked me and he wanted to give me a second chance.

In spring training in 1970 I went to Triple-A ball with the Tidewater Tides in Norfolk, Virginia. I had a so-so spring training. I didn't regain the speed I had on my fastball, but if I was able to get two or three days' rest between starts, I could pitch decently. If I had to pitch two or three days in a row, I wouldn't have the elasticity. But darn it if the soreness didn't go away.

They came to me and said, "Is your arm hurting?"

"No," I said. "My arm feels pretty good."

"We're going to send you to Memphis. Start the season there and go from there."

I was scheduled to pitch the opening game. Whitey Herzog came to me before the game and said, "Here's what we have to see tonight. First of all, all I want you throwing is fastballs and curveballs. No sliders, no changeups. We have to see the Bill Denehy fastball of old. If you can't show us that, we'll stay with you a little bit but you might as well start looking for a job as a shoe salesman."

Whitey was putting the fear of God in me, and it worked. I struck out thirteen batters. I threw the living shit out of the ball. My next start I struck out thirteen batters. I pitched five games down there. I had a two-win-and-three-loss record, but I pitched really well.

Things were going good. I had a good manager, John Antonelli, the infielder, not to be confused with the New York Giants pitcher by the same name.

Our apartment was between Graceland and the airport. A tornado touched down one night. Everything you hear about a tornado is true. You hear a train coming at you. That tornado didn't miss our apartment by much.

The tornado touched down just before it got to Graceland, popped up in the air, went over Graceland and over our apartment, and slammed down again at the airport, causing tremendous damage. The experience was terrifying. Either Marilyn or I decided to open the door to see what was going on outside. It took five or six minutes to close that damn door. The two of us were pushing as hard as we could, and we couldn't close the door. That was scary.

But what I remember most about my short stay in Memphis was a memorable contest of team depravity. We were in San Antonio, and we had to fly back to Memphis. There was a plane strike, so we were stuck in our hotel rooms until the team could arrange with Arnold Palmer, the golfer, for us to fly to Memphis in his plane. We were playing cards and watching TV when one of the pitchers made me a bet.

Each of us was to put up twenty bucks, and whoever could bring the homeliest woman to his hotel room for oral sex would win the pot. We figured that normal, straight sex would have taken too long, so we chose oral sex as the goal. Three players entered the contest, and I wasn't one of them. When one of the guys who entered the contest called to say he was bringing someone up to his room, we hid under the bed, in the closet, and on the fire escape.

"We watched as two women came to the room, and we watched as they had oral sex with two of our players. Then the guy who initiated the contest called to say, "I'm coming up with the winner." We waited patiently. Suddenly the hotel room door opened, and there he was, pushing a girl in a wheelchair. To be fair, the girl was a softball player who broke her leg and needed the wheelchair to get around. Needless to say, he won the contest hands down amid the sound of a squeaking wheelchair. We audiotaped the event for posterity, and on the plane ride back to Memphis we listened to the tape of that squeaking wheelchair rocking back and forth. We were depraved *and* hysterical.

In June I got word that the front office wanted me to drive from Memphis to Norfolk, Virginia, to pitch against the Mets in an exhibition game. I was told to pack my stuff and that they would decide what to do with me. I had pitched in seven games in Memphis. I won three games and lost four, with a 3.13 ERA. I struck out, on average, one batter per inning.

Against the Mets, I pitched well. I only gave up one run.

"You'll be on the Tidewater roster the rest of the year," they told me.

Bill Virdon was the manager of Tidewater, so I was reunited with him. My arm was better. I pitched some good games for him. One night I struck out thirteen batters in a game against Louisville, the Red Sox' Triple-A minor league team.

Another time, because of rainouts, we played four doubleheaders in a row—all were seven-inning games. We were in Winnipeg, Canada. I was scheduled to pitch the first game of a doubleheader. Bill pulled me aside and said, "I need a real favor. I need a complete game today. If we use the bullpen in the first game, we're really in trouble."

Every inning when I came in, Bill would say, "You want to try something, Bill? You want to try throwing a couple of sidearm pitches? Here's a chance. Don't worry about the report back to the Mets. We need you to get through as long as your arm isn't hurting."

I really felt Virdon was behind me. He was right there. I went out there, and it was a football score. We won the game 14–8. And I pitched a good year for him.

That year Ronnie Allen, Richie's younger brother, played first base for us. He was a switch-hitter. Ronnie and Jesse Hudson, a black pitcher, roomed right next to us on this one road trip. Every night they'd go to bed listening to James Brown. *Jesus Christ!*

I banged on the walls and they laughed.

"Get with it. Get into the spirit," they'd holler.

When we got home, Marilyn met me at the airport. She told me, "We're going to a birthday party tomorrow."

"Whose birthday?" I asked.

"It's Ronnie Allen's little daughter."

"Perfect," I said. "I'm buying the gift."

"His wife told me some of the things . . ."

"I don't care," I said. "I'm buying the gift."

We went downtown, and I bought Ronnie's daughter a set of drums. When I gave them to her, I told her, "Your daddy loves you. There's nothing that makes him happier than when you wake up in the morning to play the drums as loud as you can for your daddy. He loves that. He tells me every day this is the happiest part of his whole day, when you do that."

A couple of days later, Ronnie came to me.

"When the blacks take over this country," he said, "you're the first guy who's going, and I'm going to kill you myself."

That was the good-natured fun we had, and Ronnie was a really good guy.

I finished the 1970 season at Tidewater, and continued to pitch well. I won seven games, lost four, and finished with a 3.29 ERA. I figured that by the next year I'd be back in the major leagues.

After the 1970 season in Tidewater, the Mets asked me to go to San Juan, Puerto Rico, to play winter ball. I was assigned to the San Juan Senadores, who had an agreement to accept three players from the Mets, three from the Pirates, and two from the Red Sox. Also on the roster were pitcher Jim Coburn from the Milwaukee Brewers and Coco Laboy from the Montreal Expos.

The Mets sent me to San Juan with Leroy Stanton, an outfield prospect, and Ken Singleton, a talented young outfielder. The

Red Sox sent Jim Lonborg, Boston's star pitcher who was rehabbing from a skiing accident, pitcher Ken Brett, and a third player whose name I can't remember. The Pirates contributed three excellent young ballplayers: second baseman Dave Cash, first baseman Al Oliver, and catcher Manny Sanguillén. Laboy was the third baseman.

My wife and her brother, John, came along for the trip, and we rented singer Eddie Fisher's beautiful two-bedroom condo in Miramar, a district in San Juan. The San Juan team paid the rent on our condo plus $2,000 a month for expenses. Like all my teammates, I was given a VW Beetle for transportation while there. If the team had a road game, each player would drive his VW. After games, we'd line them up, somebody would drop a flag, and it looked like a Grand Prix race. Six or seven Senadores ballplayers drove VW bugs, roaring out of the stadium at about seventy-five or eighty miles an hour. I was in love, and I had the opportunity to play for some of the most intense baseball fans in the world.

The opening game was against Santurce, the other San Juan team. The rivalry between San Juan and Santurce was unequaled in baseball. Not even the Yankees and the Red Sox could match this rivalry. If you've never been to a game down in the Caribbean and South America, the fans down there are just crazy. They throw cups of beer at each other. They yell and they scream, and they play the guitar. A baseball game in Puerto Rico is quite an event. It's fun, but it can turn contentious and even dangerous. The fans want their team to win at any cost. They are my kind of fans.

In the ballpark there was a definite line of demarcation between the opposing fans. The San Juan dugout was down the third base line, and their fans sat from home plate down the third base line to the outfield. The Santurce fans sat down the first base line. They didn't commingle.

Santurce was managed by Frank Robinson, and featured major league stars like Reggie Jackson, Tony Pérez, Mike Cuellar, and Elrod Hendricks. Hiram Bithorn Stadium was packed to the hilt and then some. Ushers held ropes, and a large crowd stood behind the ropes strung all around the outfield. Just before the start of the game, a bank of lights went out, and the technicians couldn't get them to come back on.

"We have to call the game," said Frank Robinson, the Santurce manager.

"If we call the game," said Roberto Clemente, the San Juan manager, "we're going to have a riot."

Frank, who was a tough guy, said, "If we have a riot, we have a riot. I'm not going to have my guys play without that bank of lights."

"That's your decision," Clemente told Robinson, "but if you're going to have the game called, you're going to get on the public address system and announce it yourself. You're going to be the one to tell them."

"Let me give it another look," said Robinson. "Let's throw a couple of pitches. Maybe we can play."

The game had been going on for six innings when another bank of lights suddenly went dark. Now it was impossible for the batter to see a pitched ball.

Clemente went out to talk to the officials, and when he came back to the dugout he told the bench players, "In half an hour they're going to announce that the game is canceled, so see if you can find your families and tell them to leave now. We want you guys to stick around so the crowd doesn't become suspicious."

Most of the guys found their families and had them leave. Sure enough, after the announcement that the game had been canceled, there was a riot.

Fans overturned cars in the parking lot and set them on fire. The National Guard came in, and I could see there was really going to be a problem. I was looking out a little window into the parking lot when Clemente told the head of the National Guard, "Let me talk to the people and see if I can do something."

The head of the National Guard said to Clemente, "I'll give you ten minutes, and then we're going to have to go in and take control."

Roberto took the PA mike, and he spoke in Spanish, so I'm not exactly sure what he said, but he spoke to the crowd, apparently asking everyone to calm down and leave, and within ten minutes the rioting stopped and the parking lot was empty. My teammates and I sat there and marveled. Was he God?

Roberto asked all the rioters to go home, and everyone went home. It was like he had separated the waters. When Marilyn and I drove home that night, we could see a couple of cars still burning in the parking lot.

I had a great time playing for San Juan. One of the joys of the experience was playing for Roberto Clemente in what would turn out to be the only time he would ever manage. He was elected to the Hall of Fame posthumously, after dying tragically in a plane crash in December of 1972, while en route to deliver aid to earthquake victims in Nicaragua.

Roberto was a terrific person. He was the closest thing to a living God that I've ever found. I've never been around a man who was so well respected. The people of Puerto Rico loved and treasured him. And he was actually a pretty good manager. He was helpful, and he was kind with his ballplayers. He was fun to be around. He really went out of his way to make sure all the American players were comfortable in their surroundings.

The only thing Roberto wouldn't do was argue with the umpires. If there was a close play at second, and our guy was jumping up and down, Roberto wouldn't leave the dugout.

Finally we had to tell him, "As a manager, you have to go out there and represent us."

The next time there was an argument, he went out, and later in the season he even bumped an umpire and was tossed out of the game. Within fifteen minutes the San Juan fans had identified the umpire's car and set it on fire. Like I said, the fans take their baseball *very seriously* in Puerto Rico.

We played Caguas, which is a mountain city. When it was eighty degrees in San Juan, it was only sixty degrees in Caguas. We were playing a doubleheader, and I didn't know how cold it could get in Caguas, so I neglected to bring a sweatshirt.

Roberto had just thrown batting practice, and he came into the clubhouse to change. While doing so, he asked me if everything was okay. I told him, "It's cold out there, and I forgot to bring a heavy sweatshirt."

"Here, use mine," said Roberto, while tossing me his sweatshirt.

I put it on, and I couldn't believe it. Even though he had thrown batting practice for half an hour while wearing that sweatshirt, it was bone-dry.

Think about this. After someone throws half an hour of batting practice, do you want to put on his sweatshirt? Ordinarily not. But Roberto's sweatshirt wasn't wet. It was completely dry. *Wow!* I thought. *How did this happen?* I saw him throw during batting practice. He was out there wearing a long-sleeve, heavy wool sweatshirt. And it wasn't wet!

I pitched well for Roberto and San Juan. One week I was Pitcher of the Week, and one month I was Pitcher of the Month. Playing for San Juan gave me the chance to play on a talented team and to compete against major leaguers. One night the team was playing Mayagüez when the game was rained out, and we had a chance to use the facilities of the resort hotel where we were staying.

Jim Lonborg, Dave Cash, Al Oliver, and I had been star high school basketball players, and we were shooting hoops on the resort's basketball court.

"You want to play a little two-on-two for dinner?" asked Oliver.

I looked at Lonborg, who was six foot six, and he said, "Sure, we'll play you."

Oliver, whose nickname was Scoop, wore a pendant around his neck, and he said, "Before we play, I want to show you something." He opened the pendant, and inside was a photo of him hanging upside down while dunking a basketball.

"I was all-Ohio," said Oliver.

"Who gives a fuck?" said Lonborg, who was one tough cookie.

We kicked their ass badly, and every time I ran into either Oliver or Cash, I'd always say, "Do you remember the score of the basketball game down in Mayagüez when the white guys killed the black guys?"

Jim Lonborg was also one hell of a pitcher. Lonnie was a great teammate and a practical joker. If you were pitching, he'd nail your shoes to the floor during warm-ups or spray shaving gel into the fingers of your glove. But when he went to the mound, he was a mean son of a gun.

In 1966 Lonborg's record with the Red Sox was nine wins and twenty-four losses. Then, in 1967, Sal Maglie became the pitching coach for the Red Sox and Jim won the Cy Young Award as he led the Sox to their "Impossible Dream" American League championship.

Lonnie told me the only difference between his performance one year and the next was Maglie, who got him to start throwing at hitters. In '67 Lonnie led the American League in hit batters, and he said that was a big difference.

My catcher with the San Juan Pirates, Manny Sanguillén, was the best catcher I ever threw to. You couldn't throw the ball past him. You didn't have to worry about throwing a curveball in the dirt with a runner on third base. He had an infectious smile with that space between his teeth, so when he'd give the signal, it looked like he was always smiling at you. He was a super teammate. All the Pirates were super. Freddie Patek, another Pirate, and Manny were good friends and fun guys to be around.

The Mets put me on their roster for the 1971 season. Marilyn and I drove from Middletown, Connecticut, to St. Petersburg for the start of spring training in February of that year. We arrived in Jacksonville, Florida, around six o'clock in the evening, and we figured we'd grab a motel room and drive to St. Pete the next day. When we got to Jacksonville, there wasn't a single motel room available. We drove to Gainesville, and there weren't any rooms available there, either. So we drove the rest of the way to St. Pete Beach, getting in at eleven o'clock at night, and found not a single hotel or motel room available there, either.

All the rooms were already full for the night, so Marilyn and I slept in the car that night, parked at the beach.

We woke up the next morning and drove to a Howard Johnson's. We washed up in the bathrooms and had breakfast, and I reported to the ballpark. Then we found a nice place to live for spring training.

That year I was told I would have a good opportunity to make the team. I had a solid spring training. The Thursday before we broke training camp I was scheduled to pitch against the Dodgers. On Saturday I was scheduled to do my National Guard weekend, and I needed to know whether the Mets were going to keep me.

We would take taxicabs from Huggins-Stengel Field, where we practiced, for the ride to Al Lang Field, where we played. One day I found myself sitting in a cab with Gil Hodges, our manager.

"I've got a little predicament," I said to Gil. "Tomorrow I have to fly to Washington. I have a weekend military commitment. I need to know if I made the team." Gil put his big hand on my left knee, and he said, "Young man, your performance today will dictate whether you make the team or not."

I pitched against the Dodgers and gave up one hit and no runs in four innings. After the game, I went in to his office and I said, "I gotta believe after my performance today that I made the team."

"Yes, you did," he said. "Make your arrangements. If you need any extra baggage, make sure it's in here tomorrow morning so we can put it on the truck going to Shea Stadium. We have a ten o'clock workout Monday morning at Shea Stadium."

I was thrilled. I called Marilyn's brother John and said, "You've got to fly down here today, because I have to fly to Washington, D.C., and I need someone to drive Marilyn back." I was scheduled to fly out Friday night. John found a flight and arrived on Friday afternoon. We went back to the apartment, and there was a message on the door for me to call Bob Scheffing, the Mets' general manager. I got on the phone, and Scheffing said, "I think this is a good break for your career, Bill. We just traded you and Dean Chance to the Detroit Tigers."

My bags were going to Shea Stadium, I was going to Washington, D.C., into the National Guard, Marilyn's brother was down in St. Pete ready to drive Marilyn in my car north to Connecticut, and my contract was now in Detroit.

Welcome to the big leagues.

9

BILLY BALL

BOB SCHEFFING TOLD ME TO CALL THE Detroit Tigers' general manager, Jim Campbell, so I did, and Jim said, "Bill, we're glad to have you. We want you to come over here, but we have a roster problem. We need to clear someone off waivers, so we want you to go to the minor leagues, Toledo, and then we'll bring you to the big leagues in ten days."

Sure you will, was my first thought.

"I've already had a bad experience with people promising me stuff," I said, referring to George Selkirk's broken promise. So I said, "I'm not interested in doing that."

"We want you to come here to Detroit," he said.

"I want some sort of guarantee that in ten days I'm going to come up," I said. "I want the contract now, before I go to the minor leagues. Otherwise I'm just going home."

I figured if Detroit released me, I'd done so well in spring training that someone else would sign me. Besides, I was tired of being fucked with. I didn't tell Campbell I had to go into the National Guard for the weekend. I kept that to myself.

I flew up to Washington, checked into the barracks, and called him the next day.

"Have you had a chance to think things over?" Campbell asked.

"Jim, I haven't changed my mind. I had a really good spring. I don't want to blame you. I don't know you, but I had a bad experience in Washington with promises. I want a raise and I want a guarantee."

"We can give you $1,000 more."

"I was looking more at $3,000."

"No. A thousand is all we're willing to do."

"*How about a guarantee?*"

"We've got to figure out how to do that."

"Figure out how to do it. I'm on my way home now."

"Call me tomorrow morning," he said.

I called the next morning, and Campbell said, "Okay, here's the deal. I will sign you to a big league contract and a minor league contract. Your big league contract will have a $3,000 raise, and your minor league contract will too. That way you get your money no matter what. It doesn't behoove us to give you that money for you to play in the minor leagues. We want you to pitch up here."

On Monday morning I flew from Washington, D.C., to Tampa, Florida, and I drove over to Lakeland to join the Toledo team for spring training. I pitched well for Toledo. I won one game and lost one game in relief. In my third start, I had one of those games where I walked a batter, there was a swinging bunt, I walked another batter, there was an error, then there was another bunt, and then there was a double down the right field line that was fair by inches, and I couldn't get out of the first inning. When I was taken out, I was so angry I couldn't see straight. This was another of those rages where I was so totally out of control that I didn't know what I was doing.

I came into the dugout, picked up a lead-filled fungo bat, and completely demolished the aluminum water fountain attached to the wall.

No one said or did anything as I smashed it. Marilyn was sitting in the stands while I pounded on the drinking fountain. She was so embarrassed.

When my raging was over, I threw the bat down, walked into the clubhouse, sat down in front of my locker, and opened my first beer. It was the first inning, and I drank for nine innings.

At the end of the game Mike Roark, my manager, said he wanted to see me in his office.

"I've got some good news and some bad news," Mike said.

"The GM called down, and you're going to have to pay for the water fountain," he said. "He's going to take it out of your check." A new water fountain costs five hundred bucks.

"What could the good news be?"

"You've been called up to Detroit, and you're to meet the Tigers in Anaheim."

Suddenly, I wasn't so angry anymore.

I joined the Tigers in Anaheim for a series against the Los Angeles Angels. The team was flying down from Oakland, and I got to the hotel before it arrived. I went to the bar. It seemed the likely place to go when you don't know anybody and no one's around.

All of a sudden the guys started coming in. I recognized Tom Timmerman, Joe Niekro, Kevin Collins, and Eddie Brinkman.

I knew these guys from the minor leagues. They welcomed me. We had dinner that night, and at about 11:00 p.m. we were still at the bar. I was feeling no pain by that time, and then Billy Martin, the Tigers' manager, walked in with his pitching coach Art Fowler.

Aw, fuck was my first thought.

I didn't know Billy. Here was my first meeting with my new manager, and I was cocked. Little did I know that Billy was also cocked; Billy came over and introduced himself and said he was glad to have me.

"Really think you can help us," Billy said.

I apologized to him for having had too much to drink.

He put his hand on my shoulder, and he said, "Look, let's get things straight right now. I'm not your fucking babysitter. I'm your manager. I don't give a fuck what you do off the field or how much you drink, as long as you give me 100 percent on the field."

We bonded instantly. My attitude became *You tell me what you want done, and I'll do it.*

Right then and there, I knew I had found the right manager for me.

Even though I had never been a reliever before, Billy wanted to impress upon me how important it was for me to do my job in the bullpen. He kept talking about what we had to do to win the pennant.

"If we have to knock somebody down, we'll do it," he said.

The next day we went out to the ballpark. Before the game I was out in the outfield when I ran into Tony Conigliaro, my old Army buddy, who was playing for the Angels. Tony confided in me that he couldn't see and was having trouble hitting the fastball. He had been hit in the face with a pitch a couple of years earlier when he was with the Boston Red Sox. His face had shattered into a million little pieces, but what no one knew was that he was slowly losing sight in his left eye. It would not be long before he was out of baseball.

Tony was one of the greatest talents ever to play the game. Had he not gotten hurt, it's no telling how many pennants the Red Sox might have won. What happened to Tony was a terrible tragedy. And now Tony was telling me that he was going blind in one eye.

Before the game we had a meeting to go over the Angels' hitters. Someone brought up newspaper reports about Tony's failing eyesight. I wanted to raise my hand and say, "Excuse me. Tony and I are friends. He can't see." But I didn't speak up. I kept quiet.

Billy was sitting back in the corner. He came forward and said, "Gentlemen, we can't worry about this hitter not being able to see the ball. That's his problem. Our problem is to go out and win this ballgame, and we have to win it any way we can."

"The first time Conigliaro gets up," Billy said, "I want you to knock him right on his can. If he can't see the baseball, then he doesn't belong in the game. We're not going to babysit him and not going to lie down for him, because he may be lying to us."

As Billy was saying this, I thought back to my high school days when I enjoyed the sport of hitting batters for the fun of it. Billy and I, it seemed, were soul mates. No one threw at Tony that day.

Billy had contempt for pitchers who wouldn't throw at hitters. We had a pitcher by the name of Jim Hannan who Billy ordered to knock the first hitter down. Jim, a very religious person, said, "I can't do that." The next day, Jim was traded to Milwaukee.

We had another pitcher by the name of Daryl Patterson. Billy ordered Patterson to hit somebody with the first pitch at the start of an inning. Patterson actually threw a strike. After the game was over, Billy went after him in the clubhouse, calling him "gutless" and a few other names. The next day, Daryl was sent to the minor leagues.

A week or so later we played the first weekend series against Cleveland and bombed them; we beat them four straight games, and badly.

On Friday night, Sam McDowell was pitching against us. Sam, who was lightning-fast and had no qualms about hitting batters, hit two of our players and knocked down a few more.

I got the call. Billy put me into the game. Charlie Silvera, the bullpen coach, said to me, "Chris Chambliss is the second hitter." Chambliss had come up from the minors the week before and had gone eleven hits for seventeen at bats at that point.

"Billy wants you to knock Chambliss down," Charlie said.

The first hitter was Indians catcher Ray Fosse, best known for being run over and getting badly injured by a hard-charging Pete Rose during the 1970 All-Star game. Fosse was a big right-handed hitter. He liked the ball out over the plate so he could extend his hands, so we pitched him inside. I hadn't pitched in five or six days. Even when I was sharp I was a little wild. The first pitch my catcher Bill Freehan called for was an inside fastball. I threw it, it ran in, and it hit Fosse in the back. He charged the mound.

What do you do? There's no book to tell you. I reacted. I had never had anyone charge the mound before. As he came in to football-block me, I jumped up in the air and kicked him. Fosse ended up with seventeen stitches from his ear down to his neck. While he was rolling around on the ground, someone stepped on his hand and broke it.

I was dragged off by Sam McDowell, who was laughing.

"Take it easy, take it easy, Irish," Sam kept saying.

"Okay, Sam," I said. "You can let me go."

But I didn't mean it. As soon as Sam released his grip, I ran back into the pile. By this time the Indians' trainer had put a towel over Fosse's neck. I jumped in the air to try to hit him again, to take a coldcock shot at him, when Bill Freehan, my catcher, walked right in front of him. I knocked Bill Freehan out cold, then got dragged off of him and tossed out of the game.

Tigers outfielder Willie Horton, Billy's enforcer, hit one of the Indians pitchers with one punch and broke his cheekbone, jaw, and nose. Ike Brown, another tough character for Detroit, hit Gomer Hodge and put him on the disabled list. There were a series of photos in the newspaper the next day. In the first photo, Ike put his right hand on Hodge's shoulder. The second picture showed him turning Hodge around. The third picture was Hodge's head snapping back, and Ike's fist going up in the air. It knocked Hodge out cold, broke his jaw. We put three Indians on the disabled list after that fight. Umpire Jim Honochick said it was the worst fight he had seen in twenty-seven years in the American League.

In Detroit, we rented a fourplex in Deerfield, Michigan, with Tigers teammates Eddie Brinkman, Kevin Collins, and Dalton Jones. Marilyn and their wives were out jogging, listening to the game on headphones, when Marilyn heard, "Fosse charges Denehy, and Denehy kicks Fosse." Marilyn later told me that she went back to the apartment and was waiting by the phone, thinking I'd call to say I was okay.

What do you do in a situation like that? You go to a bar.

After the game the *whole team* went to the bar. Talk about a sign of unity.

Bill Freehan had an ice pack over his face.

"I'm going to find the bastard who hit me, and I'm going to get him back," Bill said. He was glued to the TV to watch for the culprit. The rest of us were in different parts of the bar, talking.

I was sitting at a table. The next thing I knew, four drinks hit my table.

"Where did that come from?" I asked the waiter.

"It's from the group in the corner."

I looked in the corner and saw Ike Brown, Willie Horton, Gates Brown, and Tony Taylor, our four black players.

I grabbed one of the drinks, walked over to them, and said, "Thanks, guys, but what's this for?"

Willie came out of his seat and put his arm around me.

"I want to tell you something," Willie said. "If you ever get into a fight again, you don't have to worry about a thing. I'll always protect you. But I want to tell you, from all the times I've been with the Tigers organization, this was the first time a white guy hit a white guy. We want to tell you the four of us always will have your back covered."

I was aware that Billy Martin always picked black and Latin players to hit. His choice of Chris Chambliss was yet another example. Willie didn't know that I had hit the *wrong* guy. Billy had wanted me to hit Chambliss, and I had hit Fosse by accident. I was tossed out of the game and fined, and Billy picked up the fine. That fight brought our club together. It was one of the closest-knit ball clubs I had played with during my years in professional baseball.

Later in the season we went to Boston. The call came down for me to go into the game. Charlie Silvera walked up to me and said, "Reggie Smith is their first hitter, and Billy wants you to knock him on his ass."

I finished warming up. I was by the gate at Fenway Park, and just before the inning ended, the phone rang. Charlie got a call. Billy was on the phone. He wanted to speak to me.

"Did you get my message about knocking Smith down?" he wanted to know.

"Yeah."

"Drill him," Billy said.

"Okay."

Back then they had little carts to shuttle you from the bullpen to the infield. The cart picked me up. I rode down the first base line and was let off right in front of the Red Sox dugout as John Kiely played organ music.

I went to the mound. Bill Freehan was standing there, and he said, "There's no use going over any signs. You're only going to be in here for one pitch."

Sure enough, Bill gave me a fastball sign to the inside part of the plate, and it was almost as though Reggie Smith knew it was coming, because when I got into my windup, he started moving away from the plate. He was a good foot and a half back from his original stance when I drilled him with a fastball in the lower part of the back. I got him pretty good.

Reggie took it. He said a couple of things to me. I said a couple of things to him. We were chirping as he walked down the first base foul line. The funny thing was that everyone on the Tigers team *knew* I was going to hit him. Guys told me that when I was looking in for the sign, Willie Horton slowly went into his trot from left field, and by the time I was in my windup, he was almost at shortstop. By the time I hit Smith, Willie was on the infield grass, running full speed toward the Red Sox dugout. He got to the foul line just as George Scott, the physically imposing first baseman for the Red Sox, was coming out of their dugout. All I remember is Willie pointing his finger at Scott and hearing him say, "George, you cross this fucking line, and I will kill you."

George Scott looked like he was standing on the edge of a cliff. It was as though if he took another step, he'd fall to his death, except that he'd fall into Willie Horton's arms, and Horton was going to kill him.

Smith went to first base, and he started chirping a little more. I got into the stretch position, and I backed off, and I said to him, "You want a fucking piece of me? Why don't you come over here and take your shot?"

From first base Reggie charged me, and we got into a free-for-all. I got spiked on my right leg, not bad enough to break the skin, but my pants were torn. After they broke us up, I started walking off the field. I wanted to make sure the umps would throw me out so I wouldn't have to hit when it was our turn to bat.

The umpire said, "Where are you going?"

"I'm out of here, right?" I said. "You threw me out for fighting, didn't you?"

"I didn't throw you out of the game," he said.

"I'm cut, my uniform is torn," I said. "I'm out of here."

"You're *not* out of here," he said. "You're still in here."

I finished the inning and didn't give up any runs. I was the leadoff hitter the next inning, and they were bringing in Jim Lonborg. I had just played with Jim in the Puerto Rican winter league the season before. He and I used to have contests hitting guys. I knew this was not a good sign.

I was in the on-deck circle and I had my batting helmet on, and Billy came to the top step of the dugout.

"You think you can hit this guy?" he asked.

"Fuck no," I said. "My leg's hurting. Get a good hitter in here."

"Okay," Billy said, and he put Mickey Stanley up to pinch-hit for me. As Mickey walked past me, he said, "You motherfucker. I'm taking it for you."

"No," I said, "you're taking it for the team."

Sure enough, first pitch, Lonnie drilled Mickey in the back.

The next day, just before the game started, Billy Conigliaro, who was playing right field, was warming up by throwing pitches to the ball boy down the right field line. Reggie Smith was in center field and Carl Yastrzemski was in left field. Smith and Yaz were playing catch. Billy moved closer to our bullpen and yelled, "Hey, Denehy."

I walked toward the fence, and he walked over to me. He had his uniform shirt open, and he showed me an envelope he had. Billy C handed me the envelope.

"What's this?" I asked.

"That's what I collected from the guys on the Red Sox who were glad you hit Reggie Smith."

It was mostly filled with one-dollar bills, but there were a couple of fives, one ten, and a twenty. There had to be thirty-five dollars in the envelope. I guess most of the Red Sox players didn't care much for Reggie.

After the game was over, we were on the plane leaving Boston. Billy Martin was sitting up front, and for some reason he didn't like Reggie Smith either.

Billy said, "What we might want to think about doing in Detroit is I'll put you in the game and you can drill him again, and then tell him you want to meet him under the stands after the game." Then he said, "Except *you* won't have to meet him. I'll have someone else to take care of it." He was implying that one of his thug buddies would do a number on Smith.

"I don't know if I want to do that, Billy," I said.

"Just think about it," Billy said.

On another occasion I was pitching a game in Detroit, and the Red Sox were killing us. Billy had me warm up. I took eight warm-up pitches in the bullpen. I wasn't even breaking a sweat. He put me in the ball game. The bases were loaded, there were two outs in the top of the ninth inning, and Jimmy Lonborg, my old teammate in San Juan, was the batter.

"This guy used to knock down all my hitters when I was managing the Twins," Billy said. "I want you to knock him down on the first pitch."

Well, I was going to go out to dinner with Lonnie after the ball game. We were good friends.

Billy started to walk off the mound, and I made the sign underneath my chin to Jimmy that the first pitch was going to be up and in, and he nodded to me. I took my warm-up pitches, I went into my windup, and just when I got to the point where I was coming over my head and raising my leg, Jimmy hit the ground.

I had to hurry my motion, and I threw one in the vicinity. Christ, he was lying on the ground, for God's sake!

Everyone was looking around and asking themselves, *What's going on?*

Knocking down or hitting batters was my job. Toward the end of the season in Detroit I walked into the clubhouse one day. Somebody had replaced my glove with an Everlast boxing glove. It had to be either Gates Brown or Mickey Stanley, because the two of them came up to me when I was looking for my glove and asked, "What did you do, get a new glove contract?"

I was a team player, and I would do anything to win, so I fit in very well with Billy. He wanted everyone to do his part, and I'm sure if he said to me, "I want you to grab a gun, go out, and shoot somebody," if I could have done it without going to jail, I'd have probably shot somebody.

We had players who didn't like Billy's ruthlessness. Others didn't like him because he was too hard on them. Some of the veterans like Dick McAuliffe and Al Kaline were among them.

One day Billy said to me, "On a ball club there are ten guys who would do anything for you, ten guys who hate your guts, and five guys who are undecided. The good managers get the five guys who are undecided on their side."

We lost a doubleheader in Minnesota. It was Billy's first trip back to Minnesota, where he had managed the year before. After the game we attacked the spread of food in the clubhouse. Billy walked in and saw all the guys eating; he was furious, and he tipped over the tables of food, picked up a chair, started cussing, and shouted, "You guys are a bunch of losers. All you're interested in is filling your faces." He took a chair and whipped it right over Al Kaline's head and into his locker. Al just kind of looked back over his shoulder and then looked at his locker.

You never knew when Billy might explode. One night in Cleveland a group of Detroit players were at a bar called The Theatrical. Billy was standing behind us, and he had a drink in his hand. Some guy walked right into Billy, knocked his drink over, and kept walking.

About ten minutes later the same guy, walking in the opposite direction, bumped into Billy again, and *again* he spilled Billy's drink. Billy figured out that neither time was an accident.

"Hey, asshole," Billy yelled at him, "it's one thing that you bumped into me one time and didn't buy me a drink, but this was the second time, and the least you can say is you're fucking sorry."

The guy looked at Billy as if to say, "Fuck you," and Billy coldcocked him. Billy knocked him to the ground and kicked him a couple of times. Before anyone called the cops, we were out of the bar, into a cab, and out of there.

The next day I got a call from Billy inviting me out to lunch.

It's not every day you get invited to lunch by your manager, and so I met him.

"We're going out to the house of a friend of mine," Billy said. "We're getting picked up."

A big black sedan arrived, and we got in. We were driven out to somewhere off Lake Erie. When we got to the gated community, the only thing suspicious was a guy standing guard at the gate. He opened the gate and let us in. The residence faced the lake. As we drove along the long, circular driveway in front of the house, there were three or four other guys walking around. I didn't see any guns. They were just guys walking around.

We went inside, and this nice Italian gentleman came out. I don't remember his name. His son, who was in his early twenties, was with him. We had a really nice luncheon. After lunch the father said that he and Billy needed to talk about some things. He asked his son, who was about my age, to show me around the place. We walked around. He showed me their boat launch, and I saw a couple of more guys just hanging around this guy's house. They were all Italian. Before leaving, we said, "Thank you very much."

"Good luck the rest of the season," the nice Italian gentleman said, then Billy and the man embraced, and we got back to the car. Billy didn't say who he was. He didn't say how he knew him. The encounter was like nothing I had ever experienced before. My suspicion was that he was in organized crime, but he could have been anybody. I was probably jumping to the wrong conclusion. But who knows?

10

THE BEST YEAR
OF MY LIFE

BILLY SEEMED TO ATTRACT CELEBRITIES. ONE DAY, while in Detroit, Milton Berle came into our clubhouse. *Uncle Miltie* was in our clubhouse. We recognized him. How could we not? He was perhaps one of the most famous comedians in the history of television. *The Milton Berle Comedy Hour* was one of the highest-rated shows for many years.

One of the things Uncle Miltie used to do on his show was kiss a guy. One of the Tigers players brought this up, and I said, "For fifty bucks, I'll go and kiss Uncle Miltie." The bet was made, and I went up to him, tapped him on the shoulder, and said, "Uncle Miltie," and when he turned around, I gave him a kiss right on the lips.

The look on his face was priceless. For fifty bucks I would have kissed him on his ass.

I had three roommates with the Tigers during the year. One night I shared a hotel room with the first of my three roommates, Dean Chance, who was a beauty, a celebrity in his own right. Dean had a reputation, along with Bo Belinsky, a teammate of his on the LA Angels, of being a playboy, but I never saw any of that. Dean was a really good businessman and a good promoter. After games I'd go to my room to watch TV; Dean was always on the phone, chatting away.

Dean had one of those old cell phones the size of a radio phone you carried into combat, and he was always talking to somebody on it.

One evening he said to me, "Here, call this number. It's in England." He gave me the number and told me to ask for Gil Clancy.

"Gil Clancy, the boxing promoter?" I asked.

Then I asked, "What am I supposed to say?"

"Get him on the phone and tell him I want to talk to him."

I called the number and asked for Gil Clancy.

"Dean Chance is calling from Anaheim, California."

Gil said, "Hey, Deano."

I gave the phone to Dean, who was negotiating the rights for the Muhammad Ali–Joe Frazier fight for the state of Ohio.

They were talking, and I was listening, and I was thinking, *This is really big-time.* And Dean was talking really big numbers. When their conversation ended, Dean said, "I'm a boxing promoter in the off-season, and I want to get this fight for Ohio."

The next night, after the game, we went back to our room. As I walked in, Dean was in the corner of the room over by the desk, and he was on the phone again. Sitting on my bed was one of the best-looking women I'd ever seen in my life. I recognized her immediately, but couldn't put a name to her.

"Hi, how are you?" she said. "I'm a friend of Dean's."

After Dean hung up the phone, he said, "I want you to meet a good friend of mine. This is Jo Collins."

Jo Collins was Playboy Playmate of the Year in 1965.

This is really exciting, I thought.

I started talking to her, and Dean got back on the phone, and the next thing I heard was the toilet flushing in the bathroom.

Who is this? I wondered.

The door opened, and out popped Bo Belinsky, Jo's husband.

This is unbelievable. This *was* big-time.

They left, and that was the extent of my encounter with Bo and Jo. She was absolutely gorgeous and he was very nice.

We flew home to Detroit. Our bullpen coach was Charlie Silvera, who had played with Billy on the New York Yankees. Charlie, the third-string catcher behind Yogi Berra and Ralph Houk, loved to tell stories about his Yankee days. He said that one time Yankee shortstop Phil Rizzuto was given the day off.

"Since you have the day off, Phil, why don't you come out to the bullpen?" asked Charlie.

"What's so special about the bullpen? You can't see the game."

"We're going to have Italian cuisine."

"Okay," said Phil, who loved Italian food. "I'll come out there."

There was an Italian restaurant across the street from Yankee Stadium. The bullpen was out of sight of the Yankee dugout, and a waiter from the restaurant brought a table with a red-and-white tablecloth and set up a little candelabra—a branched lamp with several candles. When Rizzuto saw the table and candelabra, he asked, "What's this?"

"It's where we're going to eat," Charlie told him.

Then, about the fifth inning, the waiter brought the food out. They lit the candles, and the waiter handed them a menu and told them about the specials. They sat down, and the waiter brought Phil a three-course Italian meal.

"We do this every day," Charlie told Phil.

Charlie told me, "Rizzuto thought it was the greatest thing in the world."

The Tiger bullpen consisted of Ron Perranoski, the former Dodger relief star; Tom Timmerman; Fred Scherman; Joe Niekro; Dean Chance; and me. Our warm-up catcher was Jim Price, who we called the Big Man, because he liked to wheel and deal.

There were these little TV sets for sale in the early 1970s. They were about four inches square and had a pop-up screen.

One of the Tigers fans was watching one of these TVs behind the bullpen dugout in Detroit, and Jim asked him about the little TV.

"Would you trade for it?" he asked him. They haggled.

"How about an autographed bat?" Price asked.

"I'll tell you what," said the fan, "I'll take an autographed game bat of Al Kaline for it." Kaline had been the star of the Detroit Tigers for twenty years. He was perhaps the greatest Tiger player since Hank Greenberg, who had played in the 1930s and '40s.

"Okay, deal," Jim said as he ran back into the bullpen.

Charlie Silvera, who was afraid that if we did anything crazy he'd get in trouble with Billy, overheard the conversation and said, "Jim, you can't do this. It's in the middle of the ball game, and you're not running to the dugout and getting a bat and getting Kaline to sign it during the game."

THE BEST YEAR OF MY LIFE

"I have to go to the bathroom," Jim lied, "and when I go to the bathroom, what I do in the bathroom, in the dugout, it's none of your concern, Charlie. Don't worry about it."

Charlie said, "If Billy sees you getting Kaline to sign an autograph and sees you carry that bat out here, he's going to know something is suspicious."

"You always bring bats out here so you can stand at the plate while these guys are warming up," Jim said. "No problem."

"Don't do it," Charlie said.

"Okay, fine."

At the end of the half inning, the Big Man ran down to the dugout. He was out of sight for a while, and he emerged from the dugout with a shit-eating grin on his face. He was holding a bat and pointing to where the signature would go on the bat. He was telling us he had Kaline's bat.

Billy had to go to the umpire to make a lineup change, and as soon as Billy left the dugout, Price ran over to Kaline in the dugout and got him to sign the bat. And before Billy returned to the dugout, here comes Big Jim Price, with a big, big, big smile, running all the way to the bullpen.

He had an autographed bat from Al Kaline. And he exchanged it for the television set. Oh, yeah.

The Tigers had some real characters on the team. One time poor Joe Niekro almost blew himself up. I say "poor" because Joe had a hellacious knuckleball and Billy wouldn't let him throw it because our catcher, Bill Freehan, couldn't catch it. Billy made Joe throw his slider and sinker, which weren't nearly as effective as his knuckler.

At any rate, Joe almost blew himself up because of a concoction Dean Chance made. Dean mixed turpentine with rock resin and boiled it. When the rock resin melted down and mixed with the turpentine, the result was a substance stickier than pine tar. Dean showed us how to loosen the stitching in one of the fingers of a pitcher's glove so we could form a little pocket, and then we took a scoop of this sticky stuff and put it in there. When we went to the mound, if we needed to get a really good grip on a breaking ball, we'd go into our glove with one or two fingers and touch this substance to improve the grip on the ball.

There was only one problem. You had to be careful making the stuff, or else it could explode.

When Deano was released, one of the last things we asked him to do was leave us some of this stuff; but he took off, leaving us goo-less. We all knew what the ingredients were, turpentine and rock resin, so Joe Niekro decided he would cook up a batch.

"Go ahead and do it and we'll share the cost," we told him. "It can't be that expensive, anyway."

One day Joe came to the ballpark, and I noticed he didn't have any hair on his arms.

When asked about it, Joe said, "The thing exploded and burned all the hair off my arms."

We were in Baltimore for a big game against the Orioles at Memorial Stadium. At the start of the game the group of us walked down the right field line to the bullpen. I was one of the last to arrive. Tom Timmerman was sitting on one of the bullpen seats, intently reading the newspaper, as I got down on my hands and knees, crawled underneath the seat, and inserted two matches into his shoe. The rest of the pen—Niekro, Scherman, Collins, Price, and Perranoski—knew I was underneath there, and they were watching me just to make sure I wasn't putting the matches in *their* shoes.

As I backed myself out from under the seating, I sprayed a trail of ethyl chloride—the stuff trainers use to freeze injuries after a player gets hit by a pitch—from Timmerman's shoe back a distance of about ten feet. I struck a match and threw it on the ground; the flame followed the trail of ethyl chloride along the ground until it hit Timmerman's shoe. His shoe caught fire.

We were waiting for Tom to jump up in the air. But nothing, until smoke started to rise, and his newspaper caught fire. Tom put out the fire while swearing and shaking his finger at us, and we were laughing like hell. What we didn't know was that when he was a boy, he had been shot in the foot, and all the nerves in his foot were dead, and so he couldn't feel anything when the flames hit his foot. I had actually burned a hole in his shoe, and I had burned his foot pretty badly. There would be no way Tom would be able to pitch that day.

Charlie Silvera just about had a stroke.

"If Billy finds out about this," he wailed, "I'm going to lose my job."

Meanwhile, Ron Perronoski told Charlie, "Don't worry about it. We'll think of something." Then he fed Charlie's fears by telling him, "I think, *Charlie*, what's going to happen, you'll probably get a couple of bullets in the back of your head for letting this happen. Billy is going to be . . ."

We concocted an idea that Tom should warm up right fielder Al Kaline before the start of the next inning. While he was playing catch with Al, he would fake a knee or ankle injury, and we'd have to take him to the clubhouse for treatment.

Tom agreed and walked out of the bullpen to play catch with Kaline, but he was limping badly, and we were screaming at him, "Don't limp, Tom. You're going to give it away. Stop limping."

Tom gave us the finger as if to say, *You fuckers. You burned my foot and now you're telling me I can't limp?*

Tom dropped to one knee, pretending he was hurt. Bill Boehm, our trainer, came out and asked, "What's the problem?"

"We need to get him into the clubhouse," said Silvera, "and we'll explain it to you later."

We took him underneath the grandstands, got Tom into the clubhouse, and told Boehm the real story. What he reported to Billy was that Tom had jumped for a ball, had come down wrong, and had slightly twisted his ankle. Charlie, meanwhile, was scared to death that Billy would come into the clubhouse to check it out for himself or ask to see his ankle.

"He can't pitch tonight," he told Billy, "but he's day-to-day."

"Get dressed and get out of here," we told Timmerman.

Billy never did find out.

My point is that when I was compared to Tom Seaver, players always said that I was a scoundrel, a guy who liked to have fun, and a guy who wasn't as serious as he should have been. That was one of those times when I probably went overboard. How was I supposed to know Timmerman had no feeling in his foot? *Jesus Christ.*

My second roommate was Tigers first baseman Norm Cash. I roomed with him for a two-week road trip. I never saw him. His bag would come to the room and you could pick it up with your tongue. I don't think there was a bit of clothing in there. Nothing.

"Make sure when it's time to go," he'd tell me, "you put both of our suitcases outside the door." Yet I would see him at the ballpark every night. I have no idea where he stayed.

The word on Norm was that he was a real womanizer, but I never saw him with a woman. I never saw him. I can't tell you where he was.

We went on a West Coast road trip. We first went to Anaheim, and before the game they were having a softball game between the Playboy bunnies and the media. We were watching. Billy was sitting there, and he said to me, "I'll give you twenty bucks. After this next hitter, I want you to go out there and see if you can put this chest protector on the catcher."

The catcher for the bunnies was well-endowed. She had to be a size forty-two.

Sure enough, I went out there with a chest protector, and try as I might, I couldn't get it over her boobs. I got a big laugh trying to get it over her head. She had her hands over her head, wiggling. Once the game started, the bunnies were gone.

Next, we next went to Oakland, and two things happened. The A's owner Charlie Finley announced he would pay you $500 if you could ride his mule. This was a *big* fucking mule.

"I could use the $500," I said to Billy.

"All right," said Billy, who arranged for me to ride the mule before the game. I got on top of the mule, and he started bucking. Then I grabbed him around the throat, and I went maybe ten feet when the animal became annoyed that I was on his back. I jumped off. But I had ridden Charlie's mule.

"Just have Charlie send me the check," I said to the PR guy.

The next day there was a note. Charlie wasn't paying. He said I hadn't ridden it long enough. Billy took care of it.

He got me the $500. I don't know how, but an envelope with Oakland A's letterhead arrived with five one-hundred-dollar bills in it.

That night, Vida Blue pitched against us. It was 1971, and that year Vida won the Cy Young award and the Most Valuable Player award. He was pitching great, and after six innings he had a no-hitter. It didn't look like we were going to touch him, so Billy put me in the game.

"We don't have a chance to beat this guy unless you can get him out of the game," Billy said.

I went to the mound, and I was thinking, *How do I get him out of the game?* My solution: I would hit him and try to bait him into a fight so the umps would throw him out of the game.

I wound up and threw the ball at Vida as hard as I could. I hit him in the knee. Perfect. He went down. He was limping. They took him out of the game. I did my job. Either Norm Cash or Dick McAuliffe got a swinging bunt off Rollie Fingers. That was the only hit we got, and we lost.

The next night, Billy put me in the game and had me knock down Tommy Davis. Now I loved Tommy Davis, a great guy and a good clubhouse guy. Tommy had a smile on his face all the time, and he was good with rookies. But I had to knock him down. I took a deep breath, and I rubbed my hand across my upper chest, hoping he would see what was going to happen. I threw an inside fastball, he ducked, and his bat came up so the knob of the bat was facing the pitcher. The ball hit the knob of the bat, rolling into fair territory, as he went down. Our catcher picked it up and threw him out at first base.

Tommy stared me down.

In Oakland we were down the first base line, and the A's were down the third base line. There was a walkway behind home plate. The next night, I walked out of the clubhouse and there was Tommy.

He asked me, "Did you throw at me on purpose, or were you told to do it?"

"I can't answer that," I said.

"Okay, you answered that," he said.

He took a step away, and then stepped forward and said, "Jesus Christ, Bill, do you know how close you came to hitting me in the face? You scared the living shit out of me. Watch what the fuck you're doing, will you?" And he walked away.

I felt bad. *Because he was a good guy.* But I had to do my job.

That summer my third roommate was pitcher Mickey Lolich. Mickey started off having a really good year, until it was June and it started to get hot. He was bitching and moaning because he never pitched well in hot weather. In cool weather he had great starts, and he had great finishes, but during the summer he always faded because he was overweight. Before one game against Kansas City, Norm Cash gave me a black beauty to give to him. Mickey struck out sixteen batters. He struck out Bob Oliver four times on twelve pitches, all fastballs. Mickey was incredible. He threw bullets. I roomed with Mickey the rest of the year, but I never saw him take any amphetamines other than the one he got from me, the one Norm told me to give to him.

The second funny thing that happened, and this happened the same week I kissed Uncle Miltie, was that Norm was supposed to be interviewed for a spot on the NBC Game of the Week. It was a Saturday, and he was to be interviewed by Sandy Koufax. They were going to pay Norm a $300 fee for doing the interview. Norm was excited, because the women were going to be able to see him.

He shaved extra-close so they could see what a handsome dude he was. When Koufax walked into the clubhouse, I went across and introduced myself, and I said, "Sandy, could I ask you one quick question?" I said, "I'm having trouble with my curveball. You had one of the best in the game. Can you explain what you did?"

Sandy took off his jacket, unbuttoned his shirt, loosened his tie, and stood in the middle of the clubhouse going through his motion, showing how he pulled down with one finger, the other finger up in the air, going through his mechanics. He explained it so well and took so much time that the time passed when poor Norm was supposed to be interviewed. Norm never made it on TV. Norm never got his $300. Norm reminded me of it for days. *For days.*

Norm would say to me, "You have a fucking pitching coach, Art Fowler, but nooooo, you see Koufax, and when it's my fifteen seconds of fame, where all the women in the world were going to see what a handsome guy I am from Texas, noooooooo, you gotta ask Sandy Koufax how to throw a fucking curveball. You couldn't have waited until after my interview? You couldn't wait until after the game? You had to ask him before my interview, and what happens? Norm Cash doesn't get on TV."

That same year, Michigan Senator Robert Griffin arranged for us to go to the White House. When we went there, we brought baseballs for President Nixon to sign. They were confiscated by the Secret Service.

"They'll get signed, and we'll get them," we were told.

We went into the Oval Office. We lined up, and our PR guy walked down the line with Nixon and introduced us. He got to me and said, "This is Bill Denehy, a right-handed pitcher from Middletown, Connecticut." Nixon knew something to say about each of us.

"Aaaah," he said, "you're from the Nutmeg State." He got to Gates Brown, and the PR guy said, "This is William 'Gates' Brown, from Ohio." Nixon had a big smile on his face, and said, "So you're Gates Brown."

And Gates looked at him and said, "And you're Tricky Dick."

Nixon loved it. He grabbed Gates and hugged him.

We had pictures taken with Nixon, and afterward Senator Griffin held a cocktail party. People from his office attended, a man and his wife were there, and this guy's wife was gaga over the stars on the team. She wanted her picture taken with Al Kaline and Norm Cash, and for some reason, I got stuck with her husband. He started talking baseball with me, I would walk across the room to get away from him, and two minutes later he'd find me, and we'd be back at it again.

In mid-August, we were playing in Baltimore. I went to the ballpark. When I got there, I was told Billy wanted to see me in his office. My first thought was, *You're going to send me down for two weeks and then call me back up. What a pain in my ass.*

MY LITTLE
LEAGUE TEAM
WON THE
MIDDLETOWN,
CONNECTICUT,
CITY LEAGUE
CHAMPIONSHIP
WHEN I WAS
TWELVE.
Bill Denehy Archive

I HAD BEEN KNOWN
AS WILD BILL EVER
SINCE I WAS A KID
WHO COULD THROW
A BALL THROUGH
A WALL. I DIDN'T
ALWAYS KNOW
WHICH WALL.
Bill Denehy Archive

I WAS ROGER CLEMENS'S PITCHING COACH WHEN THE NEW
BRITAIN RED SOX WON THE 1983 EASTERN LEAGUE CHAMPIONSHIP.
Bill Denehy Archive

photo by
Alfa Studio

Wild Bill Deneby   *The Grog*

WHEN I WAS THE COACH AT THE UNIVERSITY OF HARTFORD, ONE OF THE GUESTS I INVITED TO SPEAK AT MY BASEBALL CLINIC WAS LOU PINIELLA OF THE YANKEES. LOU WAS A GREAT STUDENT OF HITTING.
Bill Deneby Archive

I DON'T KNOW THE PLAYER ON THE LEFT, BUT WADE BOGGS, STEVE LYONS, RON DARLING, AND I HELD A PRESS CONFERENCE IN AN ATTEMPT TO ATTRACT A MAJOR LEAGUE FRANCHISE TO HARTFORD. I WANTED THE TEAM TO PLAY IN THE DOMED STADIUM I WAS PROPOSING FOR THE UNIVERSITY OF HARTFORD.
Bill Deneby Archive

TIGERS MANAGER BILLY MARTIN KEPT ME ON THE DETROIT STAFF AS THE PITCHER HE WOULD DESIGNATE TO COME INTO THE GAME AND HIT A BATTER. BILLY WAS AS CRAZY AS I WAS.
Bill Deneby Archive

Final Minor League Statistics
Top 10 Prospects: Double-A, Class A Leagues

Baseball america™

"Baseball News You Can't Get Anywhere Else"

Oct. 10-24, 1988
Price: $1.95 ($2.50 in Canad.
Now In Our 8th Year

GOODEN   CLEMENS

1983
A Classic Year

At Lynchburg, Dwight Dominates Class A Hitters

At New Britain, Roger Leads Red Sox To Title

WHEN I WAS THE PITCHING COACH FOR THE BRISTOL RED SOX, ROGER CLEMENS AND I WERE VERY CLOSE. HE WAS A RARE TALENT. HE WAS WHO I THOUGHT I WOULD BE.
Bill Deneby Archive

MANAGER CLYDE MCCULLOUGH AND ME AT AUBURN, NEW YORK. I COULDN'T HAVE ASKED FOR A BETTER MANAGER.
Bill Deneby Archive

MY DAUGHTERS KRISTIN AND HEATHER. THEY'VE GROWN UP TO BE FINE YOUNG WOMEN.
Bill Deneby Archive

IN SPRING TRAINING OF 1970, I INVITED MY PALS FRANKIE MARINO AND JOEY SCIONTI TO VISIT ME IN ST. PETERSBURG.
Bill Deneby Archive

AS YOU CAN SEE, I CLEAN UP REALLY WELL.
Bill Deneby Archive

AS PITCHING COACH AT BRISTOL, I TAUGHT MY PLAYERS HOW TO THROW AND HOW TO COMPETE. HERE BILLY MALONEY LEARNS THE PROPER MECHANICS FOR THROWING A CURVEBALL.
Bill Denehy Archive

TONY TORCHIA, THE MANAGER OF THE BRISTOL RED SOX, AND ME. IN 1981 TONY HIRED ME TO HELP WITH HIS PITCHERS WHEN I WAS WORKING FOR ENTERPRISE RADIO.
Bill Denehy Archive

ON THE MOUND FOR WOODROW WILSON HIGH SCHOOL. MY THIRD BASEMAN, PAT MILARDO, HAD SOFT HANDS AND A GOOD ARM, AND HE COULD HIT WITH POWER.
Bill Denehy Archive

I HELD A BASEBALL DINNER TO RAISE MONEY FOR MY UNIVERSITY OF
HARTFORD VARSITY BASEBALL TEAM. AMONG THE GUESTS WERE BOOSTER
ALAN BECK, A LOCAL ATTORNEY, AND THE GUEST SPEAKER, GEORGE
STEINBRENNER, THE OWNER OF THE NEW YORK YANKEES.

Bill Denehy Archive

TOPPS BASEBALL CARD OF BILL
DENEHY AND TOM SEAVER.

*Topps baseball card used courtesy of
The Topps Company, Inc. For more
information about The Topps Company,
please see our website at www.topps.com.*

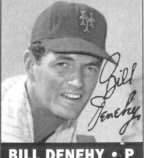
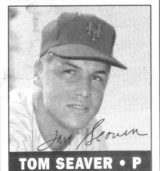

METS 1967 ROOKIE STARS

BILL DENEHY • P   **TOM SEAVER • P**

STROM THURMOND
SOUTH CAROLINA

COMMITTEES

ARMED SERVICES
JUDICIARY
VETERANS' AFFAIRS
LABOR AND HUMAN RESOURCES

United States Senate

WASHINGTON, DC 20510-4001

March 11, 1994

Mr. Bill Denehy
N.A.R.P.A.
First Union Building, Suite 700
20 North Orange Avenue
Orlando, Florida 32801

Dear Mr. Denehy:

Thank you for your letter of recent date supporting S. 674, and for the information booklet on NARDA. I appreciate having the benefit of your views, and am pleased to learn of your commitment to addressing the problems of addiction.

As you know, the abuse of alcohol and its attendant problems are a major concern facing our Country. Consider the following facts:

* the average age at which young people begin drinking is age 13;

* alcohol is the most widely used and abused drug among young people today;

* close to 50 percent of all fatal highway crashes are alcohol-related;

* an alcohol-related family problem strikes one of every four American homes; and

* fetal alcohol syndrome is one of the top three causes of birth defects---and it is preventable.

As a response to these facts, I introduced, on March 30, 1993, S. 674, the "Sensible Advertising and Family Education Act." This legislation represents an important step in educating consumers on the potential hazards of alcohol consumption. It does so by requiring the use of health warning labels in alcoholic beverage advertisements appearing on radio, television, and print media.

This bill was referred to the Senate Committee on Commerce, Science and Transportation. Hearings were held on May 13, 1993. No further action has been taken at this time.

Thank you again for writing. I believe S. 674 represents a reasonable means of further addressing the alcohol problems of this Country.

With kindest regards and best wishes,

Sincerely,

Strom Thurmond

Strom Thurmond

ST/lx

I went to Billy's office, and sitting there were two guys in black suits. I closed the door.

"We have a little predicament here," Billy said. "We need your help."

I was relieved I wasn't getting sent out.

"These two guys are from the FBI," Billy said. "This woman's husband has threatened to shoot one of your roommates tonight."

He said it was *one* of my roommates, but he didn't say which one.

I can't believe it's Dean, I thought. *I never saw him with a woman.*

I don't know if Lolich could get laid if you brought the woman in and paid her.

Norm, now he's a different story. But I didn't know for sure.

"One of your roommates met this guy's wife a couple times, and he found out about it; so he's threatening to shoot him tonight," said one of the FBI agents.

"How am I involved in this?" I asked.

The other FBI agent said to me, "Do you remember Senator Griffin's cocktail party?"

He continued, "There was a guy you were seen talking to most of the time. Can you identify him?"

"Identify him?" I said. "He was a pain in the ass. *A real blue fly.* I'd like to get him out of my mind."

"That's the guy."

"We figure if he's going to shoot him, he has to be close to the dugout."

The plan was for me not to dress for the game that night, to walk around the stands, and to stay close to the first base dugout, because the FBI figured that's where he'd have to be to shoot him. I made one observation.

"The radio guys are pretty good," I said. "They're going to see me walking around in the stands. What's my cover story?"

"That's pretty sharp," Billy said. "I'll tell you what we're going to do. We're going to announce you as the starting pitcher in two days in Detroit against the Yankees. You'll throw batting practice tonight before the game, and since you're doing that, there's no reason for you to be dressed. If they see you in the stands, they'll say you're going to pitch in Detroit."

That was the plan. The FBI guys figured the suspect would come in through a runway, and there was one to the right of the dugout.

"Keep an eye on that," I was told. We did this for five or six innings. The FBI agents and I were standing in the middle of the ballpark, and I was gazing toward that runway when I thought I'd spotted him.

"See that guy over there?" I said. "He looks like the guy, but when I saw him the last time, he had a suit and tie on." The FBI agents made a beeline over toward this guy, who spotted them and ran back down the runway. They chased after him, but he got away.

We continued to watch for him, but nothing happened. After we won the game, the FBI agents said, "Here's what we're going to do. Along the walk from the locker room to the bench, there's twenty-five yards to cross where people stand and get autographs, and we can't take the chance he might be in that crowd. We're going to swing a car around and take a bunch of guys out in a couple of cars early."

We drove to Friendship Airport, and I was told to stand at the bottom of the ramp with the two FBI agents waiting for the bus, to make sure everyone was a member of the team. I thought this was silly. But we got everyone on the plane, shut the door, and took off.

During the flight I went up to Billy, sat down, and asked for a beer.

"For what? You didn't do anything today."

"Fuck, I did more than anyone else did today," I said. "I'm soaking wet. Give me a beer."

He laughed and handed me a beer. Billy never told me which player caused the whole mess, and he never told the player about the threat. Billy told me to get lost, and I walked back to my seat.

If Billy liked you—and he liked me a lot—he was a great manager to play for. Billy may have thought Art Fowler, his pitching coach, was great. But Art was more or less a friend of Billy's. Art was a good conduit between Billy and the pitchers. But as a teacher, he didn't do much. Billy, not Art, knew how to work with me and improve my performance. Art was a really great guy, and he really kept you loose. He never let you get down on yourself. It was like having a favorite uncle on the team. But he taught me absolutely nothing about pitching.

One time in Detroit I pitched and got knocked around a little bit. The next day I was out in left field with a couple of other pitchers during batting practice. Art came out of the dugout with a paper bag over his head. He crawled on his hands and knees from the third base coaching position, down the third base line to where we pitchers were standing in left field. We were all watching him and thinking, *What the fuck is this?* Art finally got out to me, stood up, and said, "You pitched so fucking shitty last night; I didn't want anyone to know I was your pitching coach." We all laughed like crazy. Art took the bag off his head, gave me a big hug, and said, "I love ya."

One time we had a day off in Baltimore. When we got there, Norm Cash announced that one of his close friends was having a barbecue, that when we got to the hotel there'd be directions, and that everyone was invited.

"Rent a car and come," Norm told us on the plane. When the plane landed, there were two vehicles waiting by the plane, a bus for the team and a big red Cadillac convertible with a white interior and two babes in it. Norm got into the car, waved to us, and said, "I'll see you at the barbecue tonight." And off he went.

Kevin Collins, Dalton Jones, Ed Brinkman, and I got in a car. We lived near each other, were good friends, and always hung out together. We were trying to follow the directions we got from the hotel, and since the party was close to the Nike missile base where I went for National Guard duty, I knew we were going in the *wrong* direction. Dalton was driving, and we decided to cut across the median and head the other way, but we didn't realize there was a ditch in the median, and when the front of the car went into this ditch, we were stuck.

The first car that came by was from the state police. We each had had a couple of cans of beer, and the empties were lying on the floor of the car.

"What happened?" asked the cop.

"We're looking for a party," Dalton said.

Another car pulled up. Who was in it? Billy Martin.

This is not good, I thought.

Billy talked to the cop, and they walked away from each other. We were saying to each other, "We're all going to get arrested. Let's hope Billy doesn't pop the cop."

Instead, Billy walked over to us and said, "Here's what we're going to do. The officer is going to call a tow truck. They'll pull you out of here."

Billy told me how to get to the party.

We received no tickets, threats, or warnings. The tow truck pulled us out, and we went to Norm's friend's barbecue. The next day we went to the ballpark and dressed. We sauntered out onto the field, and in the dugout we noticed this guy dressed in a Detroit Tigers uniform. He was wearing brand-new spikes, had a new glove, and was just sitting there.

Who the fuck is this? we wondered.

Eddie Brinkman, who figured it out first, fell down laughing. It was the cop who had found us in the ditch. Billy had obviously bribed him.

I was only with the Tigers one year, but it was one of the best years of my life. Playing for Billy Martin was a rare privilege. Billy was better than anyone I knew in baseball when it came to learning the game—how to run the bases; how to bunt; how to figure out what the other team might do; when they might bunt, steal, or attempt a suicide squeeze; and how to manage the ball game overall.

I learned more from Billy Martin than from anybody else in the game. Billy never missed a trick; he never let anything get past him. He was like a hawk, circling around a farm field, looking for mice. He could talk to a sportswriter while at the same time watching his catcher in infield practice to see whether his throws to second base were accurate. He'd watch his outfielders to see whether their arms were strong, whether they hit the cutoff man consistently.

During the game he'd watch the pitcher, always scouting. Billy always talked about aggressiveness. That's what he preached. He wanted you to score the first run. He wanted you to scratch and crawl and always create something out of nothing—get the pitcher to balk in a run, attempt a double steal, or get the opposing team to throw the ball away. Try *anything* to cause the other team to make a mistake to get you a run.

He was always talking about taking the extra base, challenging the arms of the outfielders, knocking the second baseman down, knocking the shortstop down, not being afraid to lean over the plate with the bases loaded to get hit by the pitch.

"We have the bases loaded," he would say. "Forget hitting a fly ball. Get on top of the plate and take one for the team."

Billy had played that way for Casey Stengel, who taught him the game. Billy never asked you to do anything he wouldn't do. And if you did those things, he was tremendously loyal to you. I'm sure the way I pitched that year convinced Billy to keep me around, because I had a role to play despite my not having a good year. And I knew my role. I struggled with a bad arm, but I knew this was what I had to do to stay in the big leagues. So I did it.

We had a big stainless-steel whirlpool in the Tigers' clubhouse, and after games three or four of the guys would hop in it. Billy would grab a couple of beers, one in each hand, and he'd jump in too. Sometimes he would somersault into the whirlpool and pour beer on the guys if we had just had a good game. When we won, he was the greatest guy in the world to be around.

Billy told me that when he first got into baseball somewhere in his childhood, he associated winning with winners and losing with losers. He wanted to be a winner, and he never wanted to be a loser. And that's why he always fought to win a ball game. He was just like me.

Billy taught you how to be a winner, to accept the challenge, to fight for what is rightfully yours, and to stand up for what you believe in. More than anything else, he taught you that if you wanted something, you had to go and get it.

PART II

My Crazy, Demonic
Drinking and Drugging Years

11

STUPID AND RECKLESS

I HAD A NICE YEAR WITH THE Tigers in '71. I was with a bunch of guys who were talented and a lot of fun. I had a manager who respected me and who I respected in return. I could have been a Tiger for a while. All I had to do was not be stupid.

At the end of the season, GM Jim Campbell took me off the forty-man roster. Being on the forty-man roster doesn't mean a heck of a lot unless you're a young player. If you're a prospect, being on the forty-man roster protects you from having another team go after you. If you're a veteran player on a Triple-A roster and another team wants to acquire you, that team has to pay $25,000 to get you. That didn't happen very often.

When I found out I was no longer on the forty-man roster, I should have called Billy on the phone and told him that I wanted a shot at making the team as the fifth starter, and I'm certain he'd have given me that chance. Instead, my feelings were hurt, and I told the Tigers I wanted to go somewhere else. This was another time in my life when I acted before thinking.

Campbell told me, "If you have someone who's interested in you, have them call me." I called Bing Devine of the Cardinals. He had been with the Mets when I was there, and soon after I called Bing, the Cardinals traded for me, and I went to spring training in 1972 with the St. Louis Cardinals. With St. Louis I was having a really great spring. That was the same year Marvin Miller was voted in as the permanent head of the Players Association. He visited many of the camps, trying to get the players to vote for him.

Gussie Busch, a powerful man who owned the Anheuser-Busch brewing company and the Cardinals, called a meeting to discuss the union. He began the meeting by saying that in his opinion, a union would not be in the best interest of baseball. Of course, what he was really saying was that a union was not in the best interest of Gussie Busch and the other owners.

During the meeting, three Cardinal players spoke up. One was their star pitcher Bob Gibson. The second player was star hitter Joe Torre. And number three was yours truly. I basically said to Mr. Busch, "Your statement of whether this would be good for us or not good for us is very different from Marvin Miller's. Is it possible you guys can come and talk to us at the same time so we can get a better idea of what's really going on?"

Mr. Busch turned away from his microphone and spoke to one of his assistants. I could hear him say, "Who the fuck is that?"

When he was told who I was, Mr. Busch said, "I'm telling you what would be best for this game."

The next day, I was released.

That was Gussie Busch. He once got rid of future Hall of Fame pitcher Steve Carlton because Carlton wanted more money and he sported a mustache.

"Who the fuck is that?" is what he said after I piped up. I'll never forget it.

I called Dallas Green, the head of the Phillies' minor league system at the time, and asked for a tryout. After they saw me, they signed me to Reading, where I spent the 1972 season. Baseball went on strike that year for the first thirteen days of April, and so I had to wait to sign with the Double-A Reading Phillies.

Jim Bunning, the former Phillie pitching star and future senator from Kentucky, was the Reading manager. He was extremely aloof. He wasn't close to any of the players on the team.

My feeling was that Jim wanted to manage in the big leagues, and managing Double-A ball was somehow beneath him. Jim had pitched a perfect game with Philadelphia back in 1964. He must have thought, *Do I really need to do this?*

One game I gave up a hit during an inning. I returned to the bench after getting the third out, and Jim said to me, "How can you throw a fucking hanging slider on that count?"

I wanted to say to him, "Haven't you ever hung a fucking slider in your career?" But I didn't.

In the second half of the season, Marilyn was staying in the house we owned in Meriden, Connecticut. I was rooming with five guys in a three-room apartment. A few of the Reading players were smoking marijuana, including two of the guys I was rooming with, and I began to smoke along with them. I was frustrated because I wasn't pitching very well, and my arm was starting to really bother me again.

"Marijuana will help you relax," I was told, but more than anything I found it to be an effective painkiller. One day I smoked a joint before we went to the ballpark. I was in the outfield taking fly balls in batting practice. Every ball hit my way appeared to be six balls coming at me. I never caught one ball, but I remember trying to act nonchalant in trying not to get hit in the head by any of them.

No more marijuana before a game, I swore.

We played in New Haven, and Marilyn came to the game. After the game the girlfriend of one of my roommates asked Marilyn to follow her to the ladies' room.

She gave Marilyn an ounce of pot. My wife was *not* happy about that. She went fucking ballistic.

At the end of the season I returned to Connecticut. Marilyn settled down, while I spent the off-season partying with my hometown buddies. I hooked up with my friend Denny, whose nickname was Dobber.

Denny had had a rough time in Vietnam. He saw some deaths and had had some incidents in 'Nam that bugged him when he came back, prompting him to get into drugs and alcohol. We hit it off very well. We both wanted to have fun. We were both crazy, and that fall he introduced me to a group of friends who snorted cocaine. Dobber'd call me up and say, "Let's take the girls out for pizza at six o'clock, and after we get done we'll go to a ball game." We'd take the girls back home and drop them off. We didn't go to a ball game, and we didn't come home until the morning.

Dobber and I were famous for going downtown on a Friday night, having a "couple," and not coming home until seven o'clock in the morning. We'd stagger into his house as the sun was coming up, after a night of using. Dobber could sit there with a straight face and invent the most preposterous stories you could ever imagine about why we were out so late.

One time Dobber looked his wife in the eye and said, "Oh my God. Thank God I was able to come home this morning. I thought for a while I would never see you and the kids again. I thought they were going to kill us."

"Who was going to kill you?" she wanted to know.

"The people who kidnapped me and Bill last night. They got us into a boat in Old Saybrook. They bound and gagged us, and they took us over to Long Island. They were going to try to ransom Bill, but fortunately we escaped and we are so lucky to be alive. We love you. It was the worst nightmare of my life."

While he was telling her this story, I was sitting there thinking, *What the fuck are you talking about? The closest thing to water last night was the scotch we were drinking.*

Marilyn wasn't nearly as gullible or forgiving as Dobber's wife. One night I came crawling home about four o'clock in the morning. Marilyn was waiting on the porch of her mother's house, where we were staying that night. She had all my bags packed. When I walked in, she said, "That's it. I can't take it any longer. I've been crying, worrying about you. Get the hell out of here."

I had a four-door Honda Civic, and she had an Oldsmobile station wagon. I got in her station wagon and backed it up so it sat across Old Saybrook Road, got out, and left the car sitting there in the middle of the road. She had to run out and drive it off the highway.

It was dark, and if a car had come along, the station wagon would have been totaled. While she was moving her car, I got in my car and took off. Where I went, I can't remember.

Later I crawled back and begged her to forgive me. I don't know why, but she did.

Another morning Dobber talked about what had happened to him in Vietnam, while I talked about how I didn't make it in baseball and how I threw away my career. We cried on each other's shoulder. If he didn't have any physical injuries, he certainly had some emotional ones. I probably had both. Suddenly his eyes lit up and he said, "I know where we can get some shit. Let's go."

We got in the car and drove to a bar in a bad neighborhood of Middletown, Connecticut. The bar was supposed to be closed for the night, although there were plenty of cars around it and the lights were still on. Dobber banged on the door, and a slat in the door opened up. Dobber convinced them to let us in.

The door opened, and we went inside; the only thing we could see in there were eyes and teeth. It was that dark in there, and everyone else in the bar was African-American. Dobber talked to somebody about getting some blow, and the next thing I knew, I was grabbed from behind by some guy who asked, "What the fuck are you doing in here?"

I recognized him. He was the son of a babysitter I had had when I was a kid. He was somebody I had always liked, was a few years older than I was, and was from a great family. He was a user, too.

"Do you have any fucking idea where you are?" he asked. "They'll steal your money, knife you, and throw you in a ditch. Hold on a second."

He helped us get the blow. Of course, Dobber wanted to buy everyone a drink.

"No," I said, "we're getting the fuck out of here as fast as you came in here."

Driving back, Dobber looked at me and said, "They weren't too fucking hospitable, were they?"

I told him that going back there wasn't a good idea. He didn't understand.

After that incident, Marilyn wouldn't let me go with him. If I said, "Denny and I are going to go to—"

"No, no you're not," she'd say. "You're not going out. Give me the keys to the car."

She'd run, get my wallet, and take my credit cards and whatever money I had out of it. Marilyn tried like hell to just be the nice wife, while I was the crazy, angry, pissed-off addict. They say that addicts cause a tornado in people's lives. I can honestly say I did that to her.

In 1973 I went to spring training in Clearwater, Florida, with the Reading Phillies.

Marilyn and I rented a two-bedroom house on an acre of land one block from Clearwater Beach. It was for sale for $34,000. My mom, dad, aunt, and uncle came down to spend a week with us. We talked about purchasing the property. We finally decided *not* to buy it, because we figured I might be assigned to a club far from Clearwater, and we wouldn't get proper use out of it. I wish, looking back, I had bought it.

Jim Bunning again was my manager. I pitched well enough to make the team, and I was disappointed when they released me. Marilyn and I drove back to Meriden, Connecticut. I immediately called different teams to see if I could hook on with one of them. Since spring training had just ended, I knew there wouldn't be an opening for at least the first two months; but to my surprise, when I called the Boston Red Sox they signed me to play for Double-A Bristol, Connecticut, twenty miles from my house in Middletown. For the first and only time in my career, I could play ball and live at home.

I pitched terribly, and my arm really started to hurt again. I didn't go for shots. I figured the one thing they didn't need to hear about was a washed-up pitcher complaining about a bad arm. The highlight of the summer was the game when the PA announcer said, "And would Red Sox relief pitcher Bill Denehy please report to the hospital. Your wife is having a baby."

I got a standing ovation as I walked off the field. It was to be my last. Kristin was born the next day, June 17, 1973, on Father's Day. I arrived at the hospital and signed papers so I could witness the delivery. Marilyn had a long labor, so at about one o'clock in the morning I was starving, and asked the doctor, "How soon will this take place?"

"You've got some time; run out and grab something quick. Make sure you get back as soon as you can," he said.

Marilyn's brother John was with me, and we rushed to the far end of Main Street where my cousin owned a twenty-four-hour diner. We ordered breakfast. My cousin John screamed at me, "What the hell are you doing here? Isn't your wife supposed to have a baby any moment?"

"Yes," I said. "In fact, she's at the hospital, but I have a small window to get something to eat, so stop yelling at me and make my breakfast so I can get back to the hospital."

We ate, then we drove back, and I was there in plenty of time to watch Kristin being born.

I didn't finish the season with Bristol. My arm was hurting so bad, I could only get batters out with a prayer. After I was released, a friend of mine suggested I apply for workman's compensation to see if I could collect money from being released from a job while injured.

I applied, but the Red Sox said it was just a *seasonal* job, that they had released me because I couldn't get anyone out, and in their opinion I wasn't entitled to workman's comp. I went home and looked for an off-season job.

That winter Marilyn felt I could no longer make it in baseball. She felt that I needed to find a secure, stable job to provide the needed income to keep the house and raise our child. But I talked Marilyn into giving me one more shot at baseball.

The last opportunity I had in baseball came in 1974. I signed with the San Francisco Giants and reported to spring training in Casa Grande, Arizona. I talked to the scout who had recommended me in high school and said, "I think I can still pitch." I went out there, and my shoulder started acting up on me again, and I couldn't pitch to save my life. I can't even tell you what team I pitched against. It felt like I was throwing batting practice in a live major league game. I didn't have shit, and the Giants released me.

I was twenty-seven years old, my daughter Kristin had just been born, and I was facing the fact that I would never become a star pitcher in the major leagues. I had a wife and a baby and no marketable skills.

What the fuck do I do now?

Marilyn stayed back in our house in Connecticut. I had previously earned a $5,000 bonus from the Tigers for lasting with them for ninety days. I had used that money to buy our house. We had a mortgage to pay, so she took a temp job.

While I was in Casa Grande, Arizona, I ran into Dick Bloomfield, a former Wilson High algebra teacher. His daughter was married to Marilyn's brother. We started talking, and he told me he was doing very well in real estate. We had dinner a couple of times.

"If you don't make it in baseball, you ought to move out here and get into real estate," he told me. "I think you can make a lot of money."

After I was released, I stayed with Dick in Arizona for the weekend before returning to Meriden. Dick had a big mansion in the foothills of Tucson and owned a couple of Cadillacs, so I was very impressed with what I thought at the time was a guy who had a lot of money.

If he can make a lot of money in real estate, so can I, I figured.

"Why don't you sell your house back in Connecticut and move out here?" he said. And I did just that, even though Marilyn was dead-set against it and put up a good fight. At best, she suggested, "You should go out there for six months, and if it works out, we can sell the house." But she thought that to sell the house, then move to Arizona, was nuts.

"Rent out our house so that if your plan to move to Arizona and sell real estate doesn't work, we'll have the house to come back to," she said.

I, of course, ignored her logic and good sense.

I was finally able to sway her with grandiose stories and promised her I'd make a lot more money in real estate than in baseball. I also told her if I didn't make it in two years, we'd move back to Connecticut. Besides, what else was I going to do? I had no backup plan.

In my mind I had failed as a baseball player and needed a win. The win I thought I needed I would get from real estate, and strike it rich in the process. Marilyn, our infant Kristin, and I moved to Arizona. I passed my Realtor's exam. We moved into a two-bedroom apartment in the desert. If you live in Arizona, there's nothing but desert.

Marilyn hated her situation. She had owned her own house, and now she had to rent again. She was living in Tucson, Arizona, a place she didn't like; she was far from her family and didn't have any friends; she didn't like the hours I was keeping; and she didn't like having to raise our baby daughter by herself. Everything for her was bad, bad, bad. My daughter didn't like it that much, either. But I didn't give a shit. My mind was made up as to what I had to do.

I started drinking more, and one night Marilyn and I went to a party of real estate brokers and top salesmen, and one of the guys at the party had some cocaine, and that was the first time in a social setting that I did cocaine. I had done coke previously with my good buddy Dobber, but this was time it was different. This time I was doing coke with the jet-setters.

Eventually I became a drug addict, so obviously I liked it *a lot*. Cocaine gave me a feeling of exhilaration and a feeling of superiority to the point where I felt I could jump off a building and fly. It made me feel good about myself, strong, and mentally sharp, which is how the drug makes you feel initially. Marilyn got in my face.

"I don't like the people you're hanging around with," she said. "I want to remind you that you're raising an infant. This isn't the type of behavior a father should be engaged in."

I had gotten my hand caught in the cookie jar. But did I stop? Nooooo. *I'll be more discrete*, I thought. I certainly had no plans to give it up. The problem with cocaine is that the initial high wears off, and you keep looking for that feeling, and you think you will achieve it again. You become so caught up in looking for that high, in trying to find it again, that you just keep doing it more and more and more.

If I did one line, went my thinking, *then maybe three lines will get me there. If three lines won't do the trick, then maybe six lines will.*

Eventually, I went completely crazy.

I believe cocaine is God's message to earthlings that this is *bad stuff*, that we should not be fooling around with this at all. And from a marriage standpoint, for the next three years Marilyn and I had a very tough time. I was using, and the real estate sales I made were few and far between. One time our bank statement showed I had fifty-seven cents in the bank. That was all the money we had. And then I brokered the sale of a Tucson office building, and I got a $20,000 commission. That allowed us to go back to Connecticut on a vacation and rent a cottage on the beach.

The heat of Arizona made my arm feel better, and every so often I'd take a baseball and throw it against a handball wall at a school not far away. I felt good, and when the next spring rolled around I called Charlie Finley and asked to have a tryout with the A's. I threw batting practice one time. The A's gave me number 27, which was Catfish Hunter's old number. When I went in to throw batting practice that first time, my catcher was Ray Fosse, the same Ray Fosse I drilled when I was with the Detroit Tigers, the same Ray Fosse who rushed the mound, and the same Ray Fosse who I kicked in the face.

Ray stepped out in front of home plate, and he said, "For all you guys who don't know it, number 27 on the mound is Bill Denehy; we're trying to see whether he can still pitch. We all know he can fight."

Who had been at fault in our fight wasn't clear. There were those who said, "It was pretty stupid that Ray ran out to the mound." It wasn't like I was standing out there with a spear or a gun. Ray charged me, and I reacted. It wasn't preplanned.

I finished batting practice that first day, and Ray and I talked a little bit. We were okay.

I had one start with the A's that spring training. I pitched against the Milwaukee Brewers and didn't pitch well at all. To go out there and pitch with half the stuff I once had was unbelievably depressing. I wanted to walk off the mound because I was so fucking embarrassed. It was completely demoralizing, especially when I got to a point where I faced a good hitter and I knew that in my heyday I could have challenged him with a fastball. Even when I was with the Tigers, if I had to face Reggie Jackson, I would throw him an inside fastball—my ball sailed a little bit— and I wasn't afraid to throw him one, two, three fastballs in a row. But back then I had movement and good velocity. Now, against the Brewers, I just didn't have it.

I wanted to have a screen in front of me now if I threw an inside fastball. There was that much of a difference. I stood on the mound and asked myself, *What do I have to do?*

The worst part of it was that no one could come up with an answer of what was wrong with my arm. And so I asked myself, *When does it ever get better? Does it ever get better? Where is the end of the tunnel?*

There was no light at the end of my tunnel, no encore; my pitching days were over.

Marilyn was pregnant with our second child. As Marilyn got further along in her pregnancy, we were *sure* it was a boy, because the child was much bigger than Kristin. We had the name Sean Patrick already picked out.

On October 27, 1977, I took Marilyn to the hospital, and she went into labor. The doctor asked me if I wanted to watch the delivery. I told him that I did because I had watched Kristin's delivery, and I knew this delivery wouldn't faze me. Seconds before the baby came out, the doctor came over and he said, "Would you like to deliver the baby?"

Slowly, casually, I started rolling up the sleeves of my surgical gown, when the doctor yelled, "We don't have time for that."

I jumped into position, and within a couple seconds caught Heather Lynn Denehy and held her in my arms. I didn't hear any screams. The nurse picked her up by her feet, slapped her on her rear end, and she hasn't stopped talking since.

Times got really bad. Over Thanksgiving I was away with Dick trying to sell a property. Marilyn was home alone with a three-year-old and a newborn. She had no money and no food. And she was depressed.

After I spent a couple of hard years in Tucson, Dick's friend Don Allen bought a Century 21 franchise and made me the office manager. I had success. When we took over the franchise, we were the twenty-eighth and last office in the area. After a year, I had helped move them to number three in sales in the area. I fired my male salesmen and hired women. *Women can sell houses.*

I went to training seminars, and I like to think that I inspired and helped our people to go out, get listings, and sell. The victim of my success was my marriage. Marilyn and I weren't getting along very well. I was using pretty heavily, and one afternoon Dick and I went out to meet a broker, and when we got to his office we noticed his very attractive receptionist. Dick had brought his son, who was about twenty, along for the ride, and we said to his son, "Why don't you ask her out?"

"You think it's that easy," the son said to me, "you ask her out."

"I'm married," I said, "but there's nothing to getting a date with her."

The son and I made a bet. To win that bet I asked her out, and we went out on a couple of lunches. I was having problems with Marilyn, and this woman listened to my tales of woe and was very comforting. One day I drove to her house in a mobile home park. As we talked, I heard someone banging on the door. She opened the door and started crying.

"That's my ex-husband," she said, "and he said if you're not gone in an hour, he's going to come back and kill you."

"Fuck him," I told her. "He can't scare me away."

An hour later the ex-husband returned. I was still there, so he pulled a .357 Magnum and shot out all my car windows. He then shot the wheels, then the engine, and finally he drove off. My car was totaled.

The police came. I told them who I was sure had done it and filed a complaint.

The police drove me home to my apartment. When Marilyn opened the door, I was standing there with two police officers.

"We're bringing your husband home. He didn't get shot."

"What do you mean, 'He didn't get shot'?" she wanted to know.

"His car got shot up," said the policeman.

"Where's the car?" she wanted to know.

"I had a little problem with the car," I said.

"What do you mean, 'His car got shot up'?" Marilyn asked.

Marilyn wasn't thrilled about the explanation. After the cops left, she really let me have it, and rightfully so. She reminded me I was married. She reminded me I had a three-year-old daughter and a newborn.

I hung my head. There wasn't much else I could do or say.

"Can I just go to sleep?" I asked. "Can we talk about this in the morning?"

Three days later I was sitting in my office at the real estate company when an attorney, a young guy, came to see me. I had no idea what he wanted.

"I'm very sorry about what happened to you the other night," he said to me. "Let me get a couple of things straight. The family of the young man who is alleged to have done these things to you, and I want to say *alleged*, are really disappointed in him, and so he's now out of the country. There's no way the police will arrest him. And what we'd like you to consider is since you didn't actually see him—we read the police report—if you're willing to drop whatever charges you have pending against him, we'll send you down to the Cadillac dealer and you can have a Cadillac for a couple of days, and we'll buy you a brand-new Datsun and give you $5,000 in cash."

It seemed like a pretty good deal. I drove around in a new Cadillac for a few days, until my new Datsun arrived. Afterward the attorney paid me another visit and handed me $5,000 in cash.

"We're really pleased you decided to go along with us," he said. "This fellow's uncle would like to have dinner with you."

I agreed. I went to a bar on the outskirts of town and was met by a very nice Italian gentleman. He introduced himself as Mario and told me, "Have anything on the menu. We just want to thank you for cooperating with us. The young man has had some trouble in the past, and the family wants to make sure things are taken care of, that you're taken care of. We'll deal with him."

We had dinner, and we talked baseball. Toward the end of the meal he leaned over to me and put his hand on the top of my shoulder and patted me.

"You made a smart move," he said. "Again, we're sorry, but you'll need to stay away from the young lady and forget about this whole deal."

"I can do that," I said, "but let me ask you a question. Just for curiosity, what if I had been a prick, thought I was disrespected, and pushed this to the edge? Were you going to shoot me?"

He looked at me and shook his head sideways.

"No no no," he said. "Punks do that. If we wanted to get rid of you, we'd have taken you down to Tombstone, found an empty mine shaft, stripped you naked, stuck some dynamite up your ass, lit it, and thrown you down the shaft. If the fall didn't kill you, I guarantee the dynamite would have, and they never would have seen you again."

While the girl and I were lying on the floor of the apartment as her ex-husband was shooting my car, I said to her, "You got a gun?"

I figured I was Hopalong Cassidy—a fictional cowboy hero featured in books and movies—and that I'd go out there and duel him at high noon.

When I think back on it, all I can remember is how crazy I was.

12

A (SHORT) CAREER
IN RADIO

MARILYN AND I HAD ONE FIGHT AFTER another, and she flew to Wisconsin to spend a week with her brother. Then when her dad became critically ill, she flew to Connecticut, where she and the two little girls moved in with her parents. She filed for divorce. A week before we were getting divorced, I flew back to Connecticut. Marilyn and I spent the weekend together, and we decided to give it one more shot.

Marilyn, our two daughters, and I moved to Milwaukee, Wisconsin, and I went to work for Century 21. After a couple of years I became the director of sales and development for the Midwest region. The job paid well, I had a company car, and it was a damn good job. I wore a suit, I worked in a cubicle, I shuffled papers, and *I was dying*. I absolutely hated it.

I was interviewed on radio station WTMJ in Milwaukee. Harry Dalton, the Milwaukee Brewers' GM, heard me and called to ask if I would substitute for host Sal Bando for a week on a program called *Good Morning, Milwaukee*. During my week the show's director said to me, "I don't know what your plans are, but you ought to think about getting into broadcasting. You have a great voice, and you present yourself well."

"I'd like to do that," I told him, "but I have no idea where to start."

"There's a radio station that's starting up in Avon, Connecticut, called Enterprise Radio," he said. "The Rasmussens, who started and sold ESPN, are starting it up."

Bill Rasmussen and his son Scott apparently figured if they could succeed on TV with twenty-four-hour-a-day sports, they could do the same thing on the radio.

I called Bill Rasmussen, who remembered me from when I pitched with the Mets.

"We'd love to have you on board," he said, "but I don't do the hiring. John Chanin is our vice president in charge of production. I can get you an interview with John. If you want, you can interview, but I can't promise you anything."

The next week I flew to Hartford and sat down with John Chanin, and we had a good, long, productive meeting.

"We need a couple of talk show hosts," John said. "We're doing talk shows from seven o'clock at night until eight o'clock in the morning."

"I can fill that position," I said.

"I follow football, basketball, and golf," I said. "I'm not much on hockey, but I can read," I said. I stressed my knowledge of basketball.

"I'll tell you what," John said. "I'll ask you one question, and if you get it right, I'll hire you. If you don't, we can talk about a baseball job in the spring."

"Shoot."

"In 1960," he said, "there were two basketball players from the Ohio State Buckeyes who went on to the NBA and became all-stars. Can you name them?"

"I can name them," I said, "and the rest of the Ohio State starting lineup, the sixth man, and the coach."

"Go right ahead."

"The two players are Jerry Lucas and John Havlicek," I said. "The rest of the Ohio State starters were Larry Siegfried, Mel Nowell, and Joe West. The sixth man was Bobby Knight, and the coach was Fred Taylor."

"How about forty a year to start?" Chanin said.

"Forty what?" I asked.

"Forty thousand, you asshole," he said.

"I'll take it," I said, wanting to shout. And that's how I got my job with Enterprise Radio.

The twenty-four-hour all-sports radio network opened on New Year's Day of 1981. Among the hires were John Sterling, Ira Melman from Philadelphia, Bob Buck, and Dan O'Brien, who for years did play-by-play for Boston College. I was the only one with no radio experience. I hosted my national show from one o'clock to four o'clock in the morning on Saturdays and Sundays. Outside of pitching, it was the best job I ever had.

In late December I drove my family from Milwaukee to Connecticut and was hit by a bad snowstorm. The drive from Danbury to Middletown normally takes forty-five minutes, but that day it took me four and a half hours.

I had to report for work the next day, New Year's Day, and we went on the air live with no practice whatsoever. John Sterling was an old hand, and he had some guests lined up. I, on the other hand, had no clue as to what I was doing. I had never opened a show before.

The producer cued me, and I said, "Hi everybody, my name is Bill Denehy. Welcome to Enterprise Radio. We're going to talk about a lot of sports, about a lot of things, with a lot of people in a lot of different places."

John Chanin was in the control room, and I could see him putting his head down on his desk and pounding his fists. I was awful. I was on for three hours all by myself. I had no idea whether or not we'd have call-ins. John Sterling was able to tell stories and crack jokes to fill the time. I didn't have a clue, but because we had publicized our show, plenty of people called in. I looked down at the phone lines, and they were all lit up. At one o'clock in the morning! I was just fine talking to the callers. I just wasn't very good at ad-libbing.

After the first half hour, John Chanin had so much *agita*, he left. I went to see him at ten o'clock the next morning.

"Good news, bad news," he said. "I am relieved that you can talk sports. You handled all the callers. That was good. The bad news is you don't know one fucking thing about being a talk show host."

John Chanin was a brilliant producer and a wonderful mentor. He had worked at ABC, had worked with Howard Cosell, and had produced the Olympics. He was top-notch. He handed me some cards.

"Here's your intro," Chanin said. "I want you to read it every night when you go on the air."

He wrote down how to go to commercial breaks, and he said, "Read these things when the time comes, until you master them, and you'll be okay."

He gave me the name and number of an English professor whose job it was to put more inflection in my voice so I would talk deeper and sound better.

One night I was at my dad's house and we were talking, and I told him I needed a gimmick, maybe a nickname.

"Why don't you call yourself Wild Bill Denehy?" he said. He recalled that a long time ago there had been a pitcher in the big leagues by the name of Wild Bill Donovan.

The following Friday I went on the air and said, "Hey, this is Wild Bill Deheny," and it was only a matter of time before callers were calling me Wild Bill. Enterprise Radio sent me to Albany for a promotion and bought me a cowboy hat and a pair of cowboy boots to go along with the new nickname.

I learned a great deal from John Chanin. I was sitting in John's office when he placed a call to Tom Flores, the Oakland Raiders' head coach at the time. They were friends.

"I need to break a real big story for this network," John said to Flores. "You're in the last year of your contract, right? I'm going to announce that sources close to you told me that you're getting ready to sign a long-term contract with the Denver Broncos after the Super Bowl."

"But John, that's not true," said Flores. "There is absolutely no truth to that. I don't know where you heard that from."

"Good," said John. "Then deny it."

As I sat there, I wondered, *How much of this shit actually goes on?* Later John told me, "It happens all the time. You make up a story, put the source close to the person, cover your ass, and let it go. He can then deny it."

John assigned me to visit the baseball training camps during spring training.

"You'll have a heavy expense account," he said to me, "and I want you to use it. I want you to take a writer, a sportscaster, or someone in the business out to dinner every single night. I want you to talk up Enterprise Radio. Take a ballplayer if you have to. I do not want one night to go by where you go to dinner alone."

In my travels for Enterprise Radio I would interview a lot of players and managers. I was a former big leaguer myself and I thought current players and managers would open up to me and work with me. Little did I know that there was an underlying hostility toward the press, no matter who you were. I was taken aback whenever a player or a manager would duck an interview or flat refuse to talk to me. I found I had to work for those interviews and know when and how to approach people.

Off I went to Phoenix and the Cactus League with my producer Bob Kimball. Our first stop was to see the Oakland A's, managed by Billy Martin, my old skipper in Detroit. I called Mickey Morabito, the Oakland A's PR guy, and I asked him whether it would be possible to get a room at the A's hotel.

When we arrived, Mickey said, "Billy took care of you. Don't worry about a thing."

We went upstairs, and I was overwhelmed to see that Billy had us put in a suite.

I called Mickey Morabito.

"I'm sure Enterprise Radio doesn't want me in a suite," I said.

"Don't worry," he said, "Billy has taken care of it." Billy got me a huge discount.

Chanin wanted us to put together a special show that we were going to call *Billy Martin: The Manager and the Man*. To do the show, Billy had to sit for a lengthy interview.

The first day, Bob Kimball and I went to the ballpark and checked in with the A's. Billy was in his office, and when he saw me he had a big smile. He got up from his desk and gave me a big hug.

"Are your accommodations good?" he asked.

"Yes," I said, "I'm going to be in town all week, and we're doing a special show on you, and I'm going to need a half hour to forty minutes with you to get it done. We're at the same hotel, so whenever we can do it, that would be great."

Billy was about to hold a meeting with his team, and the reporters began filing out of the clubhouse. Billy invited me to stay for the meeting. The A's were about to play a Japanese team, and Billy began telling the players that ordinarily spring training is nothing more than getting in shape as the players work toward the start of the season.

"Today's a little different," Billy said. "We're playing against a team from Japan, and they think they're the top team. I'm only going to give you one message on how we're going to play the game today, and the message is: Remember Pearl Harbor."

Billy played that game as though the A's were playing in the World Series. He was coaching third, and he sent Rickey Henderson home from third on a short fly ball. Billy squeezed, he hit and ran, and he won the game 9–1. The score could have been 90–1.

The week was slipping away from me; I still needed to interview Billy.

Early in the evening on the last day, I went to Billy and said, "Billy, I don't want to bother you, but I must get you tonight. I'm leaving in the morning."

Billy promised we would do the interview. We sat by the pool eating hamburgers and telling jokes as the clock was ticking. At around nine o'clock, I walked back to Billy and said, "I have to interview you."

"Okay," Billy said. "Let's do it now."

Billy grabbed a bottle of scotch, and the two of us went into his hotel room. For forty-five minutes he gave me one of the very best interviews I've ever heard about managing. He poured out his feelings, talked about the game, and discussed the way he treated pitchers.

There was only one problem: He was drunk, and he was slurring his words.

After the interview, I flew to Florida and spent a week interviewing players from the Reds, the Tigers, the Braves, and the Yankees. On the final day I interviewed Dave Winfield and Ron Guidry. My last interviewee was to be Reggie Jackson.

I went up to Reggie and introduced myself.

"I played against you in Puerto Rico, and when I was with the Tigers," I said.

He looked me up and down.

"Denehy, Denehy," Reggie said. "Oh yeah, I remember you. You were the fucking head-hunter. I ain't doing no fucking interview with you."

"I never threw at you," I said.

"I don't give a shit," Reggie said. "You threw at some of my teammates, and I ain't doing any fucking interview with you. Get the fuck out of my face."

I walked away. My producer, Bob Kimball, was going crazy.

"How can we not have Reggie Jackson?" he asked.

"Relax," I said. "Give me some time to think about this."

In the Yankee clubhouse I asked Yogi Berra if he had a spare baseball. I told him I wanted it to grab a couple of autographs. He found one. I walked up to Reggie's locker, and I said, "Excuse me, Reggie. Again, I don't mean to bother you, and if you don't want to do an interview, that's fine, but my youngest daughter is four years old, and you're her favorite player. I was wondering whether at least you could sign an autograph for her, because I don't want to have to go back to her and tell her what a fucking asshole you are."

Reggie jumped up, and for what seemed like minutes we were nose-to-nose, eye-to-eye, staring at each other. Finally, he broke into a grin, and he said, "How much time do you need?"

Reggie gave me a nice interview and signed the ball. We shook hands, and I said, "I just want to tell you I never threw at you, and I want to be sure if you're pissed at me for doing anything, it's wasn't because it was anything personal with you."

"Okay," he said.

That night Kimball and I went out for dinner, and we were waiting in line at a Fort Lauderdale restaurant. In walked Reggie, Fran Healy, and two girls. Reggie saw me and walked over to me.

"Hey, how you doing?" he asked. "What are you guys doing here?"

"Eating dinner," I said.

"That's great," he said. "Why don't you join us?"

And so we all had dinner together. Reggie, my new best friend, told a lot of stories and was most affable. The check came, and as soon as it hit the table, I grabbed it.

"Let me tell you something," said Reggie. "I've never been anyplace where somebody picked up the check for Reggie Jackson. They always expect me to pick it up."

"Guess what?" I said, "Enterprise Radio is picking up your check tonight."

We paid for seven people. It wasn't cheap.

"I'll remember that," said Reggie.

When I told John Chanin, he said, "What a great move on your part."

The next morning we flew back to ice-cold Connecticut. It had been a thrilling three weeks covering spring training. Thank

God, when Kimball and I returned to Avon, the Enterprise Radio staff included a couple of really top-notch technicians. They were able to edit my taped interview with Billy Martin; they would speed up the tape at just the right spots so that Billy sounded like he had a cold rather than like he was drunk.

Next I went to cover the National Sports Festival held in Syracuse, New York. The games featured basketball, boxing, swimming, baseball, and archery. I covered basketball games, and because the games were held in Syracuse, my color man and analyst was Syracuse basketball coach Jim Boeheim. John Sterling would say, "Let's go to Bill Denehy at Manley Field House and see what's going on in basketball," and I was supposed to give a wrap-up.

John Chanin was the producer, and he'd say in my ear, "Send it back to John," and I'd say, "At the end of the first quarter, the East is beating the West 29–27. From the Manley Field House, this is Bill Denehy. Back to you, John." But I kept forgetting to mention my analyst Coach Boeheim. I was prompted by Chanin repeatedly, but couldn't seem to remember to mention Jim when I sent the broadcast back to John.

John would remind me, "Your out-cue is: 'From the Manley Field House, this is Bill Denehy with Coach Jim Boeheim. Back to you, John.'"

John got irritated with me and said, "*Bill, get a fucking piece of paper and a fucking pencil, and write this down*: 'From the Manley Field House, this is Bill Denehy with Coach Jim Boeheim. Back to you, John.'"

"Next time say it just as I read it to you."

I read from the piece of paper for the remainder of the broadcast. Every announcer at the fifteen different venues could hear this ongoing conversation in their headsets. When I got back to the hotel, every one of those people asked me, "Who is your analyst, Bill? Is it Jim Boeheim?"

One day Secretary of the Treasury Robert Simon was riding in the elevator in the building that housed Enterprise Radio. As the door opened, he was startled to see a couple of our employees playing golf in the hallway.

"Playing through," one yelled as he hit the golf ball into the elevator. They pressed the button, went down a floor, and, when the door opened, putted the ball out. We got a memo asking, "Who were those guys playing golf? Secretary of the Treasury Bob Simon was in the elevator, and he didn't think it was representative of this organization."

One night we threw a bachelor party for a guy in production who was getting married. I invited a close friend Don "the Grog" Lombardo to join us, and after the fifteen of us had dinner, one of the guys mentioned that there was a strip joint in downtown Avon, a well-to-do suburb of West Hartford.

I went, but I was bored, so I asked John Chanin, "Do you mind if we loosen things up a little around here?"

"Listen," he said, "as long as you don't get arrested or bring bad publicity to Enterprise Radio, I don't care what you do."

I told Grog to follow me into the bathroom, where we took off all our clothes except for our underwear. It was wintertime and cold outside; we wore raincoats over our boxer shorts, with socks and shoes.

We ran out onto the stage, grabbed one of the dancers, and started flipping her up in the air. We knelt down while she stood on our backs. Then she wrapped herself around the pole while we tried to wrap ourselves around her. Then the three of us fell to the stage while everyone had a good laugh.

After fifteen minutes, Grog and I ran off the stage to thunderous applause, ran back into the bathroom, got dressed, and very casually walked back to our tables to sit down. John Chanin got the biggest kick out of it. He finally realized what kind of guy I was.

Before the National Sports Festival, Chanin was working like a dog, trying to negotiate the bowl games for Enterprise Radio, and I don't know whether or not he had a stroke, but something affected one of his eyes, so he wore an eye patch. One day I asked how he was.

"Ah shit, I'm stressed out," Chanin said.

I suggested that he come to Middletown. John was on medication, so I had to convince him we weren't going to do anything horrible if he went with me. I called Marilyn and told her I was bringing Chanin to Middletown.

We drove to Middletown and arrived at La Boca restaurant. I ordered a pitcher of margaritas; Chanin reminded me he was on medication.

John laughed, and after he watched me drink one, he said, "Let me have one."

Before we were finished, he had had a few more than one.

We drove to a softball game and met my buddies in the parking lot.

They were going to a watering hole in a fairly dangerous part of town called The Fireside. The Dobber, my friend who I had partied with, walked over to our car.

"Hey Chanin," he said, "when are you going to get Denehy on a local station around here so we can call in and talk to him?"

Dobber grabbed Chanin on the cheek with his thumb and forefinger, and said, "Chanin, if you're going to hang with us guys, you've got to fucking loosen up."

And he threw two joints into the car.

"We'll see you guys down at The Fireside," Dobber said.

Aw fuck, was what I was thinking. I didn't know how Chanin felt about drugs. I was looking at him, and he was looking at me, and he picked up one of the joints and said, "I haven't had one of these since 1966 when I was with CBS."

"It will definitely loosen you up," I said.

John lit one up, and I smoked one on the way to The Fireside. So now I was loose. We opened the door, and in the doorway my friend Denny Drabek was lying on the ground in a stupor. Chanin looked at him and asked, "Is he dead?"

"I don't think so. He's passed out. Just step over him. Don't worry."

We went inside and had a few drinks with all the guys from the softball team. Soon it was two o'clock in the morning, and they were going to close the place down. "I'm hungry," Chanin said.

I suggested we go to my cousin's diner. Chanin thought we'd have to drive someplace, and said, "We have to go home. I can't stop at a diner."

I said, "It's two doors down."

We walked to Rook's Diner and ordered steamed cheeseburgers and eggs. I put Chanin in the back of the car and drove him back to Avon. I put him in his bed with all his clothes on. He had a shit-eating grin on his face.

It was four o'clock in the morning when I drove home. I was hammered. I hadn't talked to Marilyn since I'd told her I'd be home early. We had a miniature schnauzer. It barked if a worm moved. Very, very, very slowly I opened the door, and suddenly it flew open, and Marilyn was standing there.

"Where have you been?" she wanted to know. "For Christ sake, I've been crying, worrying about you. I didn't know if you were in an accident. You could have called."

She pounded her fists on my chest, and I fell backwards off the front steps into the flowerpots. I was lying among the flowerpots, and she continued yelling at me.

"And another thing," she said. "You're not sleeping upstairs tonight. You're sleeping on the couch."

I was thinking, *If you would just go away, I'll sleep here in the flowerpots.* I really didn't care. All I wanted was some peace and quiet.

Slowly I got up, walked inside the house, and lay down on the couch. The next morning I heard Marilyn say to the kids, "When you go downstairs, you're going to see your drunken father. He's lying on the couch because he didn't come home last night. Mom was crying, and so you'll be able to take a good look at him when you go into the kitchen to have breakfast."

I could hear Marilyn and my two young daughters march down the stairs. Kristin was six, Heather was three. Kristin didn't want to look at me. Heather had her right hand in Kristin's left hand, and I could see her trying to take a peek. As she walked by, I opened my eyes, and she saw me, and she gave me a little wave with her left hand as she ran into the kitchen.

Once I started partying, I got home when I got home. Apparently it's part of the disease of addiction. At one of my men's meetings, a guy from Boston said, "One of the problems with our disease is that we have glue attached to our ass. We get on a bar stool, and we just can't leave. We can't get up. We don't call. We know we should, and during the night we tell ourselves, *Call and at least tell her I'm okay.* But we don't."

"I just couldn't get off that bar stool," each member says. The story is universal.

In recovery meetings they would say to us, "If you ever want to drink again, just think about your last drunk." But I had a *great* time drinking and drugging. I felt like saying to the speaker at the meeting, "Obviously, you must have gone to the wrong parties."

I understand addiction. I understand how my life became unmanageable. I understand the fact that my body doesn't process alcohol and other drugs like a normal human being. I understand all that. But while I was doing it, I wasn't sitting in the corner of some bar thinking about committing suicide. I was on top of the bar dancing and having fun and enjoying myself.

I never got arrested. I never got to a point where I got in fights. Most of my fights occurred on athletic fields. My experience with drugs was positive. It was fun, and in my case, because of all the injuries I had, a lot of that stuff was also used as a painkiller.

On the other hand, it wouldn't be too long before my using cost me my marriage and, for a long time, kept me away from my daughters' lives. That I deeply regret.

I wish I could have worked for Enterprise Radio forever, but Enterprise Radio only lasted nine months before it went bankrupt. We heard they weren't getting enough advertising. Whatever the reason, we started hearing, "We're going to have to close down." Once the rumors started, many of our best people started leaving. I didn't realize it, but everyone at the network who had experience in the business made taped copies of their shows. That way if they applied for work somewhere else and were asked for a tape of their show, they could send one. I didn't know they were doing that or how to do it.

On a Wednesday we were told we were doing our last broadcast.

After Enterprise Radio went bust, Chanin went to work for WFAN, which belonged to the Mutual Radio Network. He said he'd try to work something out, but nothing materialized. In fact, when he went to work for the Mutual Radio Network, he didn't hire anyone from Enterprise Radio.

When I had to leave Enterprise Radio in 1981, I was stuck in Avon and felt that I had nothing.

13

BACK ON THE FIELD

EVEN WHILE I HAD MY RADIO JOB at Enterprise in 1981, I still wanted to get back into baseball. I didn't know that Enterprise would go bankrupt. That year the baseball strike ran from June 2 to August 9. The strike was *the* big story.

Roughly 40 percent of the season was lost due to the strike. Enterprise was an all-sports network, and the work stoppage in baseball would leave me with some extra time on my hands. Even before the baseball strike, I looked into finding a baseball job to occupy my time and supplement my income.

I talked to different teams, officials, and players. I networked like crazy. Bristol was only twelve miles from Avon, and Tony Torcia was manager of the Bristol Red Sox. I had played minor league ball against Tony in both Double-A and Triple-A.

I drove to Bristol to talk to the Red Sox people about giving me a job. Tony met with me, we started talking, and he said to me, "Why don't you come down some night and throw batting practice?"

I didn't work much during the week at Enterprise Radio. Unless I was assigned a trip to Boston, my only responsibility during the week was to come into the office and read the sports pages of newspapers of the big cities where they listened to my show. If someone called in from Dallas and wanted to know about Texas Christian University football, I had to know something about it. It was easy work, and after I reviewed the papers and answered any calls, I was done for the day.

I drove to Bristol and threw batting practice for Tony. There I was, hooked on baseball again. I have to admit that my arm throbbed constantly due to the damp weather. I'd wake up in the morning and within fifteen minutes my arm would ache. Even so, I loved throwing batting practice.

When the major league strike looked like a certainty, I went to John Chanin and said, "There's not going to be any baseball, especially network baseball. Why don't we do network minor league games?"

"No one's going to want to listen to that," he said.

Just then Ed Randall stuck his head in the door and said, "Did someone say something about announcing a baseball game? I can do the play-by-play, and Bill and I can work together."

Chanin struck a deal with the Red Sox that *if* the strike happened, we'd do a Bristol Red Sox game just to say we were the only sports network to broadcast a professional baseball game.

At the time the baseball strike *might* start, baseball was to be center stage in American culture. Football, hockey, and basketball seasons, both college and professional, would either have ended or be in the playoff stage of their season. So there wouldn't be much competition for airtime from the other sports.

We announced the game, and surprise, surprise, the ratings were *huge*. People called the station to thank us for giving them baseball.

We only broadcast that one game.

I don't know why, but when Enterprise Radio closed down on September 21, 1981, I went back to Tony Torcia and said, "There are six weeks left in the season. I have nothing to do. Call Boston and see if I can stay on with you, throughout the playoffs, as your pitching coach."

Boston didn't pay much, but I became the pitching coach, and Bristol made it to the playoffs as the fourth-seeded team. We faced the Glens Falls White Sox with Ron Kittle, Greg Walker, and a third hitter, each of whom had hit thirty home runs and had just killed Bristol during the regular season. The series with Glens Falls was two games out of three. The day before the opener, Tony came to me and said, "You're the pitching coach. You set up the rotation."

We had a big, strong kid in Jerome Whitehead. He threw bullets, but he was wild in the strike zone, and the Glens Falls hitters could hit a fastball. Everyone expected Jerome to pitch the opener. We also had a tall, lanky, right-handed sinker ball pitcher by the name of Howard, and his arm was worse than mine, but he could give you seven innings throwing sinkers and sliders, moaning and groaning all the way. I decided to pitch him, and he beat Glens Falls 3–2.

Jerome pitched the second game; he got whacked, and so it was one win apiece going back to Bristol. Brian Denman, the Pitcher of the Year in the Eastern League and another sinker/slider pitcher, started game three. Brian was clever. He could spot the ball, he pitched well, and we won, knocking off Glens Falls in game three of the series.

We played Reading in the championship series, beat them, and were the Eastern League champions.

I talked to the Red Sox over the winter, and they hired me to be the full-time pitching coach for Bristol. I was happy. Marilyn wasn't. I was going from the $40,000 salary at Enterprise Radio to $20,000 with the Red Sox, a 50 percent pay cut, and she didn't think that was very smart. Marilyn wanted a nice home with a picket fence, and $20,000 wasn't going to get it for her.

Marilyn was tough to live with. She was like her mother, always complaining that I didn't make enough money. One time I didn't fill up the gas tank, she ran out of gas, and I heard about it for days. Marilyn was angry at her father, who was a terrible alcoholic, and now her husband was falling into the same pattern.

Perhaps Marilyn and I might have stayed married if we hadn't been living in her mother's house. The Queen Mother, as Marilyn's mom liked to call herself, was a domineering old woman with a nasty disposition. Her late husband, a boxer, used to beat her. She seemed tough enough to go toe-to-toe with him. Marilyn's mom saw me as a washed-up old ballplayer, but she also saw in me the ghost of her dead husband. He was an amateur boxer who told her she would never have to work again, but his career never went anywhere. She became his only opponent, and their home was the ring. History was repeating itself. I told Marilyn *she* would never have to work again, and my career was cut short, and here I was, seeking refuge in using.

One night Marilyn's mom picked a fight with me, though my daughters had done their best to pull her away. When she entered the kitchen in an excitable state, I was fixing for a fight. She stood only five feet tall, but she walked up to me, raised her chin, looked into my face, and poked at me with her index finger. "You're a failure and a loser," she said, "and you will never amount to anything. I wish I had never allowed my daughter to marry you."

"You better get out of my face," I warned her. She refused to back down. My eyes were bulging out of their sockets. I put a butter knife to her throat. She still wouldn't back down.

"Do it," she snarled venomously. "I dare you."

I could have killed her. Instead, I tossed the knife on the kitchen table, pushed her aside, and stormed out of the house.

Spring training approached, and I was glad to leave the madhouse. I went to spring training in Winter Haven, Florida, for a month, and the Red Sox paid only for my expenses. I didn't even get a paycheck. My pay didn't begin until the regular season. But I didn't care. I was back in baseball, doing what I loved most.

I loved working with the pitchers, and I developed a program. I decided that if I was going to be the pitching coach, I'd be the smartest pitching coach who ever lived. That's part of my DNA. I decided to get into statistics. I wanted to know everything. If you said to me, "How many pitches should you take to warm up?" my answer would be "I don't know, but I'll tell you by the end of the season." I counted every pitch my pitchers threw during warm-ups. By the second half of the season, I'd tell my pitchers, "You have fifty pitches to warm up." And I'd determine the optimal number for each of my pitchers.

I taught my pitchers obvious things, like throwing first-pitch strikes. And like Ted Williams taught me, I tried to teach my pitchers how to think.

I taught them to throw the pitch you can get over the most times for a strike in the best location. It could be a slider, if I was talking to a slider-sinker pitcher. My pitchers gradually improved and knew what to do.

I started looking at whether the pitcher had a changeup and how good it was. What count does he throw it on? Did my pitcher throw too many pitches? I counted how many strikes he threw.

My second year with Bristol my staff included Oil Can Boyd, Mike Brown, Al Nipper, and Tommy Bolton. All four pitchers made the majors. Al Nipper had a really good knuckleball; he couldn't throw it for a strike, but he could strike out guys with it. And so I wouldn't let him throw his knuckler unless he was ahead of the hitter, and I thought they would chase it.

In the middle of the season I could see that Oil Can Boyd was losing strength, and so I forbade him from throwing between starts. Oil Can had good mechanics and good control, but he was lanky and frail. He lacked stamina, but with three days' rest had a good fastball.

Steve Shields, a big guy from Alabama, threw overhand, over the top, and had a good fastball. His problem was shitty control. As great as his curveball was, he couldn't throw it for a strike, so he gave up a lot of hits and runs and he didn't win.

"Do you want to pitch in the big leagues or do you just want to keep throwing hard and have people say, 'This guy has a great fastball and a great curveball'?" I asked him.

"I want to pitch in the big leagues," he said.

"Okay," I said, "starting tomorrow you're going to become a sinker-slider pitcher."

That summer Steve pitched ten consecutive complete games. He would've had eleven in a row, but we had a rain delay, and we couldn't send him back out there. He threw a hard sinker and a hard breaking ball. Two years later he was in the big leagues, and he was throwing over the top, throwing his big curveball again, and he was getting his ass kicked. It wasn't long before he was selling pumpkins in Alabama. Some scout or coach had changed him back to being an over-the-top pitcher. Why? I don't know, but it just bothered the shit out of me.

We also had Marc Sullivan, the son of Haywood Sullivan, a former Red Sox catcher and one of Boston's owners. Marc was a first-round pick by the Red Sox.

At the end of the year, Oil Can, a shy African-American kid, was promoted to the Red Sox, and I was asked if I would drive him up there. I drove him up to Haywood Sullivan's office so he could sign his contract. After he signed, one of the front office guys took Oil Can down to the clubhouse. I gave him a big hug, and we shook hands using the elaborate handshake the black players used. Once he left, Haywood said to me, "Sit down a little bit. I want to talk to you."

"I finally figured out why you're so valuable to our organization," Haywood joked. "You're the only guy who knows the fucking handshake."

He also had some questions about his son's ability. I told him that his son was a great defensive catcher and had a great arm, but his hitting was a question. I just didn't know whether the kid could hit. That year the Red Sox had an organizational meeting. They discussed a proposed trade that included Steve Howe, a pitcher for the Dodgers; a first baseman from the California Angels; and Marc Sullivan. The Sox asked Tony Torcia whether they should trade Marc. Tony, knowing full well that Mark was Haywood's son, gave the politically correct answer and suggested that the Red Sox keep him. When they asked me the same question, I was too stupid to go along. "I'd make that trade tomorrow," I said.

"That's the owner's son," said another scout. I argued and finally said, "Do you want me to tell you what you want to hear, or do you want me to tell you what I think?"

Well, they didn't make the trade.

The next year the team moved from Bristol to New Britain, and in June it was announced that the Red Sox' number-one draft choice was a pitcher out of the University of Texas by the name of Roger Clemens.

Roger pitched a couple of games down in Winter Haven and was promoted to New Britain. I got word from Tony Torcia that Roger wanted to talk to me. *Maybe he wants to learn a slider,* I thought.

Roger had found out I had been involved in real estate and wanted to ask me whether he should invest in a condo. I told him he should.

Clemens's first start was against the Glens Falls White Sox, who had a first baseman by the name of Russ Morman. Morman had been the White Sox's number-one draft pick. He had starred at Wichita State, and Roger said that when Texas faced him, whether he pitched or Calvin Schiraldi pitched, Morman scalded the ball.

"How are we going to attack him?" Roger wanted to know. I stalled.

Roger and I went to warm up. As we were walking out to the bullpen, Roger said, "Well, what will we do with Morman?" I stalled again.

Finally he finished warming up, and he said, "Okay, now are you going to tell me about Morman?"

"Yeah," I said. "He's the third hitter. So it's important that you get the first two hitters out and that you're not in trouble when he gets up to bat. You have to face him with no men on base. Then I want you to take a deep breath, and I want you to throw your best fastball right at his fucking face."

As we were walking toward the dugout, Roger asked, "Right at his face?"

"With your best fastball," I said.

"Okay."

Roger retired the first two Glens Falls batters, and then looked over at me in the dugout. He nodded and I nodded. He took a deep breath, and I mean to tell you he threw a beauty of a fastball right at Russ Morman's face.

He knocked his ass down, and Morman stayed down like he was part of the dirt. It had to have scared the shit out of him. Russ had

had success against Roger in college. I'm sure he was digging in, looking for a fastball over the middle of the plate, getting ready to drive it, and now a missile was coming at his head. After that, Russ Morman never got a hit off Roger Clemens.

Roger was a real team player. Later in the season our team got into a fight in Reading. Roger, who wasn't in the game, chased a couple of their players into their dugout. I had to go into the Reading dugout to rescue him. Once we got back to the safety of our own dugout, I said to him, "Roger, there are a couple rules you obviously didn't learn in college, and one of them is never go into the opposing team's dugout, because you may not come out. They can hit you with a bat. Do not go in there."

We played Reading for the championship, and in the first game we played terribly. Our manager was Rac Slider. Rac was an infielder, a fine hitting instructor, but not an overly friendly guy. At first he was standoffish with me, but as the season progressed, he began to trust me. At the end of the game Rac chewed everyone out. He told the players they didn't have any pride. He ordered no batting practice the next day. I didn't think that was a good idea. This was a young team that was uptight as it was.

I grabbed the trainer and we went up to Rac's room to talk to him. "Listen, Rac, I understand where you're coming from," I said, "and everything you said was right. I just have a feeling if we can loosen things up tomorrow, we might play better."

"I don't want to see these fucking guys until tomorrow," he said. I asked him to let me run batting practice. The next day I went out and bought an aluminum bat. I let the guys take batting practice with it. They were hitting home runs all over the stadium. Our shortstop was one-hopping the fence and our power hitters were clearing it. They had a blast, and we won the game.

We were a mediocre team, but we won the Eastern Division championship that year with Roger Clemens. After the game, Rac said to me, "I want to thank you. This is the first championship I ever won anyplace. I appreciate what you did."

At the end of our season Boston wanted to call Roger up to the Red Sox. I thought that was a terrible idea. I told the people in Boston that he needed to rest.

"Listen," I said, "in the calendar year from September 1982 through September 1983, Roger has pitched over 300 innings. I know this, because I rub his arm between starts, and he's a little sore. He really needs to be shut down."

"All we want to do is take a look, because with his control we're thinking of making him our closer next year," they said.

The top two scouts for the Red Sox at the time were Sam Mele and Frank Malzone. In their opinion, Roger could step right in and become the closer.

"I don't know whose idea that is," I said, "but I can tell you right now, in the time I've spent in the game, the only guy I've seen with better stuff than Roger was Nolan Ryan. And you don't need to make him a closer. That's a real mistake."

"I appreciate what you think, but . . ."

I thought to myself, *This guy has so much talent. He's a number-one draft choice, and with the stuff he has they're going to make him a* closer *out of the bullpen? And what the fuck do you need to send him to Boston for? The Red Sox are out of the race. Why? Because he's a new toy and you want to show him off to everyone? For Christ's sake, send him home.*

I took Clemens aside and told him to go to Boston.

"As soon as you sign your contract, speak with Dr. Pappas," I said. "Tell him how your arm feels and tell him everything you've been going through between starts. Tell him that you're tired and sore." He saw Dr. Pappas, who didn't discover any tears but did find a weakness in the back part of Roger's shoulder. The Red Sox shut him down, and he didn't pitch any more that year.

I had been the pitching coach for the Double-A Red Sox, and two years out of three we won the Eastern League championship. I had the Pitcher of the Year for three straight years—Oil Can Boyd, Brian Denman, and Roger Clemens. We also led the league in ERA those three years.

I felt I had done great work and deserved to be more than the pitching coach. My ego told me I deserved to be a manager, even though I should have realized that in the Red Sox organization no pitcher was going to be named a minor league manager.

I only wish I hadn't done what I did. It's a problem when nothing you do is ever good enough.

I gave the Red Sox my ultimatum: Make me manager or else.

My ego got in the way, aided by some nudging from Marilyn, who didn't want me to be just the pitching coach anymore.

She and I argued.

Finally, she said, "I have to be honest with you, I don't like baseball. I loved watching you perform. I was in the game, but on days you didn't pitch, it was boring."

You didn't like baseball? I wondered.

I felt confident I had done such a great job that the Red Sox would agree to my demands and make me a manager. I didn't care if I went down to the Florida State League. I just wanted an opportunity, and I was sure they'd give it to me. Instead, they let me go and hired our backup catcher to be the manager.

I know more baseball than he does, I thought. I didn't quite understand it.

They hired him and they *released* me.

It was a *big* mistake on my part.

14

I'VE GOT A DREAM

MY EGO KEPT ME FROM APPLYING FOR another job as pitching coach. I hadn't gotten any recognition for the fine job I did for Boston, and I felt I needed my name in the news. I called a couple of teams for a manager's job, but I had no takers. I couldn't believe it.

I took a job working for Farmers and Mechanics Bank in Middletown. I reviewed accounts, solved problems, and told my clients, "We love your business. Thanks very much for banking with us."

My other job was cold-calling. I'd dial, talk, and not get anywhere, and I hated it. I lasted for nine months. I came home at the end of the day and tried to do the best I could as a husband and father. There were no nights out on the town, no craziness.

I was miserable.

And then, in August of 1984, I was reading the *Hartford Courant* and saw an article in the sports section written by sports reporter Owen Canfield. The University of Hartford was going to move into Division I in both basketball and baseball.

I called Owen, asked if Hartford had a baseball coach, and was referred to Bob Chernak.

Bob took my call. I told him what I thought I could do. I talked up my resume and list of accomplishments.

He was impressed. But the only information he gave me about the baseball team was that it had had a winless record the year before. I met with the University of Hartford athletic director, Gordie McCullough, who was formerly a very successful basketball coach and then a very successful golf coach. If it had been up to Gordie, I soon found out, basketball and golf would have been the only two sports teams the university would field. Gordie didn't bullshit me. He lamented about the problems the baseball team had, and asked why I wanted the job.

I didn't tell him the truth: It was because I was desperate to get back into baseball. Even if the budget was $6,000 and my salary was $3,000, it was an opportunity. I had failed twice before, once in major league baseball and again in real estate. I needed to pull off a huge win, both financially and in the press. I intended to do something that had never been done before. My grandiose plan was to take a 0–28 team—winless in the previous two seasons—on a meager budget and build it into a College World Series champion.

Since I seemed enthusiastic about being the varsity baseball coach, Gordie said I could have the job. I was elated. Now I had to find out what I had inherited. The first employee I ran into was the equipment manager. He told me that the year before, the team had gotten new uniforms. The Hartford colors are red and white.

"I washed the uniforms in hot water, the colors ran, and now we have pink uniforms," he said.

I thanked him for his honesty.

I met with Gordie McCullough and said, "*We have pink uniforms.*"

"We don't have money in the budget for new uniforms," he said.

We argued. He promised he would *think* about doing something about the pink uniforms.

We needed new uniforms. We had to at least *look* like a team.

Before the season started I went to Herb's Sports Shop, where we bought all our equipment. "Herb" was Herb Steinfelt. I promised him that we were going to get some money the next year and I'd order brand-new uniforms. I asked for his help with getting twenty-five baseball pants and shirts with the name Hartford on them. Herb agreed. It was cheap, Little League–quality stuff, but we had a red mesh top, white pants, and red socks, so at least we had a uniform, and at least it wasn't pink. Then I got a call from Gordie McCullough. He thought I had threatened to pull our account with Herb. I told him I hadn't, that we had struck a deal, and to not worry about it. I had it covered.

When I took over at the University of Hartford, the baseball program was in disarray, we were moving to Division I play, and I didn't know how we were going to compete.

I knew I needed a dream and a plan.

My time and experience as a major league ballplayer weren't enough. Jim Keener, the sports information director, took me aside. He had been the baseball coach the year before. He led me out to the baseball field, which looked like a sandy swamp.

Jim told me how bad the facility was and that there was no money in the budget to fix it. He, like Gordie, couldn't come up with one positive thing to say about the baseball program.

My first problem was lack of adequate facilities. The gym was too small. We had no baseball field. The girls' softball field was in terrible shape. The best venue was the men's soccer field.

I had to find a new practice field. Down the street from the University of Hartford is St. Thomas Seminary, and their field was used in the summer for a semipro twilight league. I visited the St. Thomas field, and it needed some work. We didn't have any games until the spring, so I figured we could use it for practice during the fall. I'd figure something out before the spring season.

I needed some help coaching the team, so I hired three of my close friends from Middletown as assistant coaches. I hired "the Grog" as hitting instructor. He had coached in American Legion, had studied hitting his whole life, and knew everything there was to know about hitting. I made his brother Teddy the pitching coach. Teddy had managed the American Legion team in Middletown. For the past twenty years Teddy had also been the athletic director at Coginchaug High School in Durham, Connecticut. I also made him my assistant, which meant that part of his job was to keep an eye on me.

The third assistant I hired was Paulie LaBella. He had been the third base coach on the same American Legion team that Teddy had managed. He had been a very good player in high school and college.

These guys were as good as any high school coaches I could have hired, plus I knew these guys, I trusted them, and they were willing to work that first year for nothing.

They believed in my dream, but I still had to convince them. I used every favor owed to me. My goal was to build a college baseball powerhouse from scratch.

The four of us wanted to see how good or how *bad* the team was. We held a tryout. We discovered we had a JUGS pitching machine. Grog fed fifteen balls to the first hitter, and the kid didn't have a single foul tip. He didn't make contact with a single pitch.

Grog thought he was just rusty. Turns out the kid started at second base the year before and only had one or two hits all season.

Another player named Green took some good swings, fouling off a few pitches. He said he was really good in the outfield. He had sixteen at bats with fifteen strikeouts the year before. And so it went.

Every kid who tried out was like that. You could not have put together a worse college baseball team than this one. They were good kids, but they could barely catch the ball.

We had one player, John Tuso, who could throw pretty well. We had a first baseman/pitcher named Jack Tracy whose arm was so bad I bathed it in DMSO. We had a center fielder named Billy Wilson, a scholarship player who was okay. Our other scholarship player, Todd McReynolds, our shortstop, wasn't bad. He was a tough kid from a small school, and we could do something with him. Still, I just couldn't believe how *bad* we were.

We scheduled a week of fall practice, but after the first day, Paulie LaBella said we should cancel the rest of the practices. There was no way we could help any of these kids. What we needed to do, he said, was to go out and recruit some real ballplayers. Unfortunately, we couldn't do that until after the season.

We opened the season away, playing at Yale. We drove down in a transit bus—a bus that has poles down the middle so riders can stand if they have to. The bus had four seats up front for the handicapped and infirm. The coaches sat in the handicapped seats on the way down to New Haven.

We got as far as Meriden, and the bus conked out. I was surprised it made it that far. They sent another transit bus, and when we finally arrived at the ball field, people thought we were Yale students coming from another part of campus.

Even though we were a terrible team, looking back, there were the funny moments that my coaching staff and I would recall over beers.

We drove down to play Wesleyan University on a cold and drizzling day. Our left fielder was an African-American kid, a smart kid who was studying international banking. I liked to give my players nicknames, and nicknamed him Honeydew. He always had a smile on his face. He was a really good kid. About the second inning Paulie LaBella walked over to me and said, "Honeydew is waving to you."

I called time, and I walked toward Honeydew as he was walking toward me. He wanted out.

"Coach, I have to be honest with you," he said. "I'm freezing, and this isn't fun. Is it possible you can take me out of the game? I have some homework to do, and I brought it on the bus, and I'd rather sit on the bus, do my homework, and get warm." I took him out.

We played a game against Eastern Connecticut, a Division III school but a very good team. My pitcher that day came from Massachusetts, and his family and friends were at the game. He gave up eleven runs in the first three innings. Even the outs he got were screaming line drives. In fairness, we should have put a screen in front of him. He was standing on the mound with tears in his eyes when he called me out to the mound. He wanted out too.

"This is just too embarrassing," he said. "I have my family here, and my girlfriend, and I don't want to pitch anymore. You gotta get me out of here."

"Okay," I said, and I took him out.

And so it went. A fly ball would go to an outfielder, he would pat his glove, and the ball would hit the ground beside him. On one double-play ball, instead of throwing the ball to first base, the second baseman threw the ball back to the pitcher. We went to play the University of Bridgeport. John Tuso was pitching, and somehow we were winning. About the fifth inning, Paulie said, "We better win this fucking game, or else I'm going to kill somebody."

"Why is that?" I asked.

"Honeydew just went on the bus, and he threw up all over the place."

Grog overheard the conversation and began laughing. I asked him what was so funny. "I forgot to tell you," he said, "our bus driver hadn't eaten yet, so he took *our* bus and went to get a sandwich. Honeydew threw up on the *Bridgeport* team bus."

We won the game, our first win of the season. We scrambled onto our bus and got the hell out of there. Nobody on the other bus knew who threw up, and we weren't telling.

Our players may not have been talented, but they were colorful. Our second baseman was five foot one, and I nicknamed him Stump. He didn't like the nickname and suggested I call him Dirt.

"Okay," I said, "you're Dirt."

When we played Southern Connecticut, they put on a hit-and-run play with a runner on first base. The batter fouled the ball down the left field line. I watched it go foul, and when I looked back to the infield I could see that the Southern Connecticut runner was on his knees at second base, clutching his stomach. The Southern Connecticut coaches ran out to see what the matter was.

I trotted over to the runner and asked him, "What happened?"

"I was running," he said, "and then I felt this huge pain in my stomach and side. I could hardly breathe."

The inning ended, and our players ran back to the dugout.

"I slugged him," Dirt told me.

We played Amherst, coached by Bill Thurston, who also was the Eastern Conference baseball supervisor. Thurston was a real prick who liked to run up the score.

Before the game I told Thurston we were lousy and warned him not to run the score up on us.

"I understand," said Thurston. "We're just here to play."

We were losing 9–0 at the end of the third inning. Amherst had a runner on third, and Thurston squeeze bunted.

"The cocksucker lied to your face," LaBella said to me.

I gave my pitcher the signal to knock down the next hitter. This kid had never faced a situation like that in his life.

He looked in to the catcher, blinked, got into the stretch, and threw the ball ten feet over the batter's head and ten feet up the third base line.

One Amherst kid said to the batter, "I think he threw at you."

The Amherst batter charged the mound. Both benches emptied. I circled around the Amherst players coming out of their dugout, and I body-blocked Bill Thurston to the ground, really nailed his ass, and I had my forearm around his throat.

"You low fucking son of a bitch cocksucker," I said to him. "I told you not to run up the score. What's this bullshit? You gave me your word."

Every time I applied pressure to his neck, his eyes would bulge and a little bit of chewing tobacco would come out of his mouth.

For a couple of minutes I yelled and screamed at him, until they pulled us apart. No one got tossed. There's no doubt I was engulfed with rage.

We finished the game and went home, and a couple of days later I got a letter of reprimand from the ECAC baseball committee, supervised by none other than Bill Thurston.

Nothing like going before an impartial *judge and jury.*

I was called into the office of Bob Chernak, the man who had hired me. He read me the letter and asked me if I wanted to respond to it.

"Yeah," I said, "I did everything they said I did."

I told Bob what happened, and while recalling it I could feel my rage return.

I told him that when Thurston pulled that squeeze in the third inning when he was up 9–0, I figured that was bullshit, so I told my pitcher to knock their batter down, but the pitch wasn't even close. And yes, I threatened him; I yelled and screamed at him.

"Well, try not to do that again," was all Bob had to say. "I'll take care of it."

Our last game was against Fairfield, and we beat them for our second victory of the season. On the way home as we drove up Interstate 91, one of our players said, "Coach, Christ, I have to take a piss."

"Pull over," I said to the driver.

We pulled over, and ten guys got out. In a show of solidarity, we all urinated on the side of the bus.

We finished the season with a 2–26 record.

15

BUILDING FOR SUCCESS

THIS TEAM WAS AWFUL THAT FIRST YEAR, and during just about every game we played, Coach LaBella would remind me, "These are the worst players. We have to recruit. I can't take another year of this. I'm going to go crazy." After the beating we took that first year, we started to recruit on a grand scale.

We knew that the central area of Connecticut had some great talent. Since we didn't have any money for scholarships, we decided we would recruit from the Catholic and prep schools. We thought I could get some of those kids to come to Hartford, arguing that my professional background and my expertise could train some top-notch players for a pro career.

There was another important sales come-on: I would also offer them the opportunity to play under the new domed stadium we would build on campus. This stadium I was envisioning could be converted from a baseball field into a basketball arena that would seat fifteen thousand fans.

The college administration would've been shocked to hear about this domed stadium, because there was no stadium in the works.

The administration had no idea we were building such a structure, because the idea sprung entirely from inside my wild imagination. I went to the architecture department and asked for a mock-up of a domed stadium. I thought it could be a class project.

And I'll be darned if they didn't design a really good-looking domed stadium with walls and lights and all the bells and whistles. The model fit on a two-by-two wooden base and was something I could use to recruit ballplayers.

Once I had the mock-up stadium, I met with HOK, a highly respected design and construction company, builders of many stadiums throughout the country, and they showed me the domed stadium they had built in Northern Arizona. I had them present a professional proposal to Bob Chernak.

Bob wanted to know where the money was coming from. I told him we would get a title sponsor. I approached Aetna Life Insurance and its CEO Robert Fiondella, who loved baseball and loved the idea.

I also talked to Joe Buzas, the owner of the New Britain and Pawtucket Red Sox, about owning a Triple-A team in Hartford and playing in our stadium. I also talked with the Hartford Whalers hockey team about adding a separate facility where they could practice.

I had nothing in writing. I just had a great idea and everyone I talked to agreed.

"This makes sense," they said. "I can see where I'd be interested in doing this."

As part of my dream to build an NCAA champion baseball team, I looked forward to building my domed stadium in Hartford and playing our games there. When I recruited a kid, I pushed the idea that the University of Hartford was going to go big-time. I also told recruits that we were going to go on a two-week spring trip to Arizona, which we didn't have any money for. I told them we were getting brand-new uniforms, which we also didn't have any money for. And I told them we were going to put together a team of the best players in New England.

Then I'd show them the model of the stadium and tell them, "I'm hoping you'll be able to play in it your senior year." I sold them on the idea, and it worked.

I started getting acceptance letters from one kid after another. These star high school players were giving us early commitments. And I made sure when we signed a player, the commitment was announced in the local newspaper and at the Hartford basketball games. That pissed off the basketball coaches because we were getting some free press on their dime. Basketball was the University of Hartford marquee sport.

AD Gordie McCullough told me I had one scholarship that I could offer my recruits. I gave out five. I kept going back to Bob Chernak and telling him, "I want this kid, and we have to have him. But I need a full scholarship."

"Okay, you can have this kid," he'd say, "but you can't have any more." Then I'd ask him later. He'd say, "Okay, you can have this one, but no more. It's got to stop. You can't have any more."

Finally I was told, "You can't have any more because the NCAA doesn't *allow* any more."

But the college also had something called a commuter scholarship. If a student commuted to school, we would give him a $3,000 stipend to cover his commuting expenses. The other coaches scoffed.

Their attitude was, "What's a crummy three grand?"

I called Dave Darling, a friend of mine in the real estate business in Hartford. I told him that I needed a bunch of apartments for my ballplayers to live in.

He was thrilled. I was going to fill one of his apartment buildings with paying tenants. I started signing players. One boy lived in Hyannisport. When the AD finally caught up with me, he said, "I did a little checking. This isn't a commuter scholarship. The boy lives in Hyannisport."

I gave him the player's new Hartford address. He didn't buy my explanation.

Bob Chernak, Gordie McCullough, and I met, the purpose of which was to chastise *me* over my abuse of the commuter scholarships. As Bob told me what he thought I was doing wrong, I told him that a commuter is someone who goes from a place of residence to another place.

"If a guy is living off-campus and he establishes a residence, that's his residence, not back in Massachusetts," I said. "If he's paying year-round, that's his residence, and if he's going to school here, that meets the requirements for a commuter scholarship candidate."

Bob and Gordie looked at each other. "I think you're right," they said.

And that's how I got another ten kids into Hartford. That first year I brought in nineteen players, all of whom were on some type of scholarship. The funds were allocated, though they weren't allocated from the athletic budget.

The part of college life I wasn't familiar with and the part I would never master was the politics of campus life. I wasn't very popular with the other coaches at the University of Hartford, not that I gave a shit. Gordie called a meeting of all the coaches and opened the floor to any gripes.

The basketball coach stood up and said he needed a better facility. So did the soccer coach. When they got around to me, I said, "No, we're happy with everything just the way it is."

When I said that, Bob Chernak slammed his fist on his desk.

"When Denehy came here," he said, "he had the smallest budget of any of you guys. And I've never heard one stinking complaint from him or his coaching staff. They take what they've got and try to do something with it. The rest of you guys whine and bitch and moan about what you can't do. Why don't you sit with them, find out what they're doing, and emulate it."

Chernak loved us.

The rest of the department hated us.

That year I went back to Herb's and ordered new uniforms and warm-up jackets.

I ordered beautiful jackets with *Hartford* on them. I ordered striped uniforms for home games, and for away games we had gray pants with a red top and a blue top. These were first-class, major league uniforms.

Bob Chernak raised my salary to $18,000, and each of my coaches was paid $1,500. Bob called me into his office.

I had booked our two-week trip to Arizona for spring training. We were going to be at the University of Arizona for four days and then travel to Las Cruces, New Mexico, to play the University of New Mexico in a week-long tournament.

"You probably have this all figured out by now," Bob said, "but do you have any idea how you're going to pay for all of this?"

I still didn't have any money, but I told him about the upcoming baseball dinner with my booster club. We didn't have a booster club and we didn't have a baseball dinner planned, at least not yet, but I was working on it. He asked who I would get to speak at this baseball dinner. "Tom Seaver, Pete Rose, or George Steinbrenner," I said.

"Do you really think you can pull this off?" asked Chernak.

"Well, that's the goal."

He told me that one of President Stephen Trachtenberg's closest friends was Yale president Bart Giamatti.

"He's been trying to get Steinbrenner to visit the Yale campus for five years," said Chernak, "and he hasn't even been able to talk to him." He suggested I go after either Seaver or Rose.

To start my booster club I called a Hartford lawyer, Alan Beck, a friend of mine, and I told him, "We have to start a booster club for my baseball team at Hartford. Who are some of the biggest real estate guys here in town?"

He told me to call Bob Simon. I called Bob, set up an appointment, and discussed my booster club with him. I told him about the gala dinner and how I would appreciate it if he'd chair the booster club and cochair the dinner. I told him that I had someone else in mind to cochair the dinner and that he'd be able to work with this person. I figured with Bob's contacts in Hartford, he could call his friends and tell them, "Take a table of ten."

I wanted to sell out the dinner.

I had attended a sports dinner and had sat next to Nikki O'Neill, the wife of Bill O'Neill, the governor of Connecticut. The governor's mansion was a mile from the University of Hartford. I called the mansion and told the Connecticut State Police that I needed Nikki's advice, and I asked if I could meet with her. I said it was personal, that I had a favor to ask of her.

Nikki agreed to see me.

I told her about the dinner and that I wanted her to cochair the dinner with Bob Simon.

"Okay," she said. "What would be my responsibilities?"

I told her about my plan. She agreed, but said, "But you are restricted to 250 people, and not one more." I agreed. I also told her she had to invite George Steinbrenner.

She chuckled; then she agreed to do it.

Four or five days later, I drove up to the mansion and sat with her, and she said, "You asked me to call George Steinbrenner. Here's his contact number with the Yankees. He agreed to come."

She confirmed that the cocktail party was arranged for 250 people, and not one person more, because of security. I went back to Bob Chernak and Gordie McCullough and told them the good news. I figured we'd make around $35,000, enough to pay for uniforms, the trip, and then some.

What I didn't know was that the gracious president of the university, Mr. Trachtenberg, being the big shot that he was, had invited all the deans of all the colleges free of charge, so when I arrived at the governor's mansion, I got word that Mrs. O'Neill wanted to see me.

"Oh boy, Mrs. O'Neill wants to see you, and she is pissed," her bodyguard said to me.

I knew what she was pissed about. She knew what Trachtenberg had done.

"*He's responsible*," I said.

George Steinbrenner was a great honored guest. He took pictures with every person at the cocktail party, signed autographs, and at the dinner gave a nice speech. After he was done, I went up to Bob Chernak and said, "I don't think it's my job, but someone should ask George whether he'd donate his fee back to the university."

We had paid him $7,000 to speak.

No one had the balls to ask him to donate the money back to the school, so he took the fee, and the next day at a sports banquet in Cleveland, Steinbrenner gave the fee to Mike Garcia, a former Cleveland Indians pitcher who was hurting for money at the time. Around the same time, Mrs. O'Neill called President Trachtenberg and told him she was not happy about the people he had invited to the fund-raising event who didn't pay.

She told him, "I want to make sure I understand your commitment to the baseball team and all the scholarships that need to be taken care of, and that all the monies for the uniforms and for the trip are paid for."

"Of course," was my understanding of what President Trachtenberg told her.

We had a grand time in Arizona. We played a two-game series against the University of Arizona, the defending NCAA champion for that year. Everyone thought I was crazy, but my idea was that if we were going to play with the big boys, let's play the best. So what if we lost? I told recruits they were going to play the best competition in the country, and stressed that "a lot of scouts will come to see the other team play, so if a player has any ability, he'll be able to show them."

We led both games initially. But we lost 12–3 and 15–5. We weren't in either game, but Arizona was the best college team in the country. We were able to practice there, and we could see what a really first-class facility they had. One highlight of the trip came in the first inning of the first game when our leadoff hitter, Pat Hedge, hit a ball over the light tower. He just crushed it. We lost, but we did play with the big boys and showed we could compete.

We had fun, but I also made sure the players went to mandatory study hall every single day. I brought along a professor to help them study, so if anybody gave us any shit, we had it covered.

We next went to Albuquerque, New Mexico, and won one game there. We beat Colorado State. We also lost to New Mexico State and the Air Force. I didn't expect to win many games. We had one senior on the team, one junior, and *nineteen* freshmen.

We played out the season and took our lumps. We played a game against the University of New Hampshire in the coldest weather I had ever experienced for a baseball game. There were forty-mile-an-hour winds and the temperature was only ten degrees. We shouldn't have played.

Before the game I asked Paulie LaBella to throw batting practice. He refused and stayed in the dugout the entire game. *Shades of Honeydew.*

In 1986 the Hartford Hawks finished the season with an 8–34 record. We knew we had a few spots to fill; we needed a backup catcher, a top shortstop, and a few well-rounded players for depth. At the top of our list of recruits was Jeff Bagwell, who went to Xavier High School in Middletown. I once saw him hit a home run 380 feet to right-center field. I always liked hitters who could hit to the opposite field. They were tougher to pitch to than dead pull hitters. As a pitcher, I can say that with authority.

Teddy, Grog, and Paulie had coached him in American Legion ball. And I had already recruited two top players from Xavier, so we had a leg up on the other colleges who wanted him.

When we recruited Jeff Bagwell, every letter Paulie wrote to him was in longhand. The rest of the colleges sent form letters. We visited Bagwell at his home. He also excelled in basketball and soccer. Jeff wasn't afraid of a little contact. In soccer he led Xavier and set school records in goals scored. He could kick with either foot.

I met with Jeff and his parents, and I told them that I thought he had the skills to be a major leaguer. The soccer coach wanted him too. He wanted us to share a scholarship so Bagwell could play soccer and baseball.

That was something you did in Division III. It was not what you did in Division I.

I told him Bagwell would play soccer over my dead body. Bagwell played baseball.

Add one more enemy to my growing list.

In order to gain an even stronger connection to the Hartford-area baseball coaches, I put together a free baseball clinic for local high school players. I brought in Tom House from the Texas Rangers, and he talked about pitching, then I brought in Lou Piniella of the Yankees to talk hitting. Both did a super job. The clinic was a big success, and that gave us an in with the coaches in the Connecticut, Rhode Island, and Massachusetts areas. The clinic improved their players' game, and it gave us a connection to their schools. If a coach had a good player, or if he heard of a good player, he would say good things about us.

I was sitting on top of the world. And then I got thrown a wicked curveball. The rest was all downhill until I landed on the rocks below.

16

THE FALL OF THE DENEHY EMPIRE
(1985 TO 1987 AD)

BOB CHERNAK WANTED TO KNOW IF I was having a second annual sports dinner. When I said I was, he then informed me that President Trachtenberg had lined up Bart Giamatti, his close friend, to be the main speaker. Giamatti had been named the commissioner of Major League Baseball. I told Bob that Trachtenberg couldn't have made a *worse* choice.

"It won't sell," I said.

"Why not?"

"People in the front office are boring," I said.

I asked to bring in Roger Clemens. Chernak agreed with the idea, but said, "but Giamatti is to be the *only* speaker."

I told him that wasn't going to work. I still was chafing from the Steinbrenner fiasco when Trachtenberg let all his buddies attend the dinner for free. Now Chernak was telling me that Trachtenberg didn't want us to go back to the governor's mansion, and that that was off the list. He wanted us to have the cocktail party on campus.

I boycotted the banquet. I went to a parent-teacher meeting for my daughter Kristin. That's how pissed I was. The dinner was only 60 percent sold out, and the next day Chernak called me. He said the president was unhappy his buddy Giamatti hadn't gotten the recognition he felt he deserved and expected.

"Bob," I said, "months ago I told you that you can't sell chicken shit as chicken salad. No one cares about Bart Giamatti."

Looking back, I should have gone directly to President Trachtenberg myself and explained to him why Giamatti was a poor choice for guest speaker. I could have done it positively. At least I think I could have left out the words arrogant, blowhard, and boring.

It was my third year at Hartford, and a man by the name of Don Cook took over as the athletic director. When colleges change athletic directors, things happen, and not always for the best. I needed the backing of the athletic director to be successful, and from the start Cook made it clear that I was no longer to be a free spirit.

He called a meeting of all the coaches to discuss fund-raising. The year before, the other college teams were holding car washes to raise money while I brought in George Steinbrenner and raised $35,000. I'm sure they were expecting me to repeat my success from the previous year.

Cook said, "What we want to do is sit down and see what everyone is going to do this year as far as raising money for the Hartford athletic department." When he said, "athletic department," my antenna went up. I was going to raise money for the baseball team, not the athletic department. I wasn't sharing a dime with anybody else.

"This year," Cook said, "we're going to do things a little differently. We're all going to pool and split this year. If one team raises $100,000 and another brings in $10,000, we will split and pool."

There were fourteen Division I teams at Hartford, so if I raised $100,000 I would end up with a lousy $14,000.

Like hell we will, I thought to myself. Cook looked at me and said, "Since you were the biggest contributor last year, what are you going to do this year to make money?"

I was my usual diplomatic self.

"I think that's bullshit," I said. "I'm going out and getting baseball people. I don't want to take anything away from basketball or golf or soccer, but the reason people are supporting baseball is that they love baseball. They want their money used for baseball."

"Doesn't matter," said Cook. "That's the way we're going to do it, we're going to split and pool. What are your plans this year?"

"Simple," I said, "I'm not going to do anything. I'm not going to work my ass off to make money when someone else is sitting around doing nothing, and I have to split and pool. I don't know how you came up with that decision, but it's a terrible one, and I'm not going to participate." I threatened to tell the booster club what was going on. As you might guess, that didn't sit well with anyone else in that room, especially my new AD Don Cook. Gordie McCullough, the golf coach and former AD, came to my defense. We hadn't been close, but when I was able to bring George Steinbrenner on campus, he just ate that up. I was surprised when he spoke up for me at the meeting.

Cook was clearly embarrassed, and there was a lot of animosity when we left that building. I made sure that Bob Simon, head of our booster club, had a long talk with Don Cook and told him that the booster club was *separate* from the university, and that he was not entitled to any of the money they raised. Cook didn't take it well. He wanted to control everything.

We began our third season with a trip to Florida. Before the season I reminded the players, "You won't win until your third year. As hotshots as you think you are, you aren't mature enough, physically or emotionally, to be able to compete with the top guys, but you will be by the end of your third year."

The previous year—the second year of recruiting—we were competitive, improving, staying in games, and losing games by one or two runs. The first day of the third season we played St. Leo's College in the afternoon and the University of South Florida that night. Jeff Bagwell went eight hits for ten at bats and hit for the cycle. He was hitting bullets. His freshman year he hit for a .402 batting average. He was a solid hitter. At shortstop, though, I could see he didn't have enough range to play the position. A few ground balls went past him on the right, and a couple on the left, and Paulie LaBella, our infield and defensive coach, was going nuts.

Jeff wasn't making errors. He had a shortstop's arm. He just wasn't getting to enough balls. Finally LaBella put his foot down.

"We have to move him to third base and we'll try Pablo Melendez at short," he said. We had picked up Pablo from Wilber Cross High School, a school in New Haven. Pablo was a great kid. But Pablo was scared, a little shy, and he didn't hit much, so we let

Bagwell come in and play short instead. We played Pablo a little at second base. Someone had to tell Bagwell we were moving him to third base, so after a game against Toledo, I addressed the whole team.

"We have to strengthen the team defensively," I said, "and therefore we're going to move Jeff to third. Peterson will move from third to first, and Pablo is going to play shortstop. That's the lineup we're going to use. Does anyone have any questions?"

"Why are you moving me to third base?" Bagwell wanted to know.

I tried to hedge. I came up with a bullshit excuse.

Jeff wasn't buying it.

"But what's the real reason, coach?" he asked.

I snapped.

"*Because you're too fucking slow at short*," I said.

Jeff (who would go on to be a four-time MLB all-star and win the National League MVP award in 1994) broke down and began to cry. Years later he said it was the only time in baseball that someone made him cry.

We traveled to Vermont to play a series. We were playing well. And then the Vermont pitcher knocked down one of our batters, our guys charged the mound, and we got into a brawl. The Vermont coach, Mike Stone, got thrown out of the game. Their clubhouse was way down the right field line; Stone was standing outside the clubhouse door giving signals. As I went to the umpire and pointed in Stone's direction, Stone stepped inside, out of view. I told the umpire, "He's out there giving signs." The umpire didn't believe me.

Then I was tossed out for arguing balls and strikes. I assigned a bench coach, and went to sit in the bus. A couple of days later I got a call from Bob Chernak.

Bill Thurston, the head of ECAC baseball, apparently my sworn enemy, said that after I was tossed out of the game, I took my time leaving the field. He also said that in the fight I had one of the Vermont players on the ground and hit him in the face several times.

That never happened. The cocksucker was making it up. I pleaded my case with Bob, to no avail. There was no hearing and no investigation into the incident. No one from the Hartford coaching staff was interviewed as to what had happened. I got a reprimand three days later that went into my personnel file.

I wasn't smart enough to see that someone was building a case against me.

The highlight of the season came against the University of Maine, which was in first place in the Eastern Collegiate Athletic Conference. The University of Maine seemed to always go to the College World Series.

We traveled to Orono, and we won two out of the three games; it was the first time in seventeen years that a school won a best-of-three series at Maine. In the final game we had a one-run lead. Jeff Bagwell led off the seventh inning, and he hit a ground ball up the middle. The shortstop dove for the ball, but he couldn't make the play.

I signaled for the next batter to bunt, and he bunted up the first base line, and they let the ball roll, and it stayed fair. Now we had runners on first and second base. I told the next batter to bunt the ball directly toward the mound. My batter bunted the ball toward the mound, and everyone ran past the ball. Now we had the bases loaded and nobody out. Pete Daniels, a really good hitter, was up next, and he drove a base hit to left for two runs.

I then squeeze bunted on successive pitches, scoring two more runs for a total of four runs scored in the top of the seventh inning, with exactly one ball hit out of the infield. We won the game.

After the game we went over to shake hands with the Maine players, and John Winkin, the coach who brought Maine to the World Series year after year, said to me, "Nice going. I hope the next time you don't play this Mickey Mouse type of baseball."

"We just kicked your ass, coach," I replied. He gave me a stare and walked away. You could tell this was going to be a great rivalry. I added one more enemy to my ever-growing list.

After our triumph over Maine I was sure the school would put up banners and balloons, or bake us a cake for the most important win in the history of the University of Hartford baseball team. There was no cake, no balloons, and not even a "nice going" from anybody, including my athletic director Don Cook, not that I hold grudges.

The lowlight of the season came two nights later. We played the University of Connecticut in Hartford.

The winner of the UConn game would lead the Division I standings in the ECAC in New England. No one thought we would ever be in a position to even compete for first place.

In the seventh inning one of our players, Pat Hedge, struck out. The catcher got up to throw the ball to third, and Pat was slow getting out of the batter's box, and so when the catcher threw to third, he bounced the ball off the top of Pat's helmet. He didn't do it on purpose.

Pat thought the throw was on purpose, and he and the UConn catcher had words, and then they fought. After the umpires got it cleared up, the umpire came over to me and said, "If there's any more fighting, I'm calling the game and I'm going to call it a no contest."

I thought that was ridiculous. If the other team starts a fight and the game is called, we should get the forfeit victory.

"If that happens, then I'm going to protest," I told him.

I was confounded that that umpire was working the game at all. I had put him on my list of umpires I didn't want working the Hartford games, because he was friends with all the other coaches. He was on the list because he was buddies with everyone. He was friends with the UConn coach, Andy Baylock, and other coaches, and I didn't want friends of these coaches umpiring my games.

When I saw him, I thought, *Oh shit, how did he get here?*

A couple of innings later the UConn batter hit a ball to our pitcher and ran hard to first base. Our pitcher threw the ball to first on the inside part of the bag, and the UConn runner deliberately ran over our first baseman. This started another fight, and immediately the umpires ran off the field. When the fight was over, the umpires called the game.

No decision, as he had said he would rule.

I wanted to protest and was told I couldn't.

The protest would have gone to the commissioner of the Connecticut Umpires Association. This umpire was the commissioner. It was another reason I wanted him blackballed. But he was there because he was close friends with Andy Baylock, the UConn coach, and with Don Cook, our AD.

After everyone else left, my coaches remained behind in the dugout, fuming. With us were two writers, George Smith from the *Hartford Courant* and another reporter from *Hartford Sports Extra*. We were talking about the game, and I was furious at the way the game had ended.

I commented about one of the UConn coaches, "That son of a bitch. Before the fight he was yelling and screaming at me like he was trying to bait me into a fight. He's just a troublemaker. He also referees soccer, and that's something that shouldn't happen.

You shouldn't be a coach on one team and referee soccer against one of your rivals."

Then I said the one sentence in my life that I wish I had never uttered.

"The next time he comes over," I said, "someone just might bomb his car."

The reporters who were with me recoiled.

George Smith said, "That's off the record. End of interview."

We packed up, got on the bus, and left. The next morning about nine o'clock I got a call from Don Cook's secretary.

"You need to get here right away," she said. "Don needs to talk to you."

I arrived at Don's office. He was sitting at his desk, scribbling away on a pad. At the top of the pad I could see the name John Toner and his phone number. Toner was athletic director at UConn.

He asked about a story in the *Norwich Bulletin* quoting me as saying, "The next time he comes over, someone just might bomb his car."

The Norwich Bulletin, I thought to myself. *I didn't talk to anyone from the* Norwich Bulletin.

Apparently a sneaky little shit by the name of Peter Abraham eavesdropped on my conversation with the other reporters right after the UConn game was called. Abraham was ambitious, and his ambition, lack of ethics, and balls would take him all the way to the *Boston Globe*.

I argued that my comment was taken out of context and asked to see the story. Cook kept pressing me, continuing to ask me whether or not I had said that sentence about bombing the UConn coach's car. He had already confirmed that I had said it with George Smith.

We argued.

What I had said was off the record.

No matter. He also took the UConn coach's word about the fight that caused the game to be called and wasn't going to investigate any of it.

Cook fired me on the spot.

He also fired the entire coaching staff with only weeks left in the season. We were 7–15, with sixteen games left to play.

Who knows how well we would have finished?

My coaches couldn't believe what was happening.

Teddy was devastated, Don used a few invectives, and Paulie was outraged. What they couldn't believe was the rush to judgment. You'd think at least Cook would investigate, talk to the assistant coaches.

All I had said was, "The next time he comes over, someone just might bomb his car." That wasn't a smart thing for me to say, obviously, but was it *fireable*? Why the push to get rid of me? Why was it done right away? Was it because of an allegation that Andy Baylock, UConn's coach, had hit one of our players? Why wasn't anyone willing to look into that?

"That's UConn's problem," Don Cook said. "We don't care about that."

Cook and Andy Blaylock were close friends. I suspect this was Cook's way to save his friend's ass. There was one other piece to this puzzle.

The associate athletic director at UConn was at the game as head of game management. This guy was supposed to intercede if there was a fight. His job would have been to say to us, "Get out of the dugout and get on the bus."

But this guy left the game after the sixth inning, just before the fight started, to catch the last quarter of the Whalers hockey game. Perhaps if he had been there and done his job, I wouldn't have opened my big mouth. Why wasn't he fired or at least reprimanded?

And to no one's surprise, Don Cook wouldn't back our protest of the game. I was made the scapegoat for those who screwed up, while Don covered for them after the fact.

My players were shocked and mortified. They didn't know what to do. I had one final meeting with my players. I urged them to stay put and not allow the incident to be a distraction.

There would be no dome and no national championship.

After the season, Pete Daniels, a pitcher/outfielder, transferred to Eastern Connecticut. Our catcher transferred to Stetson in Florida. We lost three really good recruits, including a left fielder who chose to play for Oklahoma State. We lost a pitcher from the University of Oklahoma who decided not to transfer to Hartford. In all, five guys from the Hartford team didn't come back. My prediction came true, though. In *their* third year, Hartford got to the ECAC tournament. Had Hartford not lost those five players after I was fired, they might have gone all the way to the College World Series.

I was never so crushed and dismayed as in the days that followed. I had been fired like I was a piece of shit, portrayed as a crazy bully who came around and beat up people.

It was a repeat of what had happened after my fine job as pitching coach of the Red Sox, when I coached Bristol en route to winning two Eastern League championships. It was a repeat of the treatment I got in high school, when I slowed down the basketball game to win the state championship. This was the third time in my life I was kicked in the teeth without getting any credit for the good things I did. Add to that my blown-out arm, and anyone can understand the emotional baggage, the anger, and the resentment that built up inside me.

I was beginning to think, *Life just isn't fair.*

17

YEARS IN HELL

AFTER I WAS FIRED FROM HARTFORD, I received two phone calls. The first one came from the sports information director's office at the University of Massachusetts. Peter Abraham the *Norwich Bulletin* reporter, had a long history of crossing the line. The person on the phone said, "I want to tell you something about the writer of that story. This guy has a track record. Peter Abraham was a UMass student, a kid who reported for the UMass newspaper. He had a sideline pass, and as the players came off the field after the football games, if a player would say something critical to another player, he wrote it down and printed it in the paper. They finally had to take away his sideline pass."

I later found out Abraham had had a similar incident with Jim Calhoun, the basketball coach at UConn.

He went from UMass to the *Norwich Bulletin*, and then he slithered up to the *Boston Globe* as a beat writer. He should only choke on his words.

The second call came from somebody in the UConn athletic department who also didn't feel right about what had occurred. He said that I had been fired because the administration at UConn had demanded it. He said that if I didn't get fired— and if the protest against UConn wasn't dropped, stopping the investigation of Andy Blaylock hitting one of our players— UConn was going to drop the athletic agreements with the University of Hartford.

Finally I understood what had happened to me.

In basketball, the UConn game was their biggest contract. Hartford was getting over $200,000 a year from playing in the Civic Center, and they couldn't afford to lose that money.

Hence the need to fire Denehy, and fire him fast.

Of course, no one at the University of Hartford, especially Don Cook, would ever confirm any of this. As bad as I felt for myself, I felt *worse* for my three assistants. They had done nothing wrong, and they were canned too. My children Kristin and Heather were also traumatized. They were teased by their classmates after they saw the headlines in the paper: "Denehy Fired at U. Hartford."

When the story broke, I was getting divorced. I had filed divorce papers because I didn't feel Marilyn had supported me enough in my career. My drug addiction was also beginning to drive a wedge between us. Being fired from the University of Hartford didn't help matters.

I remember one night Marilyn and I were getting ready to go to a cocktail party, and I was smoking a joint. We got in another argument.

Marilyn hated my pot smoking, and regularly flushed my pot down the toilet when she found it. I'd go to McDonald's in the morning because the coffeepot wasn't working, and I'd come back high.

I wasn't happy. She wasn't happy.

I couldn't hold a job because of the drugs and because of my temper.

I couldn't meet Marilyn's needs, and she couldn't communicate with me. She was like her mother, who nagged at me constantly. I just couldn't handle that. I didn't play well with others, and it cost me dearly.

While we were trying to figure out whether or not we should get divorced, I'd come over to the house and have dinner. I'd see the kids, and the next thing you know we'd get in a fight and she'd run upstairs. Later she told me she would sit on the bed waiting for me to come upstairs and console her, but I'd be out the door on the way to score some dope with a friend of mine, the Great Baldini, as he was called. At the time I couldn't see the part I played in her misery.

All those years I shit all over her, partying and doing crazy things like selling our house in Connecticut and moving her across the country to Arizona, where she was socially isolated. She had every right to be angry and frustrated. But I was "Wild Bill Denehy," and I needed someone to stand with me and fall on the sword if she had to. I know now it was unbelievably difficult for her. For my kids it was emotional torture, because they had to explain to their friends at school when asked, "What happened to your dad? How come he got fired?" They didn't have an answer, and I am not sure I had one either.

If I had been fired at an insurance company, it wouldn't have made the paper. But I was fired on the front page of the sports section of the *Hartford Courant*.

The way it sounded was, boy, this crazy motherfucker sure *deserved* to go before he did or said something *really* bad. My self-esteem was so low I should have considered committing suicide. But that never occurred to me. Instead, I went in the other direction. I became angry and resentful. All I could think of was getting even with the people who screwed me. My dad taught me one very simple rule in life.

"You don't fuck anybody," he said, "and you don't let anybody fuck with you."

Simple advice, yet I had gotten fucked. The firing made me so crazy; I couldn't deal with an impending divorce. All I could think about was getting back at those people from Hartford.

I went to my recreational shrink, the Great Baldini, whose real name is Robert. The reason he's called the Great Baldini is that he shaves his head. He has ears like Mr. Spock, and when he gets pissed off he talks in a high-pitched voice. The Great Baldini was five years ahead of me in high school. He played basketball at rival Middletown High, and I met him playing in a recreational league with a bunch of friends. He was a good guy to have as a friend.

He literally saved my life. So did his marijuana, which he smoked because he had been in a serious car accident and was in a lot of pain. He got me to try it to calm me down.

I lived in a rage. I never really wanted to kill anyone, though I would invent forms of torture to use on the men who caused my humiliation. I would have been very happy to see Don Cook and Andy Blaylock waterboarded or put in a sweat box, or limping around like cripples or worse.

The Great Baldini would look at me, open a box underneath his couch, roll a joint, and listen to my venom as I said the most bizarre things while we puffed away on his primo marijuana. And then we'd have another one, and after five of them it became "Fuck it. Do you have any cookies?"

In truth, this was a time when drugs saved me from doing something really stupid. I *really* wanted to get back at those people because I didn't deserve the way I was treated.

I sued the University of Hartford for false firing, and my attorney said to me, "You need to go see a shrink right now."

"Okay, I'll go," I said, and I went to a shrink.

I would fixate on and rant about "*those motherfucking people at Hartford.*"

The therapist would say, "We're not talking about Hartford," and "I want to know what's going on in your life. Are you going to get divorced? How are your children? How are you feeling?"

I couldn't get through ten minutes of our session without saying, "*Those motherfuckers in Hartford . . .*"

I did this for a year. Finally, one day the psychiatrist threw the yellow pad down on the table, looked up at me, and said, "All right. Let me make it simple for you. You got fucked. Okay? Do you understand? There might be some legal way to redeem that, but no one is going to apologize to you. You need to go on with your life. You got fucked. *How's that?*"

The Hartford firing happened in May of 1987, and Marilyn and I divorced in November of 1987. They were two huge losses that year. My daughters were hurt the most. I was living with my parents while they and Marilyn were living with Marilyn's mother. I didn't visit them as often as I should have. My daughter Heather once wrote to me, "I have a person who fathered me, but I don't have a father."

Meanwhile, I worked construction in the Hartford area. I knew people in the construction business. The union rep knew my family, so it was easy for me to get a job as a laborer. The first laborer job I got was working on the capitol building in Hartford. I was assigned to a foreman as his helper. One day I poured cement. On another day I cleaned up the side of the building. One day I used a sledgehammer to chip away at the cement around a huge sewer pipe. It took me the better part of a day to hammer away at it, and it was great therapy.

After the capitol building was finished, I got a job working on a power plant south of Middletown. After the third week, a union meeting was called, but I had to see my attorney about suing the University of Hartford for letting me go without a hearing. I skipped the union meeting.

The next day, my foreman walked up to me and punched me hard in my shoulder with his fist.

"Where the fuck were you last night, Denehy?" he said. "We had a union meeting. Understand. When you're new around here, you attend the fucking union meetings."

"I had a previous appointment," I said. We argued, and he hit me in my shoulder again.

My anger was beginning to rise. He pointed his finger at me.

"*Who the fuck do you think you're talking to?*" I said. I grabbed a push broom, turned around, and swung it at him. I started out swinging at his head, but in a moment of clarity I thought better of that. Instead, I hit his kneecap, jumped on top of him, and started beating him. I had him in a headlock and went after him like a shark in bloody water. It took about five guys to keep me from killing him.

I had snapped. If he had reacted calmly and rationally, no problem. But when he started screaming, I lost it.

I was sent to the office, where I was fired, and I threatened the superintendent that I would sue if I didn't get unemployment. He agreed to say he was letting me go because of lack of work, and I became eligible for unemployment. Was it a big deal? No. But he shouldn't have fucked with me, or I wouldn't have raged.

I worked construction all of 1988 and the early part of 1989. I also played softball, but all the while I was still angry. Once I threw the ball at an umpire's head and just missed.

Our softball team won three city titles in Middletown. We played hard and we partied hard. And all the while I raged.

18

GETTING HIGH IN FLORIDA

I GOT A JOB WITH A RADIO station in Springfield, Massachusetts. I don't remember who owned the station, but the owner previously had worked at a station that was part of the Enterprise Radio Network; he had heard me do my talk show, and he knew about my time at the University of Hartford. He hired me to do sports. My time slot was nine o'clock in the evening to midnight. I was also supposed to go out and sell ads for the station.

I knew I could sell ice to an Eskimo. But when I was selling insurance or real estate or ads on the radio when it wasn't for me but for a company, I was a terrible salesman. I lacked structure. If you give me a list of stores or accounts I need to oversee, fine.

Put me in a car to visit those accounts, I can do that too. But if I have to generate my own list, make my own appointments, and follow through, that doesn't click for me.

I did my sports show for a while, but there was a problem. Unlike the Enterprise Radio show, where the phone lines were always lit up, I had to generate calls at the Springfield station. Every day I had to come up with something controversial or clever to get people to call in. I had some regular callers. But there was a lot of downtime, and I had no one to work with. I'd have been damn good, but I was alone, and if calls didn't come in, I wasn't one to ad lib and make it entertaining.

I suggested that instead of doing sports at night I become the morning commute sports guy from six o'clock to nine o'clock in the morning. I thought I could talk about the news from the night before, talk about sports and weather, and call the newspaper guys for conversation.

The owner agreed, and I did the show in the morning for a while, but the problem was that I'm a night guy. I hated to get up in the morning. I didn't miss any work, but when I got done with my shift, I didn't go out and make sales calls. I went home and took a nap.

The Sunday of the Super Bowl, the Great Baldini invited me to the home of some friends in Naugatuck, just a few hours from where I was living in Springfield. We were waiting to watch the game, and there was some pot smoking going on. Another couple brought in chocolate brownies. After I smoked a little pot, I ate three or four of the brownies.

When they finally noticed me, somebody said, "No. No. What are you doing? *They're loaded with marijuana.*"

Within an hour I was comatose. I was slurring my words. I was all fucked up. After the game ended, I realized there was no way I could drive back to Springfield, and I doubted I could even drive the next morning. I called the owner of the radio station and I told him I was at this party, and I had eaten something and had food poisoning. But he knew I was high.

Two days later I came in for my normal shift. After my shift, the station owner asked me to step into his office.

"You can't fool me," he said. "I smoke too, but I don't miss any work, and you were all fucked up. I had to come in for you. I had to cut short my plans. And so you're fired."

Again.

Marilyn still spoke to me even though we were divorced. We still loved each other, but I was too messed up for her. She wanted a settled family life. I needed to find myself.

After I was fired in Springfield, I moved back in with Marilyn and the kids for a little while. The kids, now teenagers, couldn't figure out our relationship, because it was so unhealthy. Then I got a call from John Chanin, my former boss at Enterprise Radio. Chanin was the vice president and director of operations for the Florida Radio Network. He offered me two jobs.

A new professional league was starting in Florida called the Senior Professional Baseball League, made up exclusively of former major leaguers. John wanted me to work as an analyst beside Lou Palmer, who would do the play-by-play. I would also host a talk show with Lou from four o'clock to eight o'clock in the evening on Friday, Saturday, and Sunday nights at Disney World in Orlando.

I needed a job I liked, and it sounded like a great opportunity. I flew to Orlando. Marilyn and the kids weren't pleased that I was taking off for Florida. We were divorced, but she hadn't wanted to get divorced. I can't say I ever stopped loving her, but I needed some space. I was angry, frustrated, and pissed off, while she wanted and needed a normal family life with a husband and father. But that just wasn't who I was at the time. I didn't listen. I wanted Marilyn and the kids to move down to Florida with me, but she put her foot down.

After I left for Florida, abandoning her and the girls, she hated my guts. She wouldn't let the girls talk to me on the phone. She thought I should stay in Connecticut and make a life there, and she was really hurt when I took off. Marilyn felt, *Go to Florida and leave his two girls? Who does that? Who runs away from the responsibility and goes so far away? He's going to miss very important parts of their lives.*

But I needed to get away. I needed to do something that meant something to me. I needed to be somebody again.

The Senior League was a fun time. I loved doing those baseball games. Lou Palmer and I were in Winter Haven, home of the Winter Haven Super Sox, and they were playing the Orlando Sun, who had three Cruz brothers playing for them.

Lou was a real, true professional. He was always prepared. He'd come to the game with his *Baseball Register*, and he'd have notes from the league. I'd show up with a blank scorecard.

That night Lou made mention that it was only the second time three brothers had played in the same outfield.

"Everyone knows, Bill," he said, "that the others were the Alou brothers.

"But there are four Alou brothers, Lou," I said.

"No, just three," he said.

"No, no, no," I said, "there are definitely four."

"You want to name them?"

"Sure, Lou. There was Matty, Felipe, Jesus . . ."

"And the fourth one?"

"Bob," I said. "Bob Alou."

"I can't believe you suckered me into that one," Lou said.

The *I Love Lucy Show*, which aired in the early 1950s, starred Desi Arnaz as Ricky Ricardo. Ricky was a bandleader who played the song "Babalu." I can't believe he fell for it.

It was a fun time in Florida because I was doing baseball games. And in Florida it's real easy to connect with drug dealers.

I also did some college baseball games for the Sunshine Network with Paul Kennedy, who still does the pregame show for the Orlando Magic. There were times when I'd smoke a joint on the way to the broadcast, and I'd broadcast high.

We were doing a playoff game between Florida Southern and Tampa, and my job at the end of the game was to interview the winning coach. My out cue was "Thank you very much, coach. Congratulations on the win today. The next stop is the regional finals. Let's go back up to the booth with Paul."

But I couldn't remember Paul's name. During my interview with the winning coach, I wasn't listening at all to what he was saying because I was desperately trying to remember Paul's name. Just before I had to sign off, I remembered Paul's name. Boy, I was sweating bullets.

I became involved in a lot of using. I met a mortician, and I used to get my marijuana from him, and sometimes we'd do coke together. I needed to get my mind off the ordeal with Hartford, where I hadn't yet reached a settlement. I was over at his house and we were looking for marijuana, but we couldn't find any; we looked for coke, and we couldn't find any, so he made a call.

"Have you ever done LSD?" he asked.

It would have been too embarrassing to have said I had never done LSD, so I said, "Let's do it."

He grabbed my keys, hid them, drove off, and came back, and we did some LSD.

He had a huge fish tank in his house, and I stayed up all night long staring at the colors of the fish and at the weeds in the tank.

My drug habit got worse as I started using more and more. I'd have my coffee with a joint. Then I'd have a joint midday, a joint in the afternoon, and another joint at night. When I was working, I kept to the same schedule.

The Senior League lasted a season and a half. It ended on Christmas Day of 1990, when the Fort Myers franchise folded. Fort Myers had two owners. One was a DuPont, and the other was said to be a cokehead. When DuPont discovered his partner was putting his profits up his nose, he folded the team. When Fort Myers went under, the league crumbled. The league gave a lot of former major leaguers a second chance to play the game they loved. I felt bad for them when the announcement came that everyone had to go back home.

I was called into the office of the Florida Radio Network one day and told the station had been sold to conservative hatchet man Pat Buchanan, who decided he wanted more of a politico-religious message, so he was cutting out sports.

I was out.

I was still doing some games for the Sunshine Network, so I applied for a job at WFAN in Tampa. I wanted to be their morning guy from nine o'clock to noon. But I was supposed to troll for sponsors for the program and book my own guests, which is very time-consuming. I got up every day to have my coffee and a joint, and I'd drive from my home in Orlando to Tampa, and I'd scramble to get guests for my show. I badly needed an assistant, and I knew someone who I was sure would be perfect for the job. I hired a woman named Lisa, who I knew from the University of Hartford.

She was living in New Jersey at the time, and she flew to Florida as a favor to me. She was a great producer, even though she wasn't getting paid. She was persistent in finding guests. She would call anybody and get them to come on the show. Lisa was living with me, working for nothing, and after a few weeks I went back to the radio station and told them I wanted them to hire Lisa to be my assistant. They said they didn't have the money to hire her.

I told Lisa I'd do my best to work something out.

Our top on-air performer at the time was Nancy Josephson, the "Sports Babe." The station manager came back and said, "We can have Lisa come in and produce both your shows."

"But the Sports Babe gets to pick her guests before you do," he said.

That was ridiculous. My show aired before hers. And since Lisa didn't have a car, I would have had to sit around during the Sports Babe's show so I could drive Lisa back to Orlando.

I went on the air, and I said, "We have a major decision today. My boss has to decide whether to keep Lisa on as my producer, because if they don't hire her, I'm quitting."

An hour into my program, the program director ordered me to go to the main office.

Then he said, "I'm going to take over for the rest of the show."

I was sent to the main office.

They fired both me and Lisa.

After we were fired, Lisa took a job at Hooters. One morning she was leaving to go to work, it was raining, and while she was standing on the porch she yelled, "Look."

Standing in my carport I could see a shaggy, soaking-wet dog.

The dog looked like a schnauzer, but it must have weighed ninety pounds. I gave the dog a couple of pieces of bread, and it ran into my house. Now I had a drenched dog lying on the floor in my house eating bread.

"See, she likes you," Lisa said. "Promise me you won't chase her out until I get back."

"Oh, great. Thank you," I said.

I gave her another piece of bread, and for the next eight hours the dog and I stared at each other; the dog was in the corner and I was in my chair watching TV. I felt like I was in a *Frasier* episode where his dog, Eddie, incessantly stares at Frasier's father while he watches TV.

The next day I took the dog for a walk, hoping someone would claim her. The day after that the dog went into heat, I took her to the vet to get her fixed.

The next day the vet called to tell me that the operation had gone very well. He also called to say that she was a very valuable dog, an Otterhound. I could have made a lot of money if I had bred her, but of course now it was too late. So now I had a fixed Otterhound.

Every time I'd feed her, she'd sit in the corner of the room and stare at me. We would have stare-offs. Finally I decided that I had to come up with a name for her. John Chanin and his wife came over to the house. I served them drinks, and the dog was frisky and knocked over John's drink with her tail.

"You stupid fucking schmuck," I yelled. "Watch what you're doing."

Ah, I had my name.

I called my dog "Schmucko."

I didn't know Yiddish. I had no idea that "schmuck" in Yiddish means "penis."

I bonded with Schmucko.

I had a lease on a Mercury Cougar, and just as the lease was expiring the thermostat blew. Ford claimed the car wasn't under warranty, but I decided I wasn't going to pay to have it fixed. Since my lease was soon to be up, I stopped making payments.

One night I drove to an Orlando bar called BJ's. When I got home, I hopped into bed. In the middle of the night outside my bedroom window I heard *clank, clank, clank*. I didn't know what it was. Schmucko didn't even bark.

I went back to sleep, and the next morning when I went outside, my Mercury Cougar was gone.

I thought to myself, *I was out last night. Where the hell is my car?*

I got on my bike and rode over to BJ's. The car wasn't there. I came back home, and then I realized, *Somebody stole my car!* I yelled at Schmucko for not barking, and then I called the police to report it stolen.

"Your car wasn't stolen," the cop told me. "It was repossessed."

"No," I said. "*God has my car.*"

The cop started laughing.

I bought a Datsun. There we were, me and Schmucko, just the two of us, riding around in my new car.

Whenever there was a change in the weather, my shoulder would throb. If I played golf, I usually took four Aleve before I teed off, two more at the turn, and two more at the end of the round. One of those cold fronts came through, and my shoulder was just aching. I was out of weed, so I called my supplier.

"I got just a little," he said. "If you need something for a quick trip, come on over."

I went over to his house. He had the remnants of two joints. He said he was making a buy that night—his dealer was coming over to his house—so we smoked and waited for his supplier to call. After the call came, he said, "Bill, there's something funny about this . . . . I'm apprehensive about dealing with this guy.

"Why don't you go home?" he said. "I'll cut a deal. It'll take a little time to clean it up so I can sell you some. I'll call you, and you can come and get it around seven.

"You really need to go home," he said.

I got home around five o'clock. The joint I had smoked was wearing off fairly quickly. Soon it was after seven o'clock, but I didn't want to call my supplier because the drop was being made at his house. Finally, when I was crawling up the walls in agony, the phone rang. It was my supplier's wife.

His new dealers turned out to be narcs, and her husband was arrested. I asked if I could bail him out. If he hadn't been so insistent on my getting the hell out of there, I'd have been arrested too. He didn't go to jail, but he had to pay a stiff fine and got probation. After the bust, his inventory dried up.

I was still doing TV work, but not much. I was going crazy. I was *still* pissed off at Hartford, and Marilyn continued to hate me and wouldn't let me see my two kids. My drug habit was growing by leaps and bounds, until I was *way* out of control.

One of the tricks I learned was to take a cigarette, pull some of the tobacco out, take some marijuana, douse it with cocaine, and stuff it all back into the cigarette casing to fill the gap. The combination of nicotine, cocaine, and marijuana knocked me on my ass. One time I went out dancing with Lisa, and while she was on the dance floor she pulled out one of my cigarettes and lit it up.

I took a couple of drags and felt the effects immediately. There were poles on the dance floor, so I wrapped myself around one of those poles like an anaconda. I couldn't move. If I had let go, I would have landed headfirst on the floor. Somehow I got back to my seat, and I sat there in a mystified state until I returned to some semblance of normalcy.

On July 4, 1991, I got together with six of my druggie friends. We scored marijuana and coke, some beer, and some scotch, and over a six-hour period we went through it all.

I was lying on the floor of my bedroom, my heart pounding, looking out onto the patio, and saw a foot-long, skinny snake. I prayed: *God, if you help me not die today, I will not do drugs ever again.* But I figured if I could just cut out the cocaine; that would be acceptable.

A few hours later I woke up. The snake was gone.

Okay, I made a commitment, I thought. *I won't do cocaine anymore.*

And I didn't.

In June of 1992 I went back to Connecticut to visit my kids. I was still using. I went to watch my younger daughter Heather play softball. During her games I stood behind the center field fence smoking pot. I had reached an agreement with the University of Hartford regarding my termination. Part of the deal was that I can't disclose specifics of that agreement. One thing I can tell you: They didn't give me my job back.

On the last day of the week-long softball tournament, I took my two daughters to breakfast.

"Is there something we didn't do this time that you'd like to do the next time we're together?" I asked them.

Heather said, "I'd like to play catch."

Her words hit me like a ton of bricks that weighed heavily on my heart. I was an ex-major leaguer, yet I was so screwed up, so fucked up, that I couldn't spend fifteen minutes playing catch with my daughter.

"The next time I come back here, we'll do that," I promised.

That day, June 15, 1992, I got on the plane to go back to Florida. I vowed that I would never use again. It's been twenty-one years and counting, and I've been in recovery ever since.

19

IN THERAPY

I NEEDED HELP, AND I TURNED TO Leo Cyr, the head of the Major League Baseball Alumni Association. I told Leo what I was going through, and he sent me to a seminar on alcoholism and drug abuse at the Glen Bay Hospital in Orlando. He told me to speak with Ryne Duren and tell him about the drugs, the pills, and the cortisone, and that I had stopped.

I went to the seminar and talked about my life, my pain, my drinking, my drug use, and what happened to me.

John Brandenberg, the director of Glen Bay Hospital, and Dr. Irving Kolin, the medical director, walked over to me after I spoke. "That was great. You talk well," said John. "Would you be interested in doing work with us in community relations?"

"What's that entail?" I asked.

"Going into the schools and talking to the kids about not doing drugs."

We agreed to meet. The next day we met, and I told him everything. I was honest to a fault. I wanted him to know just how bad my drug problem had been.

"Do you know why people do drugs?" Brandenberg asked.

"No, why?"

"Because they work," he said. "We have pills for everything. People take drugs because they work. We just have to find out why *you* do it. I'd like you to enroll in the Glen Bay Hospital outpatient program."

"I'm not working right now," I said. "What's it going to cost me?"

"We want you to work with us in community affairs, so it won't cost you anything," he said. "We can continue to educate you. This will be like a scholarship."

The next day I enrolled as a patient at Glen Bay Hospital. It was the end of my five-year descent into hell. When I checked in, they wanted a history. I was required to report to the hospital every day at five o'clock in the afternoon, and I had to be there every day from six o'clock until nine o'clock in the evening.

They paired me up with someone who had a similar history of addiction. I was introduced to Anthony, who we called Tony.

"He has a cocaine and heroin problem. You have a cocaine and marijuana problem. You both are really angry men, so you ought to get along. Shake hands."

We bonded instantly!

Tony was an intimidating presence, an enforcer for the mob. He was a former military man. He told me he would get himself arrested on purpose so he could go into the jails and intimidate witnesses. If you were supposed to testify against someone in the mob, he'd walk up to you and say, "I just want to tell you how close we can get to you. Here I am, standing right next to you in jail."

He usually didn't have to do or say anything else. His presence was enough to scare the shit out of witnesses. He said he had had to beat up a couple of people, but he never killed anyone.

I met Tony's mother, who was a peach. She ran a fencing operation. One time I was visiting Tony at his mother's home. We were having breakfast, the phone rang, and his mom picked it up.

"For God's sake," she said. "You know the damn program. Drop the van off up the street. Drop the keys off inside the mailbox. We'll get back to you with a number. Now do like I told you."

This was Tony's mom. His mom loved me because I was friendly with her son, and because she had problems with his drug abuse. Tony and I went out that day, and when we returned, her house was filled with top-of-the-line designer clothes. She owned a neighborhood department store. The top floor was for the community so people without a lot of money could get some nice clothes. She ran two-for-one specials. She would take me downstairs where she had the top-notch designer stuff and let me take what I wanted.

I took golf shirts, sweaters, pants, whatever I needed off the racks.

I began therapy my first day at Glen Bay Hospital. Our group would meet from six o'clock to nine o'clock in the evening, with a five-minute smoke break.

Our group consisted of people with various problems. Tony and I had alcohol and drug issues, but there were also people with gambling problems. Other attendees were food addicts. We had a stripper with a sex addiction and a flight attendant who was both bulimic and alcoholic.

In those therapy sessions I began to understand addiction. The first thing I learned was the medical aspects of the disease, something they don't discuss nearly enough in most drug programs. Alcoholism was recognized as a disease by the American Medical Association in 1956.

"Why is this called a disease?" we were asked.

We were told that there are five components of the disease: It has symptoms; it can be diagnosed; it's progressive; it can be treated; if it's not treated, the disease can, and often does, lead to death.

Ballplayers are always talking about the *problem* they have with alcohol.

My sponsor told me, "Picking your nose in public is a *problem*. We alcoholics have a *disease*."

Once you learn that you have a disease, you ask, "What do you have to do to cure it?"

The obvious answer is abstinence. You have to stop using. Except that it's incredibly difficult to do so because of the underlying causes of the disease.

I went into rehab on July 7, 1992. It was supposed to be an eight-week program, but because I was so *very* willing and open-minded to change, it took me *thirteen weeks*. Some are sicker than others, and some take longer than others.

I learned how badly people suffer from addiction. Gamblers Anonymous has the highest rate of suicide of any of the more common forms of addiction. Gamblers often feel that since they have fallen so far into debt, the only option left is to kill themselves.

One of the women in the group was an overeater. She said she'd get up at six o'clock in the morning to bake herself a chocolate cake. And then she'd eat it before she went to work. She said that she was poor as a child. When she started babysitting and going to people's houses, she ate chips and other junk food, and then she started gorging herself, eating everything in sight. She just couldn't stop eating. And then she'd purge.

The stripper in the group was a "coke whore." She loved to strip down in front of people and get paid for it. She said that sex was like eating candy. She just couldn't get enough of it. She wanted to stop her drug addiction because the Department of Children's Affairs was threatening to take her daughter away.

Years after I listened to the people in the group talk about their sex addictions, I read about Tiger Woods, one of the greatest athletes in the world, who was also a sex addict. I wasn't sympathetic toward him at the time, but from the people I spoke with in therapy years before, at least I understood how horrendous a sex addiction can be.

Somewhere in each person's background there's some kind of abuse, whether it's emotional or physical. Our therapist would tell us, "Emotional abuse is worse than physical abuse, because it gets in your mind, and you replay it all the time."

Physical abuse may be painful, but you can get over it more quickly. The emotional abuse stays with you until you can get some therapy. There were different reasons why these people were in therapy, but whatever the reason, we knew that whatever form of addiction we had, we had to stop. Toward the end of my therapy sessions I was told, "We have everything under control except the anger and the resentment. We have to do something about that."

One day Vicky, my therapist, said she wanted to do an anger exercise with me to see if she could break the pattern. She had Tony stand behind me and two good-sized guys stand on either side of me, as she stood on a chair right in front of me.

She said, "I'm going to take you back to one of the situations you had in high school. You talked about the fact that you devised a defense that won your team a big game, but your coach took all the credit for it. I'm going to be the basketball coach, and I'm going to start yelling at you, and let's see what happens."

Standing on the chair right in front of me, she started pointing her finger at me and screaming, "Who the hell do you think you are? You're just a player. I'm the coach. You're sticking your nose where it doesn't belong. I ought to sit your ass down."

I didn't know what was happening to me, but slowly my eyes started bulging. Whenever I'd sink into one of these rages, it was as though someone pulled a window shade over my eyes. I could still see out; I was still cognizant of what was going on, but at the same time I had no idea where I was or what I was doing.

All of a sudden I began moving toward her in a threatening way. The three men held me back; they had me by the arms, but it was all they could do to restrain me. I wasn't saying anything. I just had this look on my face that said *I'm going to tear you in half.*

To break the spell, Vicky began to clap her hands and yell, "Bill, Bill, it's Vicky. Come out of it. Come down. I'm not the coach. It's Vicky."

The shades over my eyes lifted as I calmed down. I was sweating like a pig.

"What's that all about?" I asked her.

"Wow, you really went into a rage," she said. "Fortunately you didn't act out, but you were seconds away from that. You need really heavy work."

Later the group explained to me in great detail the reaction I had. But at the time I experienced it I wasn't conscious of what I was doing.

Today there's a lot of talk about anger management. I don't think that would have worked for me. All I know is that when I get frustrated and disappointed, I can go ballistic. Some people say it's instant insanity, while others dismiss that theory. But I can tell you from my experience that it's real. I know how quickly it happens. Telling me to count to ten doesn't work. By the time I got to three, I'd have the other guy on the ground, choking the life out of him.

Later in my therapy I learned that there was something in my system that really made me angry, and that something, I believe, was the cortisone the baseball doctors had shot into my body for so many years. They were literally giving steroids to a semicrazy person. Talk about fueling the fire. It couldn't have been more destructive to me and those around me.

When I had one of my rages, I wouldn't know what I was doing. I had no idea. And afterward I'd have no memory of it. When I raged, my reaction was the same as the one I had had when Vicky provoked me in the therapy session. I thought people were kidding me when they told me how I had acted.

Therapy was a deadly serious affair, but that didn't stop me from finding the humor in it. A couple of the patients had trouble dealing with grief. Loved ones had died, and they couldn't handle it. In therapy we also said good-bye to our old addicted selves.

Our therapist set aside a special room close to her office, made a makeshift casket, and played funeral music, and we were supposed to go into this room and grieve for our old self. The old addicted Bill, the old angry Bill, was dead, and we were going to grieve for him.

The afternoon before my grieving-for-old-Bill ceremony, I needed to fumigate my apartment to get rid of Schmucko's fleas.

I called Vicky and said, "I have to bring Schmucko with me."

"Okay," she said, "Sneak her in. Go to the side entrance at six o'clock this evening, and I'll open the door for you. Run the dog in and put her in my office, and we'll have some water for her."

I set off the flea bombs in my apartment, then I put Schmucko in my car, and the two of us went to therapy. A lot of patients were already there when I arrived with Schmucko.

I was sitting with her when one of the patients, a rabbi's wife, asked me, "Is that your dog?"

"Yes."

She asked, "What's the dog's name?"

"Schmucko," I said.

"Do you have any idea what a *schmuck* is?

"I have no idea, but that's my dog's name."

As an Orthodox Jew and a rabbi's wife, she got quite upset about my dog's name.

Things settled down. Soon it was time to go into the special room and grieve over our dead selves. Tony and I walked in together, and when we saw the mock casket and heard the funeral music, we both began laughing under our breath, our shoulders bouncing up and down, until we no longer could hold it in.

Vicky made us go outside, and she locked the door behind us. It started pouring rain, and Tony and I were banging on the door. When she finally opened it, we were soaking wet.

"Dry off the best you can," she said. "You have to get through this thing."

We walked back in, and no sooner had the door closed in the grieving room than we began laughing again. She threw us out again.

We never did pass the grieving test.

Another time, Tony and I had to get a physical exam. We were waiting in the therapy room with a man named Henry. He was a victim of domestic violence at the hands of his wife. He was a nerdy little guy who wore glasses. His wife kept beating him up.

The three of us sat patiently in the waiting room when the female doctor walked in.

Tony and I decided to have a little fun with Henry.

"This is the first time I've ever had a female doctor give me a physical," Tony said. "I wonder if she grabs your balls."

"I can't wait until we bend over and she sticks a couple fingers up my ass," I said.

I could see Henry was listening to every word.

I went in first, and the exam was no big deal, but when I came out I said, "It was unbelievable, Tony, when she stuck her fingers *up my ass*, it was like the greatest sensation you're ever going to have."

Henry asked to go to the bathroom.

Tony went in for his physical, and when he came out he was waiting to say something crass to Henry, but Henry hadn't come back.

A nurse went into the bathroom looking for Henry, but he wasn't there. Henry had bolted.

Vicky brought us into her office.

"What did you guys say to Henry to make him leave?" she asked.

We denied that we had said anything.

Henry never came back, and we never saw him again. I often wonder if he ever stood up to his battering wife.

We had group and individual sessions. Group sessions would break up, and each patient would meet with his or her own therapist, where we would talk about family dynamics and how addiction is genetic, how it can be passed on to other members of the family, and what causes it.

Glen Bay Hospital had a special family weekend. I brought in both my daughters, separately, to talk about family dynamics and so they could understand what went on with my addiction.

Overall, the therapy was a really good, positive experience for me. At the end of the thirteen-week therapy I was hired to work for Glen Bay Hospital as a full-time community relations coordinator.

Meanwhile, in the *Orlando Sentinel* there was an article written by Brian Schmitz about the pitcher Steve Howe and his drug abuse. Howe had relapsed again. In the article, Schmitz asked, "How many chances are the Yankees going to give him?"

The article was rather negative, and it annoyed me.

I knew Brian, so I called him.

"I read your article this morning," I said. "There's a lot of information in there that's just wrong, and I want to comment on it."

After I explained why addicts relapse, Brian said to me, "You seem to know a lot about it. Are you in recovery yourself?"

It was the first time anyone outside of therapy had ever asked me that question, and I was torn as to what to do. On the one hand, those in recovery are supposed to be anonymous. On the other hand, this was an opportunity to talk straight about addiction and its true nature.

What should I do? I asked myself. No one from the hospital was around for me to ask. I also considered what recovery literature said about the importance of being honest about your disease, so I said, "Yes, I am. I'm in recovery."

We started talking about how I got into recovery.

I gave him all the information about my addiction and how I got into recovery on June 15 and went into rehab on July 7, so I had six months of abstinence and recovery.

The next day I picked up the *Orlando Sentinel* and was shocked to find that the article he wrote about me was on the front page of the sports section. At first I was taken aback. Then I read it, and was pleased at how positive the story was.

The *Orlando Sentinel* is owned by the Tribune Company, and that day the story also ran in the *Chicago Tribune*, the Fort Lauderdale paper, the *Detroit Free Press*, and the *Los Angeles Times*. The *New York Daily News* picked it up, too. My hometown paper, the *Hartford Courant*, also ran the story. If I had any anonymity left, it was only in my head. When I visited Glen Bay Hospital after the article ran in all those papers, the therapists were up in arms. They went berserk!

"I got confused," I said. "I didn't do it on purpose. I didn't mean for this to happen."

John Brandenberg, director of Glen Bay Hospital, was pleased because I had mentioned the hospital in the story.

Brandenberg suggested that I host a radio show called *Comeback* on a small Orlando station. On the show we would talk about addiction and have a doctor on the air to answer medical questions. I would also invite professional athletes in recovery to come on the show and talk about their experiences.

Dr. Ray Dupres, who was short in stature and would get up on his tiptoes to berate me, expressed his displeasure. He didn't think giving me a radio show was such a good idea.

After he chewed out my ass, I thought, *You little cocksucker, I'll prove to you I'll make it.*

I turned his negativity into a positive.

For my first show I brought on Dr. Dupres as my guest, because I needed to convince him the show would be a positive, not just for the hospital, but also for me. I wanted to show him I wasn't coming on as a recovery guru, but only as host of the show. The show wasn't about me, and I was determined to make sure he knew it.

I invited various sports and entertainment figures. Ryne Duren, the Yankee pitcher, came on the show. Dr. Irving Kolin, who treated Eddie Fisher for a cocaine addiction, came on, and Eddie came on the show too. We had Otis Nixon, center fielder for the Atlanta Braves, as a guest. Otis talked about his cocaine addiction. My therapist, Vicky, came on the show and talked about women overeaters.

The show aired from one o'clock to two o'clock on Saturday afternoons. We were on opposite college football. We wondered what kind of audience we would get. From the very beginning, people were interested. I'd sit down five minutes before the show was to go on the air, and all of our phone lines would already be lit up.

Once my name got out there and people heard about the show, I got calls from people in Gamblers Anonymous and Cocaine Anonymous.

"How can we help you?" they wanted to know. "If you need a speaker, call us."

The show ran thirteen weeks, and my best show aired the Saturday before the Super Bowl. The topic was gambling addiction. I had people calling in who talked of losing fortunes and of attempting suicide. One listener called in and said, "Do you know the one thing during the Super Bowl that is bet on the most?"

"The final score?"

"No," he said. "The number-one thing bet on at the Super Bowl is the coin flip. You have the best odds at 51 percent of getting tails. Tails comes up more often than heads."

During the time I was doing *Comeback*, I was struck by the impression made on my listeners by my guests like Ryne Duren,

Eddie Fisher, and Otis Nixon. I thought to myself, *What if there was an organization that featured such speakers?*

I approached John Brandenberg with my idea.

We talked, and I came up with the acronym NARPA, the National Association of Recovering Professional Athletes. Glen Bay Hospital would be the host. I couldn't have started NARPA without the help of the hospital staff. I couldn't do it on my own, and I didn't have any money coming in. They gave me an office, a phone, and a secretary. Ryne Duren was named chairman. I would serve as president and executive director.

Our goal was to educate the public about the disease of addiction. We figured it would be a great way to combine resources and provide access to different rehabs and educational groups. I went to California and spent a week at the Betty Ford Center. I was assigned to different groups, including one composed of officers from a major metropolitan police department.

"When our boys go crazy, they have guns," I was told. "We have to get them with a SWAT team, and we have to get them quickly, and do it without the media knowing we're doing it. Under cover of night we go and grab them and shove them into rehab."

There were stories from many different professions. I was sure I could put together a group of professional athletes who could spread the word about addiction to the public. Through word of mouth we contacted and got the acceptance of 131 former professional athletes in recovery.

The athletes could give a little background on the history of drugs and alcohol. After talking about the history of addiction, a player could then share his own story. The only thing we were lacking was a connection to the professional sports leagues.

It was important to have the backing of the NFL and Major League Baseball. If we could get that, I knew we could be a roaring success. We first approached the NFL. I spoke with

Dr. Daniel Brown, who was the head of the substance abuse program there.

He wasn't receptive to the idea.

Major League Baseball stonewalled us too. We couldn't even get the courtesy of an answer.

Sam McDowell, who pitched for the Cleveland Indians and whose alcoholism was well known, was the coordinator for the baseball commissioner's office. Sam was on NARPA's board of directors. He would never give us an official reason why baseball was shutting us out, but he did suggest it might be better if we changed our name from the National Association of *Recovering* Professional Athletes to the National Association of *Responsible* Professional Athletes. I told him that if baseball embraced us, we'd be glad to change the name. NARPA just barely got off the ground. We got some nice letters from supporters, including Senator Strom Thurmond, whose daughter was killed by a drunk driver.

Senator Thurmond wanted to pass a law that said every beer can had to have a warning, but the beer companies responded that if the bill passed they would pull financial support from sports, so we would never see sports on TV ever again.

We planned some golf events to raise money, but we needed the major corporations to back us, and that never happened. Glen Bay Hospital shut down unexpectedly in 1995. The corporation was buying up hospitals in Ohio and Florida, they overreached, and the company went under. Once again, a job I loved was taken away from me.

But this time, at least I had my recovery.

20

ANGER MANAGEMENT

WITH THE CLOSING OF GLEN BAY HOSPITAL, I had to put away my disappointments and find a job. I went to the local Edwin Watts golf store near my home and filled out an application. My timing couldn't have been better, because the Professional Golfers Association show was at the Orlando Convention Center, and that was the year Callaway came out with the Big Bertha driver. Golf shops across the country wanted them, and the fastest way they could get them was by ordering through Edwin Watts.

Edwin Watts was setting sales records. I was hired as a greeter at their Orlando store. I was the lowest employee on the totem pole, but because of the sales volume the store needed someone to work shipping, and so my greeter's job lasted about a day and a half. My dad had been director of shipping for International Silver, and so they figured that shipping must be in my blood.

A couple of hurricanes shut down the Edwin Watts warehouse in Fort Walton Beach. We took all their golf clubs, and we became a quasi-warehouse. It was crazy and stressful. We shipped packages to cities all over the world.

My manager, Sven, was a perfectionist. To Sven, there was no such thing as an honest mistake. A couple of times I'd make a mistake with an order, and his language invariably would be "What's the matter with you? Are you stupid?"

What a fucking asshole! I'd think, but I held myself back from saying it.

The first few times he went off on me I told him I'd appreciate it if he didn't use that kind of tone and language with me. But he was my boss, and for a while I could take his abuse. On a personal level, though, we were friends and golfed together.

One time a golf pro playing in a tournament in San Juan, Puerto Rico, called. He had broken his wedge and needed another one sent to him overnight.

I was given the order, but accidently sent him a left-handed club rather than a right-handed one. The guy called Sven and was all over him. Then Sven came to me. He was very sarcastic. He said I had made a jackass out of him and asked, "How fucking difficult is it?"

I called the golf pro on the phone to apologize.

"Excuse me, sir," I said. "Can I ask you one question? I made the mistake, and I'm sorry I made it. Who's winning the Puerto Rican League?"

"Santurce, I think."

I asked him to check and he looked in the local newspaper.

"It's Santurce. Why do you ask?"

"I used to play for the San Juan Senadores. I played for Roberto Clemente. You'll have your wedge tomorrow," I said. "It was my fault."

"Oh, no problem," he said. He invited me to play some golf if I was ever in Puerto Rico.

Sven came back to shipping to ask me if I had called the guy back and if I knew I was getting fired.

"He said the next time I come to Puerto Rico to give him a call and we'll play golf together."

Dead silence. Sven walked away shaking his head.

Another time I sent a woman the wrong club and she complained to Sven about it.

"This is it," he said. "This is two times in a year. This woman is ranting and raving and wants her money back," he said. "I think I can calm her down, but if we have to pay, it's coming out of your check. You need to call this woman."

I called her.

"Mrs. Jones," I said, faking a Hispanic accent, "I'm Guillermo Denehy from the Edwin Watts golf shop. I am so sorry you got the wrong club. This is my fault. Lay it on me. I can't tell you the pain I'm in, and I'm so sorry for you, even though it might cost me my job."

"It's not going to cost you your job," she said. "Who told you that?"

"They told me you were upset."

"I'm not that upset," she said. "For God's sake, I would never do that. Don't worry. That's ridiculous. Just send the other club."

She called Sven back and said, "Why are you threatening to fire that nice man for sending the wrong club? And besides the fact you threatened him, my daughter is dating a Hispanic guy, and

I don't appreciate you taking advantage of him just because he's Hispanic."

She hung up.

Sven later told me, "You may think you're funny, and you may think you're tough, but I just want you to know if we ever got in a fight . . ."

I put my arm around him and told him that he wouldn't have a chance. That was our relationship. I didn't want to fuck with him only because I was afraid I would kill him.

The next incident occurred because one of our part-time salesmen couldn't write legibly. Ricardo was from Rome and was in the United States because he thought it would be the fastest way for him to get on the PGA tour. Meanwhile, he made money by selling golf clubs. One day he had $89,000 worth of equipment to ship to Italy by boat.

I had asked him to write out the address legibly so I could read it. But I couldn't read what he wrote, so I held the shipment, and it missed the boat to Italy. Ricardo found out and called me a fucking asshole. I was holding a box cutter in my hand with the handle facing him.

I baited him to grab it. "Because as soon as you grab it," I said, "I'm going to slice you up like a piece of Italian sausage, pack you away, and send you back to fucking Italy."

Richardo ran to Sven and told him, "He threatened to kill me."

"You can't be threatening employees," Sven said to me.

But I ended up getting fired because I wouldn't enable an employee who was addicted to painkillers.

A manager, a guy named Ed, had been in a terrible car accident. His back was fused and he was in terrible pain. He befriended doctors who ordered golf clubs, and the doctors would prescribe painkillers for him. Even after a doctor moved out of Orlando, he'd still order his clubs from Ed, who would take his old clubs as a trade-in. When the doctor sent an old club back, he would also send Ed bottles of pills. Since I was in receiving, I saw the bottles of pills that came in.

Ed was taking more pills than he needed, because there were days when he'd come in slurring his words. We would put him in his office and keep him there until the pills wore off. I complained to Sven because I was in recovery and because I didn't want to be involved with Ed's receiving pain pills from out of state.

"We have to protect Ed," Sven said. "Ed is in a lot of pain."

One day Ed was a little loopy, and we got word that Edwin and Ronnie Watts, owners of the store, were coming over for a surprise visit. We had to get Ed out of there, and fast.

After the Watts brothers left, we returned and Sven said, "Everything is cool."

"No," I said. "Everything is not cool. I won't participate in any more cover-ups. Ed needs help, and you as the manager ought to do something about it."

This argument happened on a Wednesday. Three days later, I was fired.

I was told that I couldn't get along with some of the employees. The real reasons were that I made several threats, I challenged people to fights, and I wouldn't try to help cover up Ed's problem with pain pills.

They were afraid I would turn Ed in for his drug use.

They talked about taking out a restraining order on me to keep me from returning to the store. And yet, they also gave me two months' severance pay, which doesn't usually happen when a person gets fired. I wasn't fired because of my rage. I was fired because of drugs, but they weren't my drugs.

The irony was that for eight months I was going to recovery meetings on Wednesday nights and telling the people in the meetings about what was going on in the golf shop. Everyone told me to get out of there and to find another job.

After being fired, I still had problems with rage. One day I was sharing a story at one of my meetings when one of the other men in the group, Little Ed, a sarcastic guy from Boston, commented that I didn't know what I was talking about. That was a big no-no and crossed the line.

One of the unwritten rules of twelve-step meetings is that there's no cross talk. You're not supposed to disagree with something someone has shared. You're not supposed to debate something someone says. Instead, you are supposed to say, "My experience is . . ."

I followed up his comments with "First of all, you're cross talking. What I said is my experience. Number two, you repeated something I said *wrong*, so why don't you take the cotton out of your ears and stick it in your mouth?"

He didn't like it and challenged me. I mean to tell you, Dick Butkus never ran across a room faster than I did to get to this guy. Four guys cut me off. One of them was a patient we called "Missile Mike." Ed hid behind another guy as he whined, "He's going to kill me. He's going to kill me."

Suddenly, I came to my senses. I thought to myself, *Okay, why am I doing this?* I have sixteen years in the program. I'm still getting these raging outbursts. I pray, share at meetings, do the Twelve Steps, yet nothing has seemed work on my rage.

Missile Mike told me later that when I turned and looked at him, my eyes were the scariest thing he had ever seen in his life. He said it was like I was a demon. My eyes, he said, were bulging, piercing. He also said I was crazy.

I just wish those nuns in Catholic school hadn't hit me with their rulers all those many years ago.

About five years after the incident in the twelve-step meeting I spoke to Dr. Billy Thompson and told him about my rages. He thought I had a chemical imbalance. He prescribed Selexa, an antidepressant, and almost immediately it settled me down. After a few changes in dosage we hit the right formula, and it's been smooth sailing ever since, for the most part, and it has proved to me that addiction is centered in the mind and is a mental illness.

Several times in recovery meetings I've heard people make comments that were untrue and which royally pissed me off.

Except for the incident with Little Ed, my rage usually crumbles and softly fades away.

21

MOM

MY MOTHER—WHO WAS EIGHTY-FIVE YEARS OLD and living with me—started to show signs of forgetfulness, and began to deteriorate rapidly. Her younger brother had recently died, and due to a coroner's strike we could not find out the cause of death or get his body from the coroner for burial. Every day she would ask, "When are we going to Connecticut? When's the funeral?" After we returned to Florida following the funeral, she would get up in the middle of the night fully dressed, turn the light on in my room, and say, "Aren't you out of bed yet?"

Her erratic behavior continued.

Some nights she'd get up in the middle of the night and do the laundry. Sometimes she would leave the stove on. I needed to get a job, but I also needed to keep an eye on her. She started to get cabin fever and would take Schmucko on long walks several times a day. In the beginning it was okay because somehow she'd find her way back, or the dog would lead her back home. But one time I got back from my twelve-step meeting and she was gone. I searched the apartment complex and found her at the far end of the complex.

Three weeks later she disappeared again; this time I couldn't find her. I finally had to call the police. They found her and Schmucko ten blocks away. A cop brought her back and filed a report. He said, "We could file charges against you for leaving a mentally handicapped person alone. She shouldn't be left alone." He suggested I find a nursing home for her and that I ought to call a case worker. He said he would put a picture of Mom on their computer in case she went missing again. Then he left. Twenty minutes later he returned to take a photo of her and Schmucko.

One afternoon my mom said she needed a bra. We went to the women's department at J.C. Penney. She picked out a couple of bras, went into the dressing room to try them on, and came out with one bra cup on a breast and the other one on top of her head. She was naked, crying, and confused. I found a woman to help her put on the bra. That's when I knew she needed more care than I could give.

I called a case worker who visited and asked if she could go into the bathroom with my mom. Twenty minutes later they came out, and she said, "I want to tell you what went on. A lot of people who work with relatives with Alzheimer's get frustrated and hit or beat them. I had to check for bruises. She didn't have any, so I know you've been taking care of her, but she really needs to go to the nursing home pretty quickly."

I got her into a nursing home. I was told she was at the start of the disease and that as she got worse, she would have to go into the Alzheimer's unit. She was with the normal population for exactly two days when I got the call. She had walked out into the hallway at two o'clock in the morning, completely naked, wanting to know where the shower was. The staff got her dressed. A day later they found her in the game room choking one of the other patients who she claimed made a pass at her. This was the violent stage of Alzheimer's the staff was worried about.

I got Mom into one of the best Alzheimer's units in the state and she got really good care. They were so on top of things that if she fell at three o'clock in the morning, they'd wake me up to tell me she had fallen but that she was fine.

I went to see her the last day she was alive. It was about lunchtime, and she couldn't eat on her own. I had to put the food in front of her mouth, she'd chew, and I had to rub her neck and give her some water so she could swallow. I got her a chair. She was petting Schmucko, and the last thing she said to me was "How much longer are you going to stay around here?"

"A little while longer," I said. "I have to get the dog back. She hasn't eaten."

"I hope you stay long enough," she said. "I think my son is coming to visit me today, and I'd like you to meet him. He's really a nice guy."

She didn't even know who I was.

One time I took Schmucko to the vet for her regular shots, but there was an epidemic of distemper in the vet's clinic. Schmucko contracted it, and within a week she was so sick I had to put her down. I cried over her death for days. Then one morning I got a phone call. The woman on the phone said, "Mr. Denehy, this is the Alzheimer's unit. Your mother passed away this morning."

That night Mom had woken up to go to the bathroom, gone back to bed, and died peacefully.

Because I was in recovery at the time, I was able to be there for her, to treat her well, and to help her during her final days.

I'm not sure I could have or would have done that if I hadn't been in recovery. I had a lot of support from my recovery group, especially while dealing with her Alzheimer's.

I bawled like a baby for having to put down Schmucko, who I had for the first fourteen years of my recovery. Yet I knew my mom was going to die eventually, and when she did, I didn't even shed a tear.

My uncle Bernie (my mother's brother) had passed away before my mother did. When he died, Marilyn called me to ask if she could attend his service and grieve with my family. She came for the funeral and attended the after-service luncheon, where she reunited with my family.

Later, when my mother died, Marilyn called and asked if she could fly down and participate in my mother's services. She stayed with my older daughter Kristin, and on the day of the funeral mass, the last thing I said to both of them was "Make sure you pick me up on time so we don't get to the church late."

"What are they going to do," Marilyn said, "start without us?"

They *did* start without us. When we got to the church, the priest paused the service to announce, "Here's Mrs. Denehy's family. They finally arrived!"

Not long after the funeral, Marilyn started going to twelve-step meetings. She had started drinking heavily after our divorce, and then again after her mom died in 1993; she had stopped for four years, but started up again. She began a therapy program in October of 2003, and we individually began to work on our anger, resentments, and grudges that we held against each other. I didn't know when she visited me in Florida that she was hitting bottom. She was able to control her drinking while in Florida before returning to Connecticut.

Marilyn had carpal tunnel syndrome that put her out of work. She was on workman's compensation, which allowed her to sit at home all day and drink. She finally decided that she needed to do something about her drinking and that she needed to focus on herself for a change.

"It was time for me," was the way she later put it. And because she saw the change in me through my program, she had the courage to begin recovery herself. She says that alcohol destroyed our family, and now the program has brought us back together. Today we talk about the possibility of getting together again. She says that when she retires, she'll move to Florida and we'll live together.

To reunite our family is my idea of a perfect game.

After my mom passed away, I took a public relations job with Universal Studios. It was just a job, but at least I was getting medical benefits. I was also learning to teach a program called Natural Golf, and I was making a little extra money.

I was still having trouble controlling my rage.

On a Tuesday I went to a Publix supermarket. I went to the deli department and asked them, "Do you have your fresh-made peanut butter?"

A woman behind the counter told me they hadn't made it yet.

I returned the next day; no peanut butter. I returned two days later, but still no peanut butter. I asked the woman why after three days she didn't have any peanut butter. She said they were busy, it wasn't a popular item, and that she was working on a big order and couldn't get to it. *I snapped.*

I struck the top of the glass deli counter with my fist, and I yelled, "Is it that fucking tough to throw some fucking peanuts into the fucking grinder and make some fucking peanut butter for three fucking days in a row so I can get some fucking peanut butter and get the fuck out of here? Is it that fucking tough?"

She called the supermarket manager, and he took me into his office. We argued. He told me I lost my temper and that I couldn't use that language.

"You bet your ass I lost my temper," I said. "'Cause this is the fourth fucking day that I've come in here."

A cop walked in.

The manager talked to the cop.

"They want to arrest you for disturbing the peace," the cop said. Fortunately, he didn't want to write up a disturbing the peace citation over some peanut butter. The cop took me outside and asked if I was cooled down enough. I was. Then I told him, "I get the rage." He went back into the supermarket to talk them out of filing charges.

When he returned he said, "You have a TRO against you." This wasn't true, but he said, "You can't come here for six months. Stay away as long as you can, and if you come back, don't do this again. Christ, if I wrote this up over peanut butter, I'd never hear the end of it. Go on your way."

On reflection, I wasn't right in the head. I suspected I was mentally ill. I would get crazy things in my head, and I wouldn't be able to shake them.

One time bad guys in my neighborhood were robbing customers in store parking lots late at night. They would beat up old people and rob them. That just pissed me off.

I decided I would use myself as bait, walk around in store parking lots, hoping I would get jumped. I had a screwdriver in my belt, and I figured that if I was attacked, I was going to kill them.

My friends told me I was nuts.

I worked part-time for a company at Universal called Sports Memorabilia. If I worked there for ninety days, I would get medical coverage. Two weeks before my ninety days were up, the company chose not to sign their lease agreement with Universal and declared bankruptcy.

I was paying my rent, but I wasn't making much money. After I found out that Sports Memorabilia was going under, I woke up one morning completely blind in my right eye.

I hadn't had a hint. I hadn't had floaters. I didn't feel any pain. One day I could see fine, and the next day I was blind in my right eye. So I called John Chanin, who was living in Orlando.

"We'd better take you down to the emergency room at Sand Lake Hospital," he said.

I told them that I didn't have any insurance, but I thought that the hospital staff was obligated to look at it and treat it.

"You have a completely detached retina," I was told.

"We have to send you to an ophthalmologist. He's going to have to look at it."

"Aren't you going to do something here?" I wanted to know. "I'm here. Don't ophthalmologists visit here?"

"No, you have to sign off here and go to him." They warned me that the longer I waited to have the operation, the less chance I would have to regain my sight.

Once I signed the form, I had admitted that the hospital had treated me and given me a diagnosis, so they were free and clear from having to operate on me and to pick up the cost of the operation. I made an appointment with an ophthalmologist, who refused to see me because I didn't have any insurance.

"I can't see," I said.

"I understand that," he said, "but it will cost several hundred dollars for me to do a full test. Who's going to pay for it?"

Even after everything I had been through, it was, perhaps, the lowest day of my life. I was going blind. Treatment might save me, but I had no money for treatment.

I went to another doctor, and the woman in charge of billing told me the same thing. If I didn't have insurance, there was nothing they could do for me.

I told her I was a former major league baseball player and that I intended to contact the Baseball Assistance Team.

"I need this operation," I said. "Can't you help me out?" I was desperate.

"Why don't you get one of your rich baseball friends and have them help you out?" she said. I would have liked to have stuck a knife right between her eyes, that little fucking bitch.

They wouldn't do anything, so I called my recovery sponsor, and he told me to call a charitable group called Shepherd's Hope. The woman there referred me to the County of Orlando and an organization called PECAN. If you're a resident and you need an operation and have been a good member of the community, they'll pay for it. They directed me to go to Shands Hospital in Gainesville.

"You need this operation right away," I was told by Dr. Shalesh Kaushul.

Dr. Kaushul worked for hours to reattach the retina in my right eye.

"Have you been in any fights or had any trauma recently?" he wanted to know.

It had been almost thirty years since I had been in a fight. As for trauma, I had been involved in three car accidents, but nothing severe. He said he had assisted in the operation to reattach boxer Sugar Ray Leonard's retina.

"Yours is worse than his," he said.

We were trying to figure out what possibly could have caused this. I returned to him for several visits, and during one of those visits I said to him, "I know this is crazy, but when I was playing ball, I had an awful lot of cortisone shots."

Several interns were standing around us, and one of them asked, "What kind of cortisone?"

"Cortisone shots in my shoulder."

"Can you remember how many?" she asked.

"I can remember the exact number," I said. "I had fifty-seven in twenty-six months."

She laughed, but not in a good way.

"First of all," she said, "I can't believe anyone would give you that much cortisone. The American Medical Association says you shouldn't have more than ten in a lifetime. No more than three in one area. *And you had fifty-seven?*"

"I won't say it was a notch in my belt every time I had a cortisone shot," I said, "but I counted them."

"I'm sure your blindness was caused by the cortisone," she said. "One of the things that cortisone does is cause fragility of the eyes."

Cortisone is a steroid, and I am convinced that it caused the physical damage and was also responsible for my rages. They couldn't restore the eyesight in my right eye.

The other eye was fine. I could still drive and take care of myself. When my daughter Kristin got married, I flew to California, and as I was flying I felt pain in my left eye. I returned to Orlando. One Saturday morning I was going to see friends and play a little golf. When I didn't bring out my clubs, a friend asked me where my clubs were.

"You're taking me to the hospital," I said. "I have fluid in my left eye."

I called Shands in Gainesville, and they told me to get there as soon as possible. I had a hole in the retina of my left eye, and I had to have it operated on. I also had something called galloping glaucoma. If you get that, you end up losing your sight quickly. After eight operations, vision in my left eye was 20/100. I could only see shadows of objects unless they were six inches away. I was still completely blind in my right eye.

When I filed for Social Security disability, they denied me. They said I really just had impaired vision, that I wasn't completely disabled. They said I could still work. I don't know what kind of job they thought I could do.

I found out later that even soldiers returning from Iraq had to wait months for disability.

I needed income desperately. I pawned my two minor league championship rings and the ball Richard Nixon signed when I was with the Tigers. I called the Baseball Assistance Team (BAT) for help.

I sent my medical records to BAT, which is housed in the baseball commissioner's office, and they approved me. For eighteen months BAT gave me a grant to pay my rent and utilities. They also gave me a little money. Without BAT, I wouldn't have had any money whatsoever.

I'll always be grateful to them, though I have no idea who actually made the decision. But at the same time I felt like I was begging.

I appealed my Social Security disability. I called Senator Bill Nelson, who got involved. Senator Nelson got me an appointment with a psychiatrist. She discovered I also had ADD, and she found out I was a visual learner, not an auditory learner, and that my blindness compounded my problem.

We started talking about my relationships with others, including my fellow workers. I told her about the peanut butter incident, the fight at the construction site, and my fights at Edwin Watts.

She concluded that I had an "antisocial work disorder."

"At age sixty-two," she said, "I don't see anything we can do to train you for a job. You're losing your vision, so you can't work on a computer. I don't see where you would qualify for being able to work."

"Okay," I said. She was just telling me what I had told the Social Security people.

"I want to ask you one question," she said. "I'm not a sports fan. But there's no chance you could play baseball again, is there?"

I reminded her I was sixty-two years old and that no one over age forty played major league baseball.

When she asked if I could coach, I told her I had previously been a pitching coach but that I would need to be able to see.

Then she said, "One final question. If I could say to you at the end of this interview that I could give you the perfect job, what would it be?"

I thought about it for a minute.

"First of all," I said, "I'm very patriotic. I love this country and the time I spent in the Army National Guard. If I had my dream job, it would be as a sniper. Think about this. You go out in the field, and you can be 700 yards from a target, and the bullet can pop that guy's head off like a watermelon. All for the United States of America! That would be the perfect job."

The psychiatrist dropped her glasses from above her nose to below it, and said, "Okay, I think I have enough."

I left. My sponsor was with me. I told him what had transpired.

"You're lucky they didn't throw you in a rubber room," he said.

But I got my Social Security disability.

BILL'S PRAYER

*Lord our God you are patient with sinners
like me and accept our desires to make
amends. We acknowledge our sins and are
resolved to change our lives.*

*Help me remove the character defects of
anger, resentment, jealousy, self-seeking,
self-centeredness, impatience, controlling,
and dishonesty.*

*Help me become forgiving and inspire me
into thinking and acting upon what I
do for others.*

*Protect my family and guide me to
a Christian life through your direction.
Help remove worry from my thinking.*

*Give me strength against temptation and the
courage to handle frustration and faith and
trust to accept, in all of my actions
THY WILL (not mine) BE DONE.*

*Humbly, not egotistically, I'm grateful
that through your vision you have allowed
me to become clean and sober, and that you
have granted and I have accepted serenity
into my life.*

Through Christ my Lord, Amen.

22

WHERE'S MY PENSION?

IN 1981 THE MAJOR LEAGUE PLAYERS ASSOCIATION made a deal with the owners that all players who were in the big leagues for just one day beginning in 1980 would receive their pension. Those who played before 1980 would have to have been major leaguers for five years to receive a pension. I was one of 874 former major league ballplayers who were left holding a very empty bag.

I played before 1980. I was in the major leagues for three and a half years. I don't get a pension. Why did this happen? Because, according to Marvin Miller, who was then the head of the players' union, there wasn't enough money to include us. When I asked Miller about it in the mid-1990s, he very brusquely told me, "Sometimes when you make a decision, the lower people in the union suffer.

"Our job," he said, "is to take care of the upper echelon."

My first thought was, *I thought we were all supposed to be in this together. I thought my vote was just as important as everyone else's.*

Why are the Marines so great? Because they never leave a Marine behind! If a Marine falls, you go back and get him.

Miller; Bob Boone, the National League representative; Doug DeCinces, the American League representative; and Steve Rogers and Mark Belanger, who were working for the players' association, fucked us badly.

My biggest concern was the medical coverage that my membership in the players' union would have provided.

The other concern was that many of us are disabled because of the league's drug policy. I was unbelievably abused by baseball's medical profession. Cortisone left me blind. When a letter was sent out to former players asking who else was in a similar situation, we received two hundred replies.

I have to believe it's only the tip of the iceberg. I was told that many would not respond because they were grandfathers who were telling their grandkids not to use drugs. They didn't want to come clean and admit they had used drugs to stay in the game.

These players were suffering from shame. We filed a lawsuit against Major League Baseball asking for a pension and demanding medical coverage. We won the first round, but the suit was appealed in California and the appellate court overturned the decision. The court said that an industry has the right to set its own standards for pensions. If they voted you out of the union, the court said, you weren't entitled to anything.

The appellate court ruled that those fighting for medical coverage had a better case than those who demanded admission to the players' association. The court said we could sue separately for medical coverage.

I know that behind the scenes players like Sandy Koufax, Bob Gibson, and Sam McDowell have been telling the baseball commissioner, "We have to help these guys."

Baseball responded with crumbs. So far we have received two yearly payments from baseball of about $4,250.00. The money was sent by baseball as a charitable contribution.

A writer called and asked me about it. I decided to be diplomatic. "I'm very grateful that baseball finally has decided to pay us something for the time we played," I said.

I felt kicking a gift horse wasn't cool.

I *am* grateful. But when Alex Rodriguez is getting 27 million dollars a year, I ask myself what it would cost to take the 874 players left without a pension and make their lives a little easier. What I receive isn't much. And there's still nothing left for medical care.

Looking back on my life, only two things still make me want to put my fist through a pane of glass.

The first is the accountant I went to for help in getting an eye operation, who said to me, "Why don't you get your rich ballplayer friends to help you?"

You fucking bitch.

The second was when I went to Major League Baseball and told them that I had gone blind because of all the cortisone shots, and they said to me, "We wouldn't do that. We love our players. Besides, there are no records that that ever took place."

Was that a nice way of calling me a liar?

We're still treating addiction as a "problem." Some say Josh Hamilton is still fighting his *problem of addiction.*

At a recovery meeting not long ago, one of those in attendance said that the forty-eight-year-old son of one of his best friends had died of pancreatic cancer. But he said, "We all know Tommy really died of alcoholism."

"Instead of saying he died of cancer or of a long illness, wouldn't it be better if they said he died of alcoholism?" I asked.

How many times have you read, "He died of alcoholism"? *Never, never, never.*

My goal is to continue to educate the public about the disease of addiction. This book is a first step. I also go to recovery meetings and sponsor other men, ten in all. I'm known in the room as Baseball Bill. I have twenty years and counting without alcohol and other drugs.

I've reestablished my relationships with my ex-wife Marilyn and my talented daughters Kristin and Heather. Marilyn tells me how proud she is that I'm finally becoming the man and father these kids deserve.

But stories like this don't always have a happy ending. People can and do die from addiction. They kill themselves. I somehow survived. In Marilyn's eyes I have come through with flying colors. She has, too.

Today Marilyn and I, and our daughters, have a great relationship. After looking back over my life, I would say my biggest and proudest accomplishment is my family.

And for that I am very grateful.